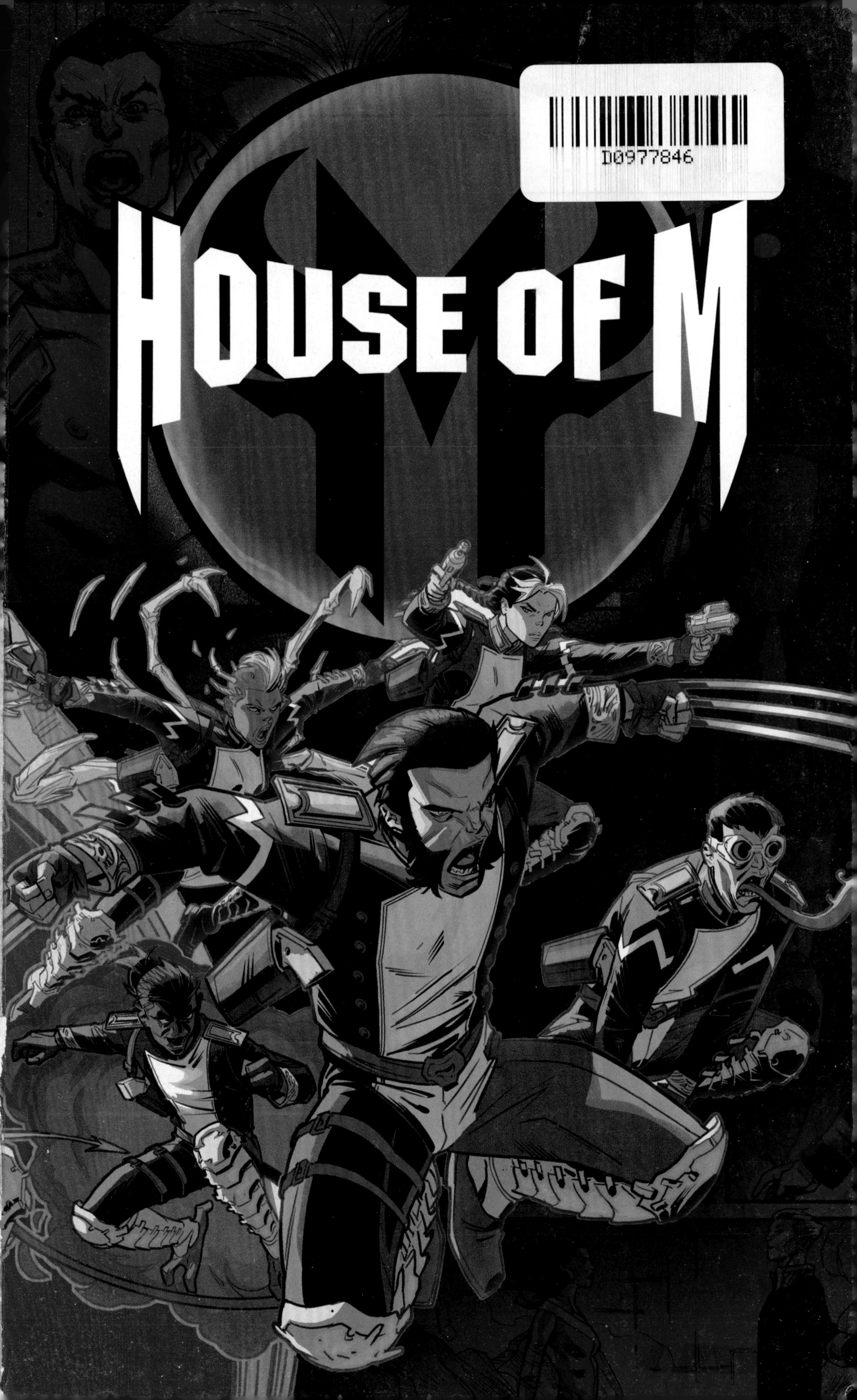
HOUSE OF M

HOUSE OF M

DENNIS HOPELESS & CULLEN BUNN
WRITERS

MARCO FAILLA (#1-2) & ARIO ANINDITO (#3-4)
ARTISTS

MATTHEW WILSON
COLOR ARTIST

VC'S JOE CARAMAGNA
LETTERER

KRIS ANKA
COVER ART

CHRISTINA HARRINGTON
ASSISTANT EDITOR

KATIE KUBERT
EDITOR

COLLECTION EDITOR: JENNIFER GRÜNWALD
ASSISTANT EDITOR: SARAH BRUNSTAD
ASSOCIATE MANAGING EDITOR: ALEX STARBUCK
EDITOR, SPECIAL PROJECTS: MARK D. BEAZLEY

SENIOR EDITOR, SPECIAL PROJECTS: JEFF YOUNGQUIST
SVP PRINT, SALES & MARKETING: DAVID GABRIEL
BOOK DESIGNER: JAY BOWEN

EDITOR IN CHIEF: AXEL ALONSO
CHIEF CREATIVE OFFICER: JOE QUESADA
PUBLISHER: DAN BUCKLEY
EXECUTIVE PRODUCER: ALAN FINE

HOUSE OF M: WARZONES! Contains material originally published in magazine form as HOUSE OF M (2015) #1-4 and HOUSE OF M (2005) #1. First printing 2016. ISBN# 978-0-7851-9872-7. Published by MARVEL WORLDWIDE, INC., a subsidiary of MARVEL ENTERTAINMENT, LLC. OFFICE OF PUBLICATION: 135 West 50th Street, New York, NY 10020. Copyright © 2016 MARVEL No similarity between any of the names, characters, persons, and/or institutions in this magazine with those of any living or dead person or institution is intended, and any such similarity which may exist is purely coincidental. **Printed in Canada.** ALAN FINE, President, Marvel Entertainment; DAN BUCKLEY, President, TV, Publishing and Brand Management; JOE QUESADA, Chief Creative Officer; TOM BREVOORT, SVP of Publishing; DAVID BOGART, SVP of Operations & Procurement, Publishing; C.B. CEBULSKI, VP of International Development & Brand Management; DAVID GABRIEL, SVP Print, Sales & Marketing; JIM O'KEEFE, VP of Operations & Logistics; DAN CARR, Executive Director of Publishing Technology; SUSAN CRESPI, Editorial Operations Manager; ALEX MORALES, Publishing Operations Manager; STAN LEE, Chairman Emeritus. For information regarding advertising in Marvel Comics or on Marvel.com, please contact Jonathan Rheingold, VP of Custom Solutions & Ad Sales, at jrheingold@marvel.com. For Marvel subscription inquiries, please call 800-217-9158. **Manufactured between 11/20/2015 and 12/28/2015 by SOLISCO PRINTERS, SCOTT, QC, CANADA.**

10 9 8 7 6 5 4 3 2 1

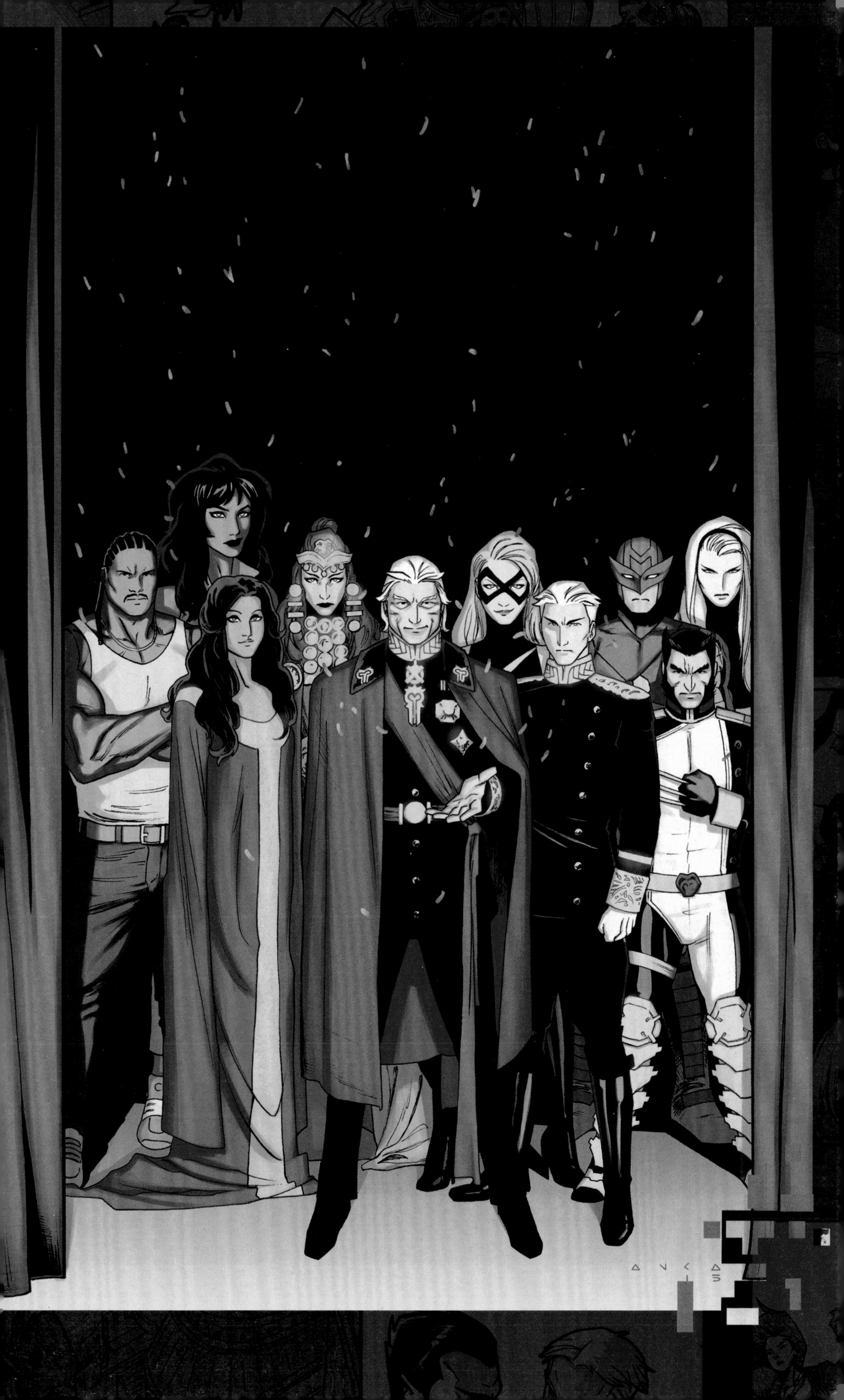

THE MULTIVERSE WAS DESTROYED!

THE HEROES OF EARTH-616 AND EARTH-1610 WERE POWERLESS TO SAVE IT!

NOW, ALL THAT REMAINS...IS **BATTLEWORLD**!

A MASSIVE, PATCHWORK PLANET COMPOSED OF THE FRAGMENTS OF WORLDS THAT NO LONGER EXIST, MAINTAINED BY THE IRON WILL OF ITS GOD AND MASTER, VICTOR VON DOOM!

EACH REGION IS A DOMAIN UNTO ITSELF!

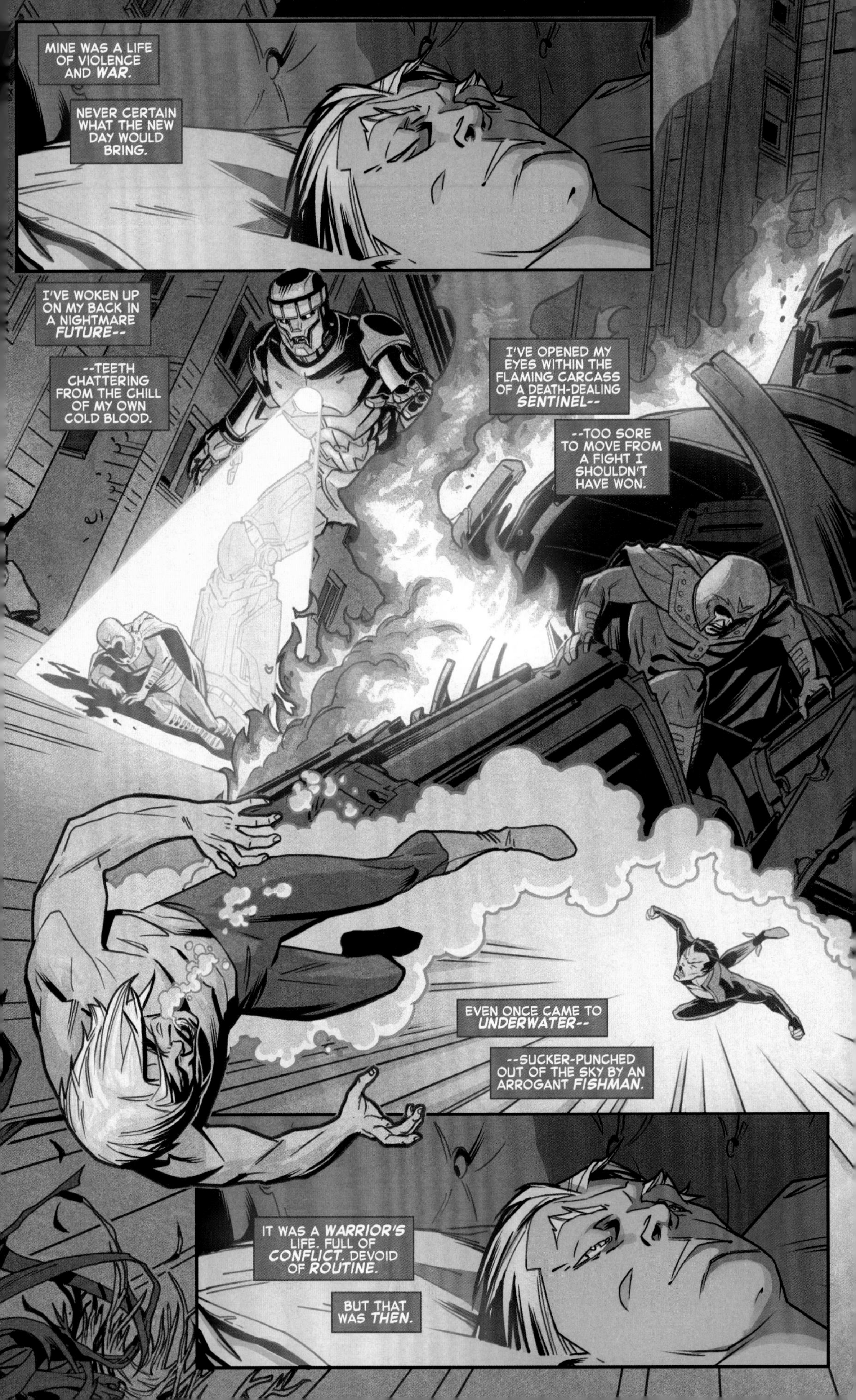
MINE WAS A LIFE OF VIOLENCE AND WAR.
NEVER CERTAIN WHAT THE NEW DAY WOULD BRING.
I'VE WOKEN UP ON MY BACK IN A NIGHTMARE FUTURE--
--TEETH CHATTERING FROM THE CHILL OF MY OWN COLD BLOOD.
I'VE OPENED MY EYES WITHIN THE FLAMING CARCASS OF A DEATH-DEALING SENTINEL--
--TOO SORE TO MOVE FROM A FIGHT I SHOULDN'T HAVE WON.
EVEN ONCE CAME TO UNDERWATER--
--SUCKER-PUNCHED OUT OF THE SKY BY AN ARROGANT FISHMAN.
IT WAS A WARRIOR'S LIFE. FULL OF CONFLICT. DEVOID OF ROUTINE.
BUT THAT WAS THEN.

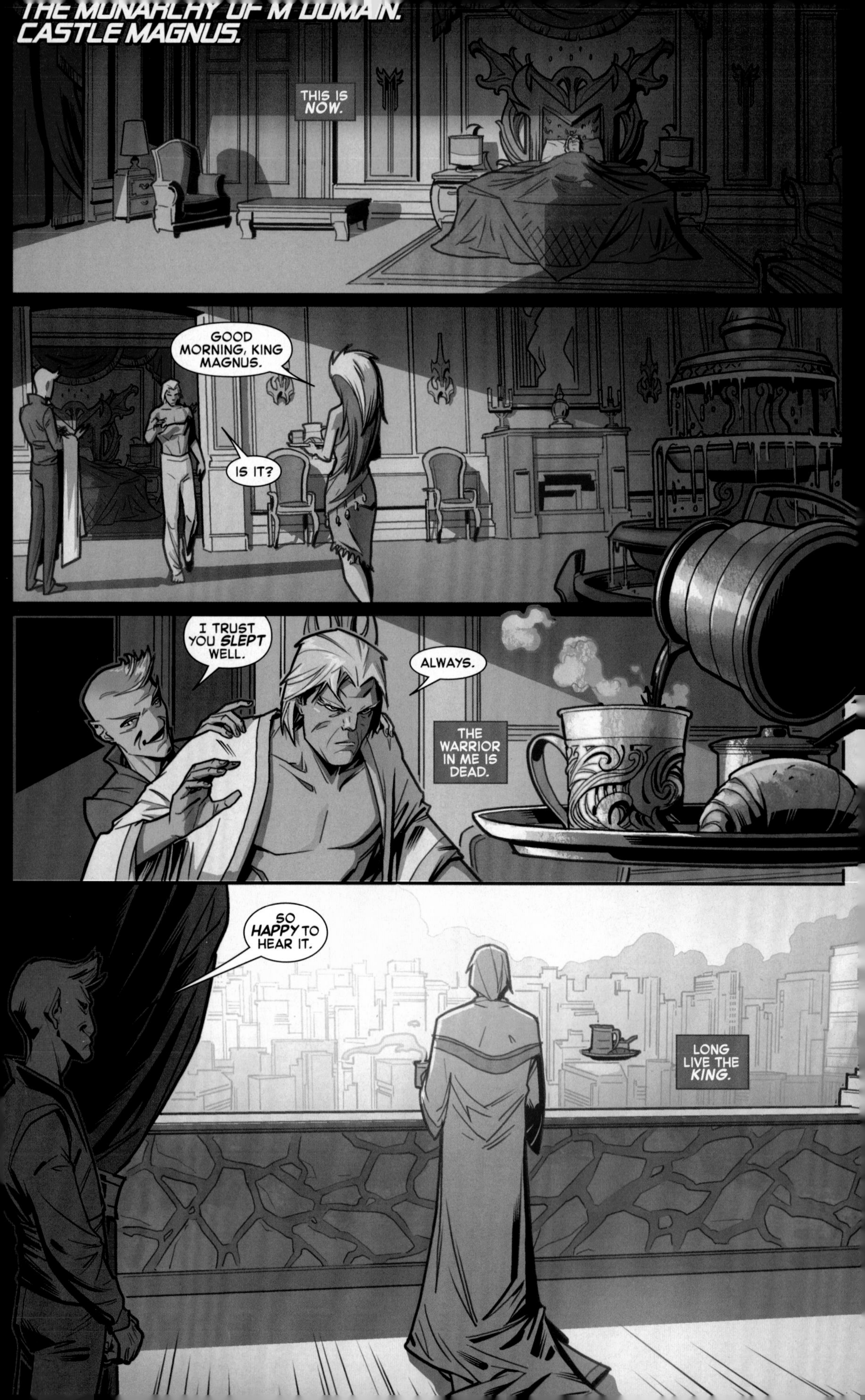
THE MONARCHY OF M DOMAIN.
CASTLE MAGNUS.
THIS IS NOW.
GOOD MORNING, KING MAGNUS.
IS IT?
I TRUST YOU SLEPT WELL.
ALWAYS.
THE WARRIOR IN ME IS DEAD.
SO HAPPY TO HEAR IT.
LONG LIVE THE KING.

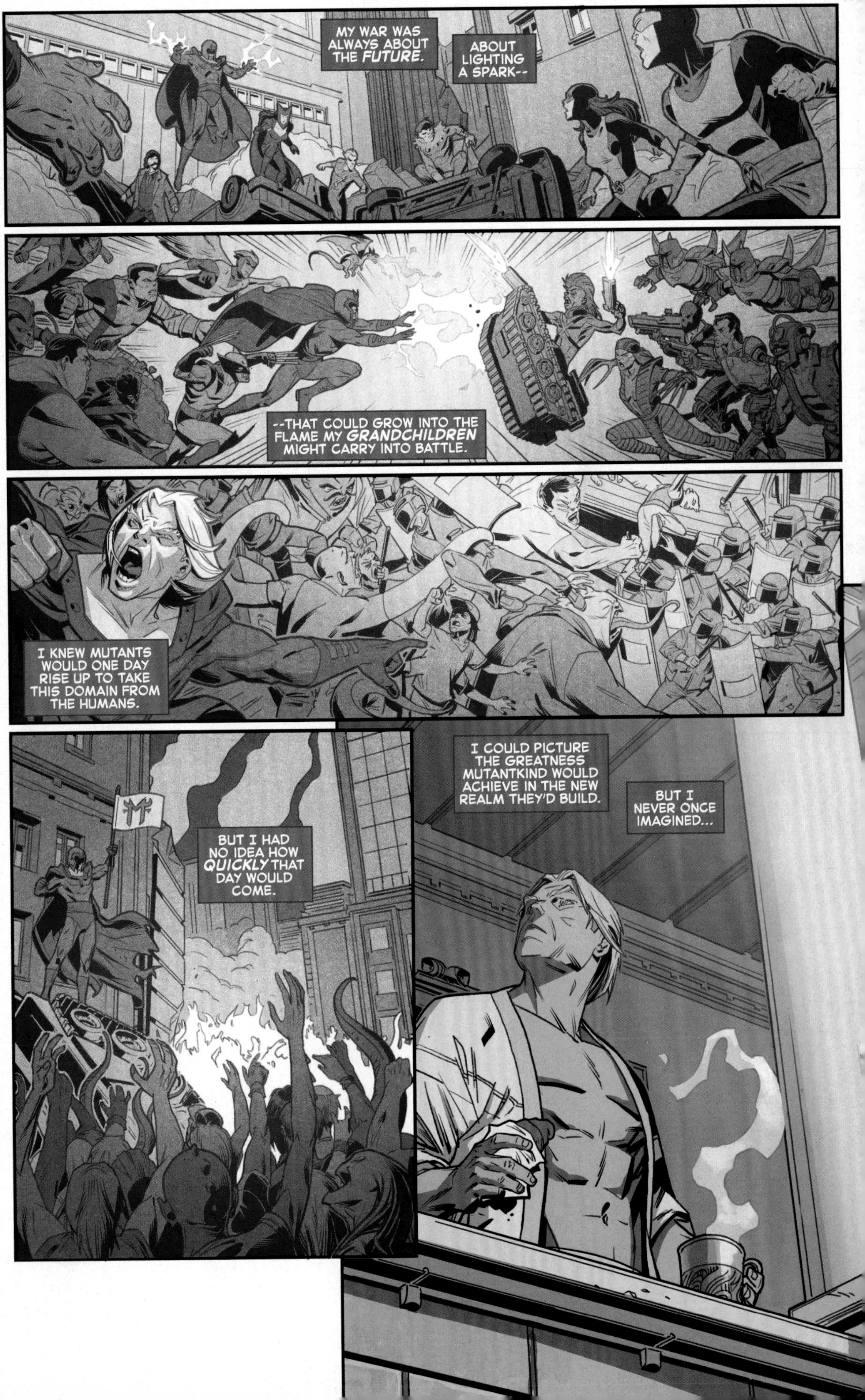
MY WAR WAS ALWAYS ABOUT THE *FUTURE.*
ABOUT LIGHTING A SPARK--
--THAT COULD GROW INTO THE FLAME MY *GRANDCHILDREN* MIGHT CARRY INTO BATTLE.
I KNEW MUTANTS WOULD ONE DAY RISE UP TO TAKE THIS DOMAIN FROM THE HUMANS.
BUT I HAD NO IDEA HOW *QUICKLY* THAT DAY WOULD COME.
I COULD PICTURE THE GREATNESS MUTANTKIND WOULD ACHIEVE IN THE NEW REALM THEY'D BUILD.
BUT I NEVER ONCE IMAGINED...

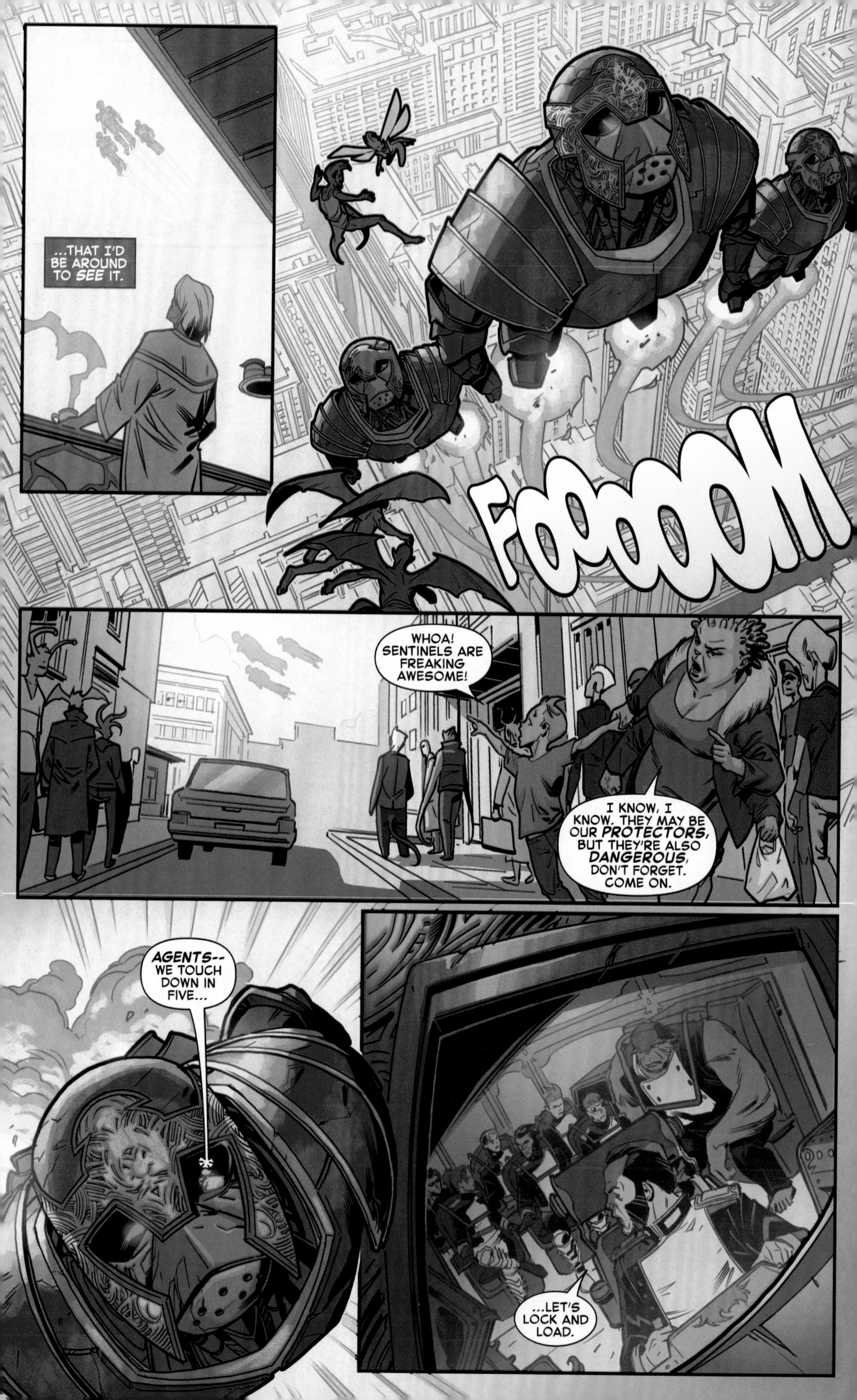
...THAT I'D BE AROUND TO SEE IT.
FOOOOOM
WHOA! SENTINELS ARE FREAKING AWESOME!
I KNOW, I KNOW. THEY MAY BE OUR PROTECTORS, BUT THEY'RE ALSO DANGEROUS, DON'T FORGET. COME ON.
AGENTS-- WE TOUCH DOWN IN FIVE...
...LET'S LOCK AND LOAD.

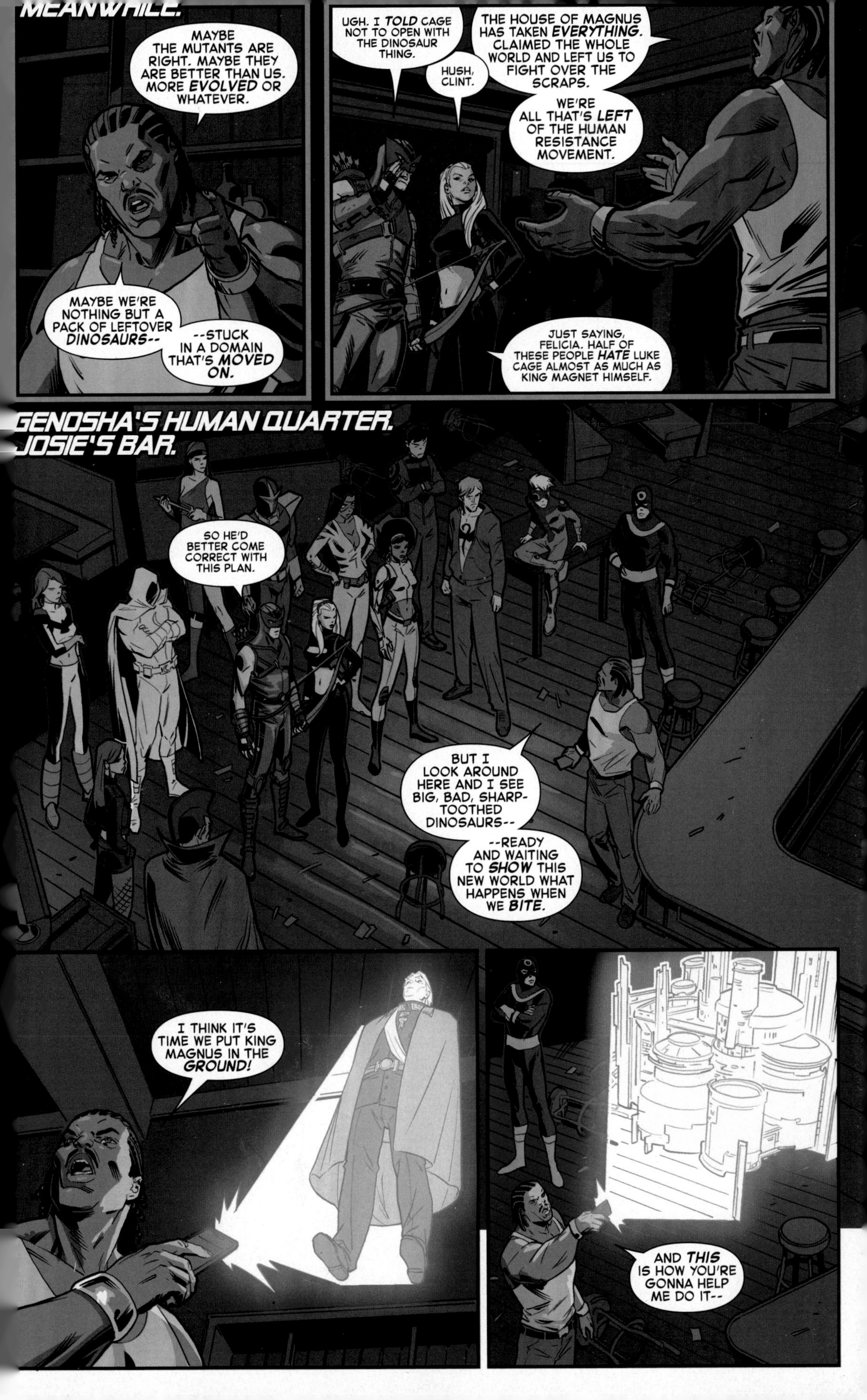
MEANWHILE:
MAYBE THE MUTANTS ARE RIGHT. MAYBE THEY ARE BETTER THAN US. MORE EVOLVED OR WHATEVER.
MAYBE WE'RE NOTHING BUT A PACK OF LEFTOVER DINOSAURS--
--STUCK IN A DOMAIN THAT'S MOVED ON.
UGH. I TOLD CAGE NOT TO OPEN WITH THE DINOSAUR THING.
HUSH, CLINT.
THE HOUSE OF MAGNUS HAS TAKEN EVERYTHING. CLAIMED THE WHOLE WORLD AND LEFT US TO FIGHT OVER THE SCRAPS.
WE'RE ALL THAT'S LEFT OF THE HUMAN RESISTANCE MOVEMENT.
JUST SAYING, FELICIA. HALF OF THESE PEOPLE HATE LUKE CAGE ALMOST AS MUCH AS KING MAGNET HIMSELF.
GENOSHA'S HUMAN QUARTER. JOSIE'S BAR.
SO HE'D BETTER COME CORRECT WITH THIS PLAN.
BUT I LOOK AROUND HERE AND I SEE BIG, BAD, SHARP-TOOTHED DINOSAURS--
--READY AND WAITING TO SHOW THIS NEW WORLD WHAT HAPPENS WHEN WE BITE.
I THINK IT'S TIME WE PUT KING MAGNUS IN THE GROUND!
AND THIS IS HOW YOU'RE GONNA HELP ME DO IT--

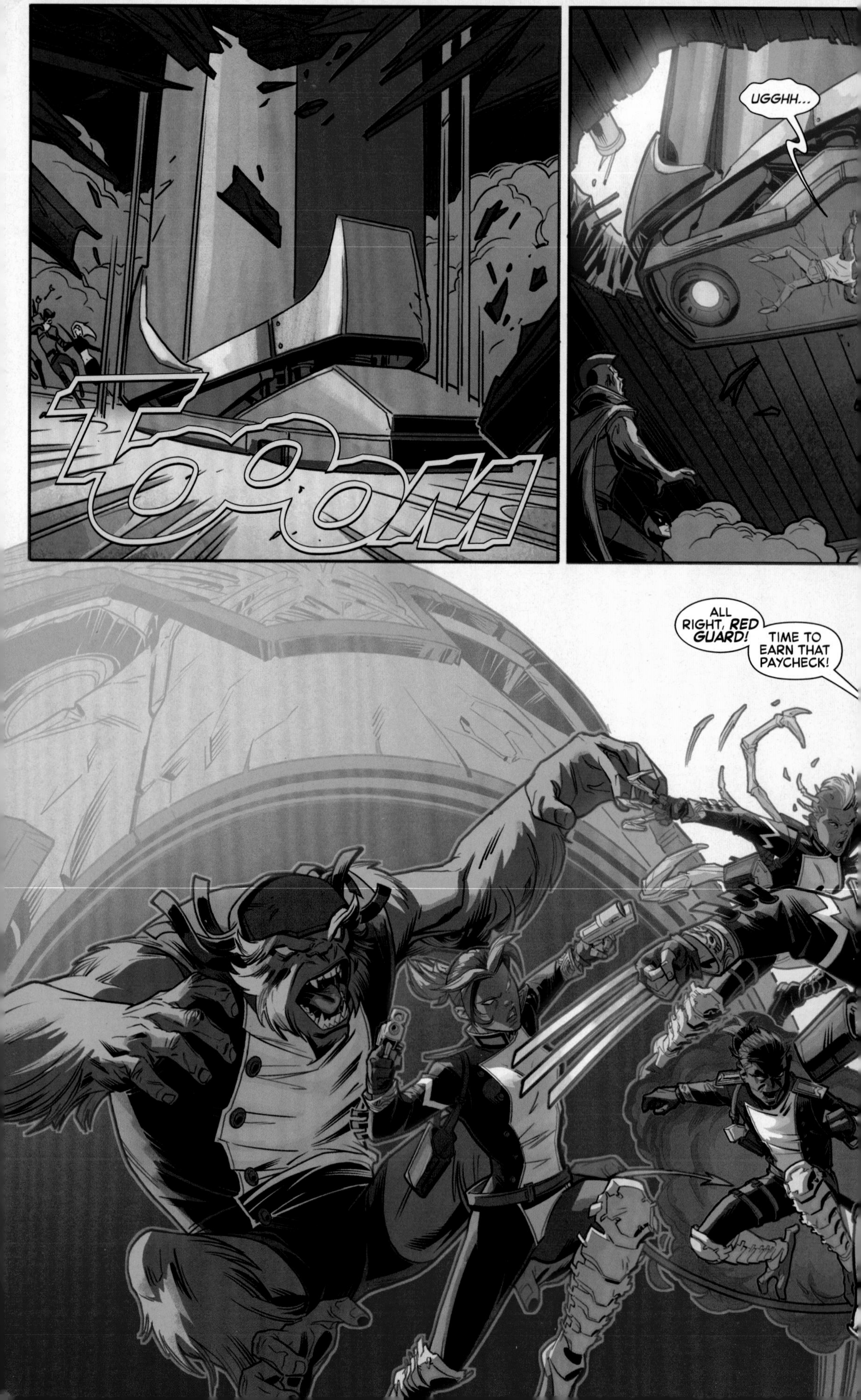

TOOOM
UGGHH...
ALL RIGHT, RED GUARD!
TIME TO EARN THAT PAYCHECK!

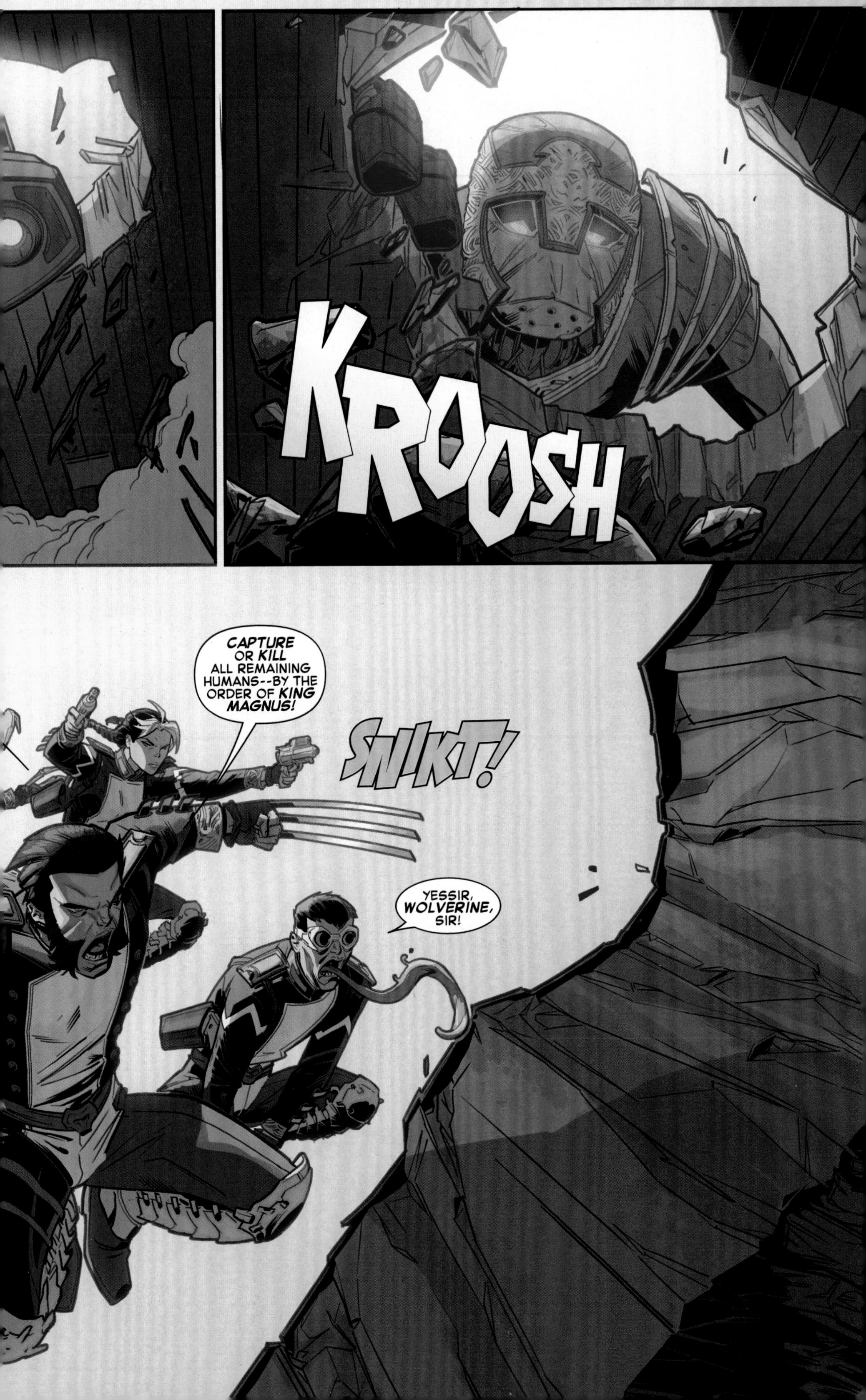
KROOSH
CAPTURE OR KILL ALL REMAINING HUMANS--BY THE ORDER OF KING MAGNUS!
SNIKT!
YESSIR, WOLVERINE, SIR!

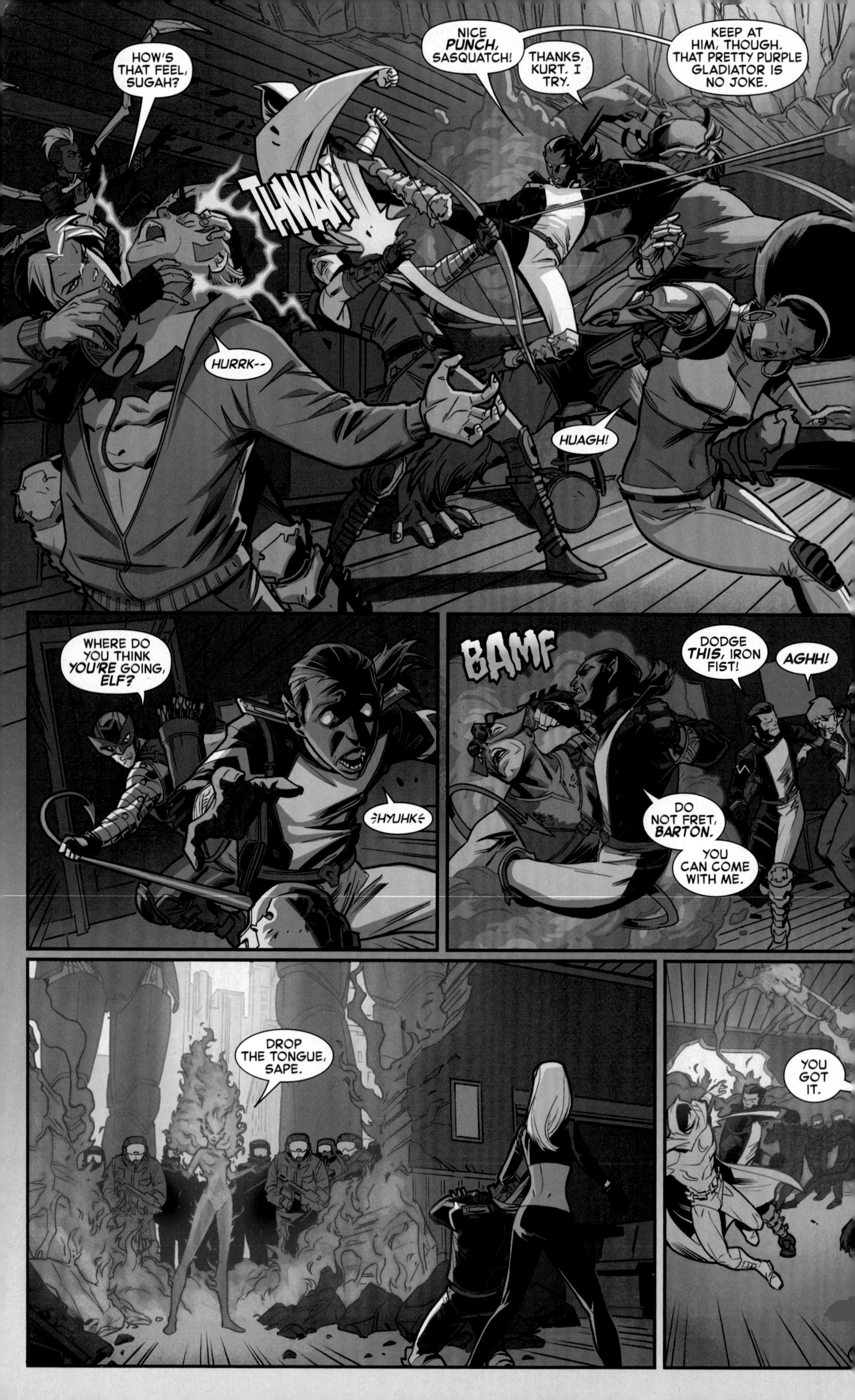
HOW'S THAT FEEL, SUGAH?
NICE PUNCH, SASQUATCH!
THANKS, KURT. I TRY.
KEEP AT HIM, THOUGH. THAT PRETTY PURPLE GLADIATOR IS NO JOKE.
THWAK!
HURRK--
HUAGH!
WHERE DO YOU THINK YOU'RE GOING, ELF?
HYUHK
BAMF
DODGE THIS, IRON FIST!
AGHH!
DO NOT FRET, BARTON.
YOU CAN COME WITH ME.
DROP THE TONGUE, SAPE.
YOU GOT IT.

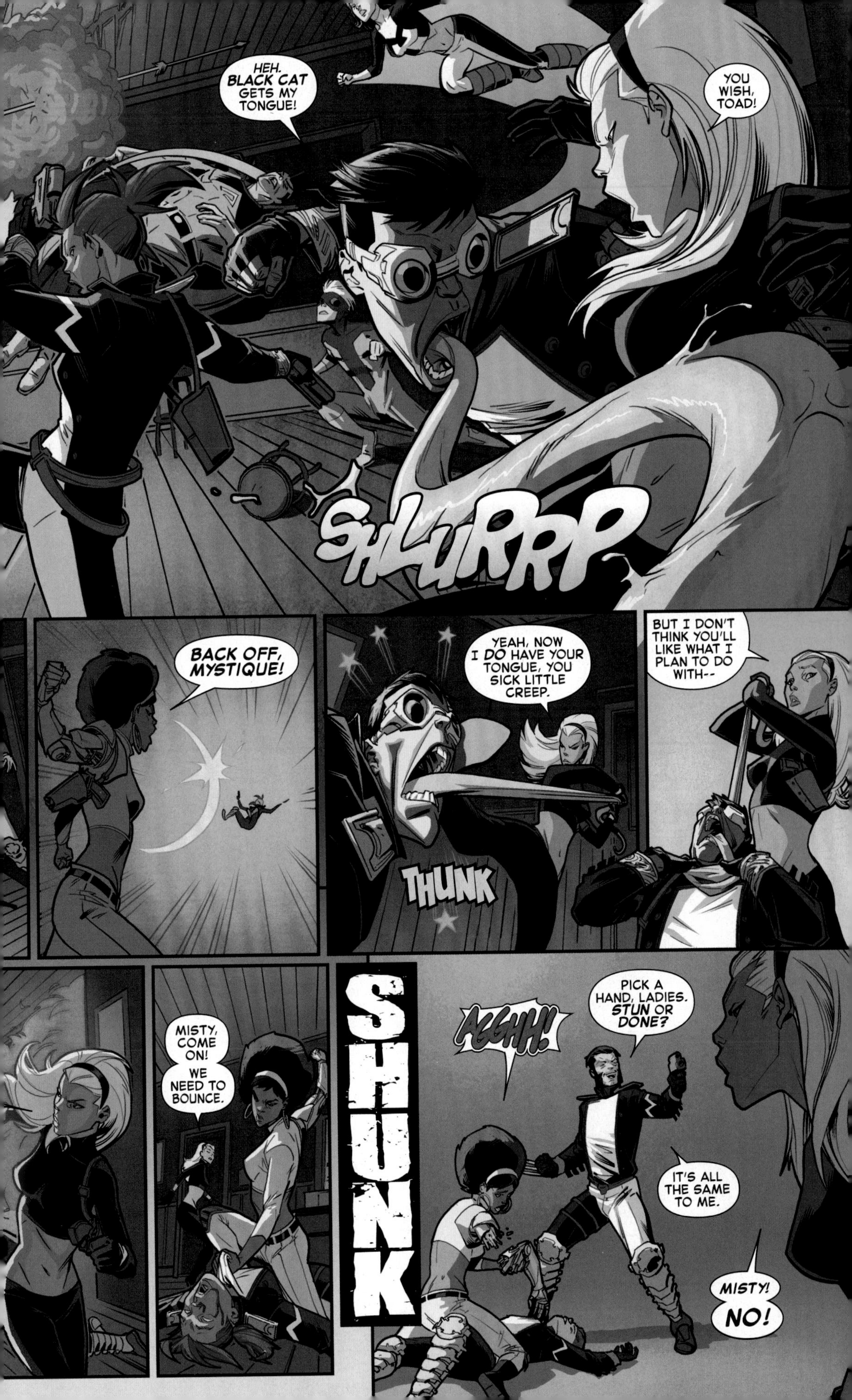
HEH. BLACK CAT GETS MY TONGUE!
YOU WISH, TOAD!
SHLURRP
BACK OFF, MYSTIQUE!
YEAH, NOW I DO HAVE YOUR TONGUE, YOU SICK LITTLE CREEP.
THUNK
BUT I DON'T THINK YOU'LL LIKE WHAT I PLAN TO DO WITH--
MISTY, COME ON!
WE NEED TO BOUNCE.
SHUNK
AGGHH!
PICK A HAND, LADIES. STUN OR DONE?
IT'S ALL THE SAME TO ME.
MISTY!
NO!

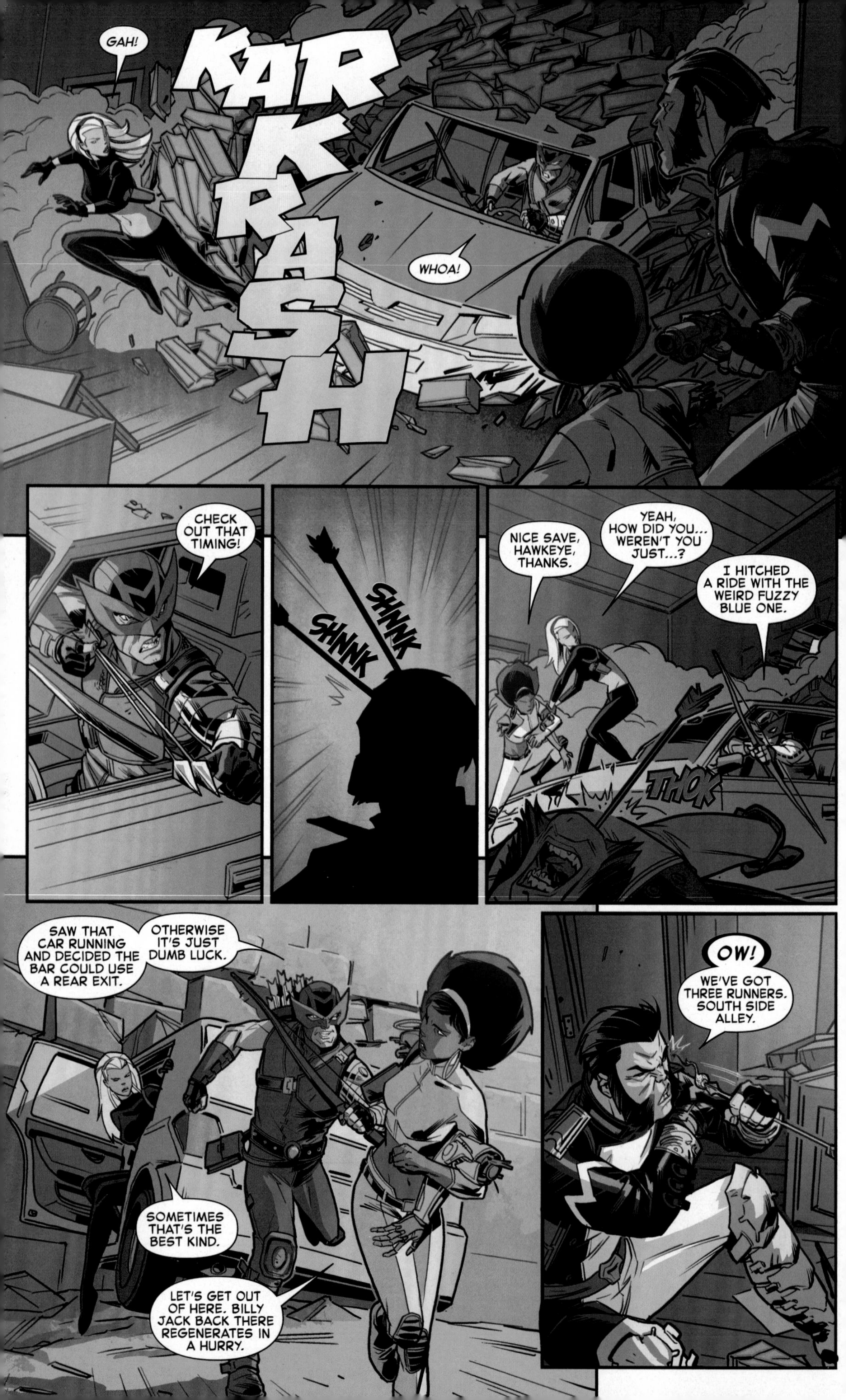
GAH!
KAR-KRASH
WHOA!
CHECK OUT THAT TIMING!
SHNNK
SHNNK
NICE SAVE, HAWKEYE, THANKS.
YEAH, HOW DID YOU... WEREN'T YOU JUST...?
I HITCHED A RIDE WITH THE WEIRD FUZZY BLUE ONE.
THOK
SAW THAT CAR RUNNING AND DECIDED THE BAR COULD USE A REAR EXIT.
OTHERWISE IT'S JUST DUMB LUCK.
SOMETIMES THAT'S THE BEST KIND.
LET'S GET OUT OF HERE. BILLY JACK BACK THERE REGENERATES IN A HURRY.
OW!
WE'VE GOT THREE RUNNERS. SOUTH SIDE ALLEY.

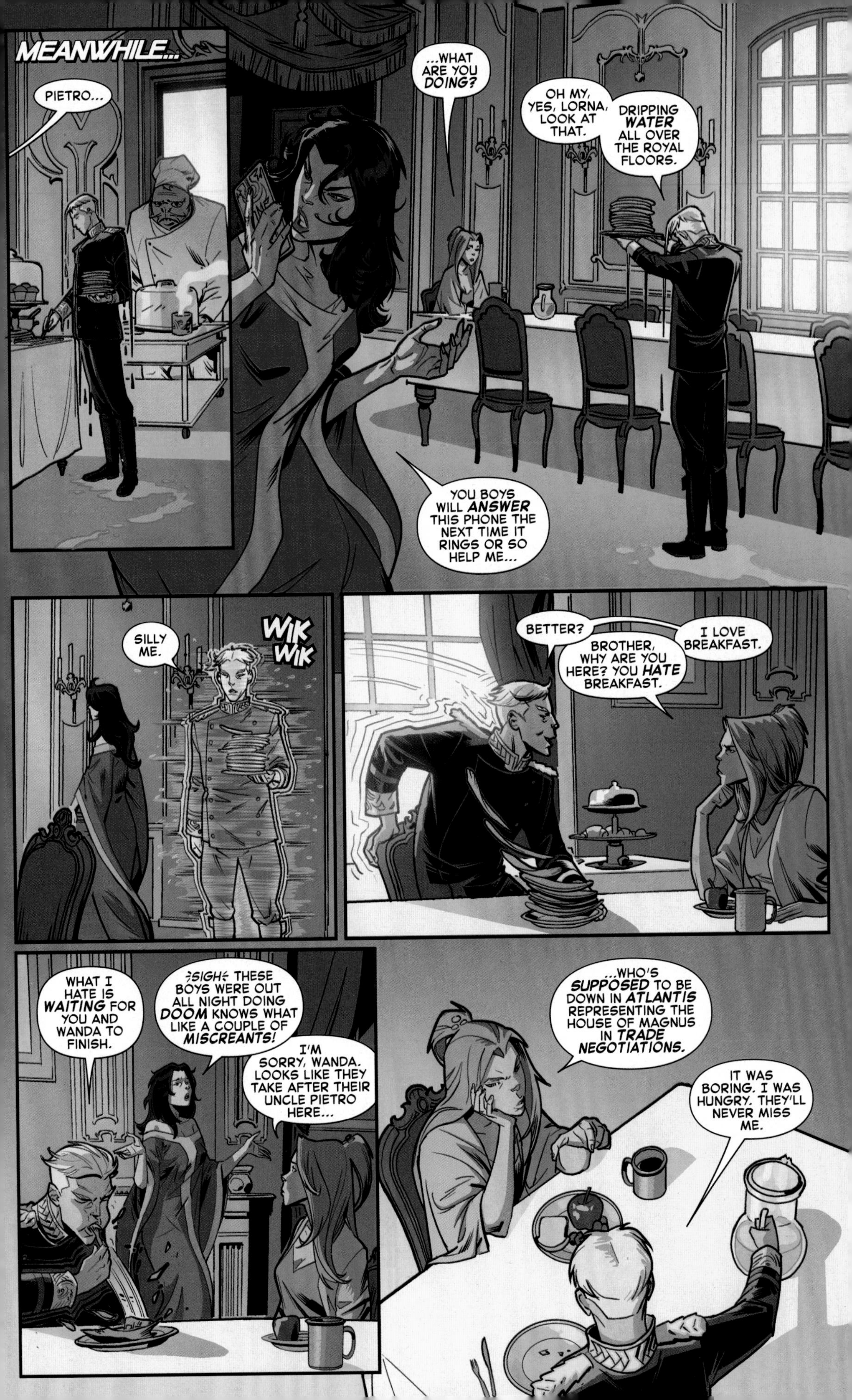
MEANWHILE...
PIETRO...
...WHAT ARE YOU DOING?
OH MY, YES, LORNA, LOOK AT THAT.
DRIPPING WATER ALL OVER THE ROYAL FLOORS.
YOU BOYS WILL ANSWER THIS PHONE THE NEXT TIME IT RINGS OR SO HELP ME...
SILLY ME.
WIK WIK
BETTER?
I LOVE BREAKFAST.
BROTHER, WHY ARE YOU HERE? YOU HATE BREAKFAST.
WHAT I HATE IS WAITING FOR YOU AND WANDA TO FINISH.
SIGH THESE BOYS WERE OUT ALL NIGHT DOING DOOM KNOWS WHAT LIKE A COUPLE OF MISCREANTS!
I'M SORRY, WANDA. LOOKS LIKE THEY TAKE AFTER THEIR UNCLE PIETRO HERE...
...WHO'S SUPPOSED TO BE DOWN IN ATLANTIS REPRESENTING THE HOUSE OF MAGNUS IN TRADE NEGOTIATIONS.
IT WAS BORING. I WAS HUNGRY. THEY'LL NEVER MISS ME.

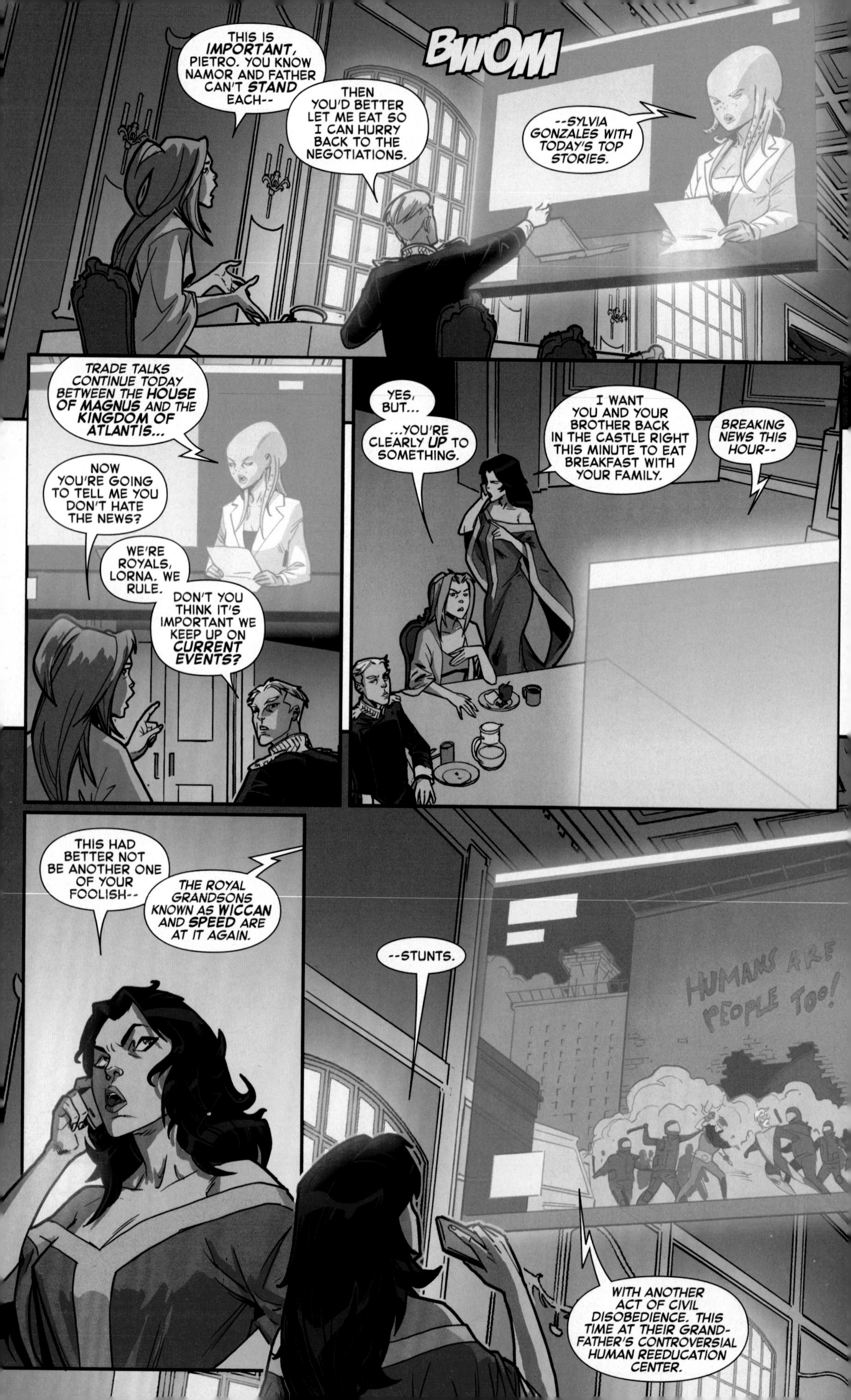
THIS IS IMPORTANT, PIETRO. YOU KNOW NAMOR AND FATHER CAN'T STAND EACH--
BWOM
THEN YOU'D BETTER LET ME EAT SO I CAN HURRY BACK TO THE NEGOTIATIONS.
--SYLVIA GONZALES WITH TODAY'S TOP STORIES.
TRADE TALKS CONTINUE TODAY BETWEEN THE HOUSE OF MAGNUS AND THE KINGDOM OF ATLANTIS...
NOW YOU'RE GOING TO TELL ME YOU DON'T HATE THE NEWS?
WE'RE ROYALS, LORNA. WE RULE.
DON'T YOU THINK IT'S IMPORTANT WE KEEP UP ON CURRENT EVENTS?
YES, BUT...
...YOU'RE CLEARLY UP TO SOMETHING.
I WANT YOU AND YOUR BROTHER BACK IN THE CASTLE RIGHT THIS MINUTE TO EAT BREAKFAST WITH YOUR FAMILY.
BREAKING NEWS THIS HOUR--
THIS HAD BETTER NOT BE ANOTHER ONE OF YOUR FOOLISH--
THE ROYAL GRANDSONS KNOWN AS WICCAN AND SPEED ARE AT IT AGAIN.
--STUNTS.
HUMANS ARE PEOPLE TOO!
WITH ANOTHER ACT OF CIVIL DISOBEDIENCE. THIS TIME AT THEIR GRAND-FATHER'S CONTROVERSIAL HUMAN REEDUCATION CENTER.

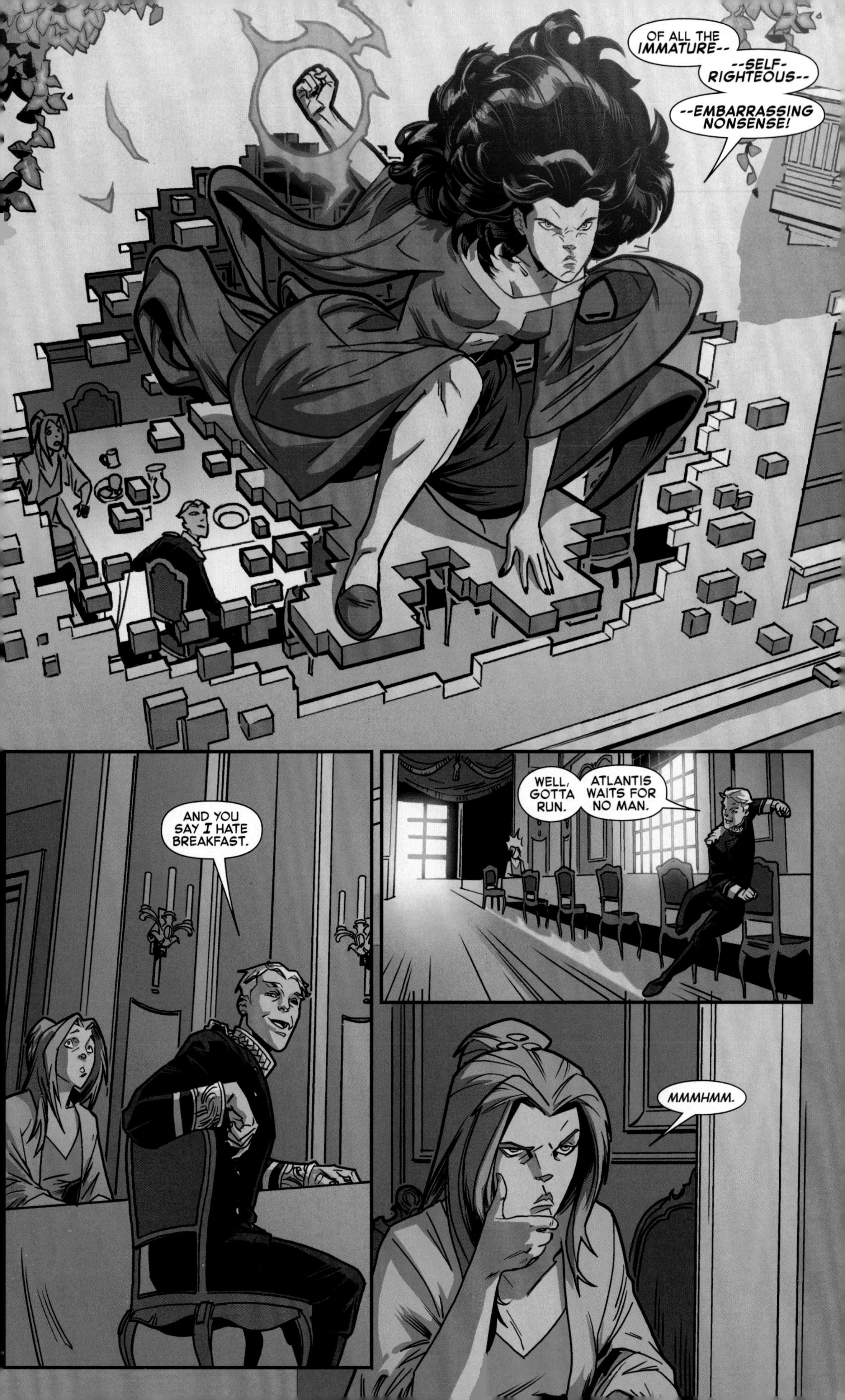
OF ALL THE IMMATURE--
--SELF-RIGHTEOUS--
--EMBARRASSING NONSENSE!
AND YOU SAY I HATE BREAKFAST.
WELL, GOTTA RUN.
ATLANTIS WAITS FOR NO MAN.
MMMHMM.

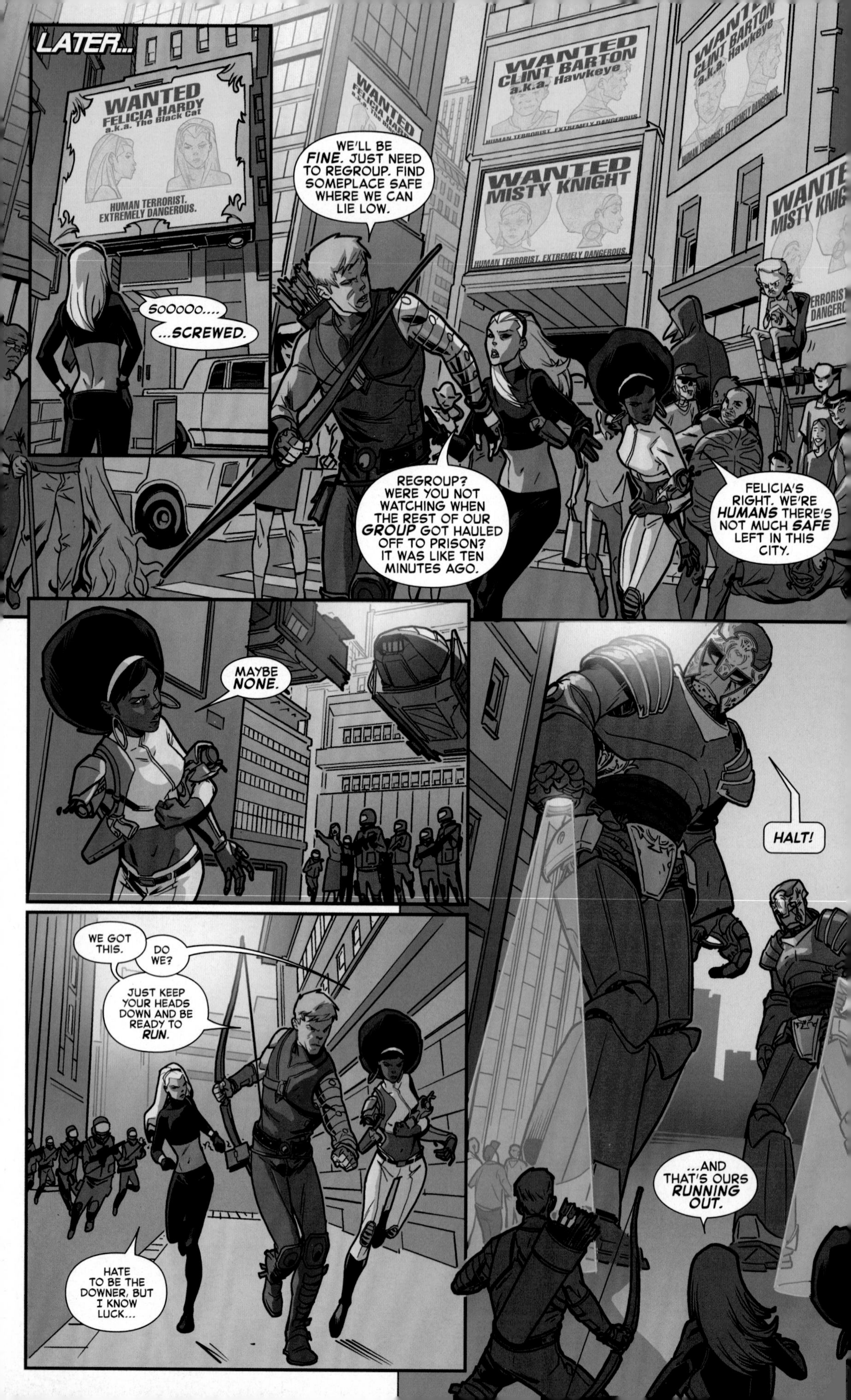
LATER...
WANTED
FELICIA HARDY
a.k.a. The Black Cat
HUMAN TERRORIST. EXTREMELY DANGEROUS.
SOOOOO....
...SCREWED.
WANTED
CLINT BARTON
a.k.a. Hawkeye
HUMAN TERRORIST. EXTREMELY DANGEROUS.
WANTED
MISTY KNIGHT
HUMAN TERRORIST. EXTREMELY DANGEROUS.
WE'LL BE FINE. JUST NEED TO REGROUP. FIND SOMEPLACE SAFE WHERE WE CAN LIE LOW.
REGROUP? WERE YOU NOT WATCHING WHEN THE REST OF OUR GROUP GOT HAULED OFF TO PRISON? IT WAS LIKE TEN MINUTES AGO.
FELICIA'S RIGHT. WE'RE HUMANS THERE'S NOT MUCH SAFE LEFT IN THIS CITY.
MAYBE NONE.
HALT!
WE GOT THIS.
DO WE?
JUST KEEP YOUR HEADS DOWN AND BE READY TO RUN.
HATE TO BE THE DOWNER, BUT I KNOW LUCK...
...AND THAT'S OURS RUNNING OUT.

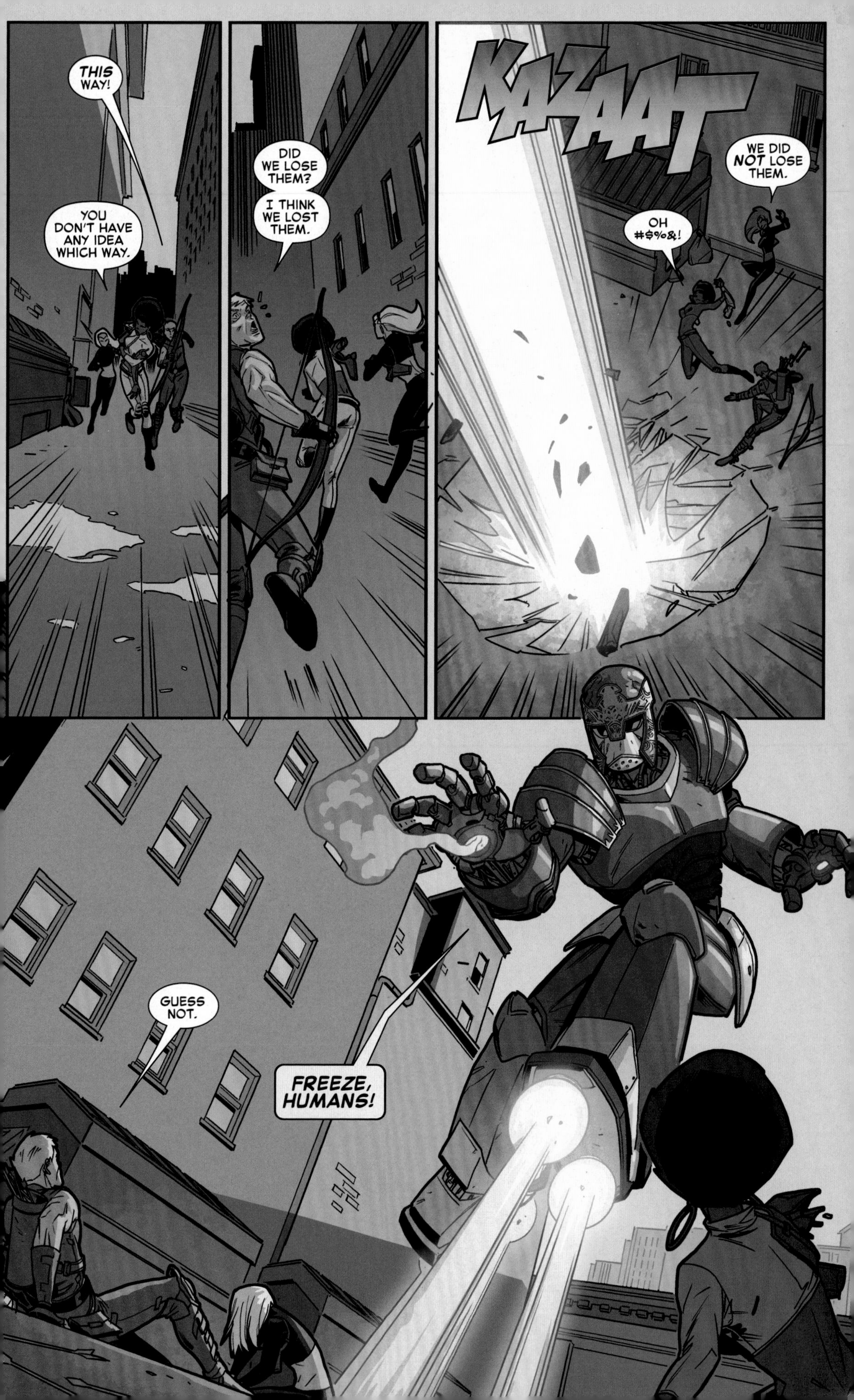
THIS WAY!
YOU DON'T HAVE ANY IDEA WHICH WAY.
DID WE LOSE THEM?
I THINK WE LOST THEM.
KAZAAAT
WE DID NOT LOSE THEM.
OH #$%&!
GUESS NOT.
FREEZE, HUMANS!

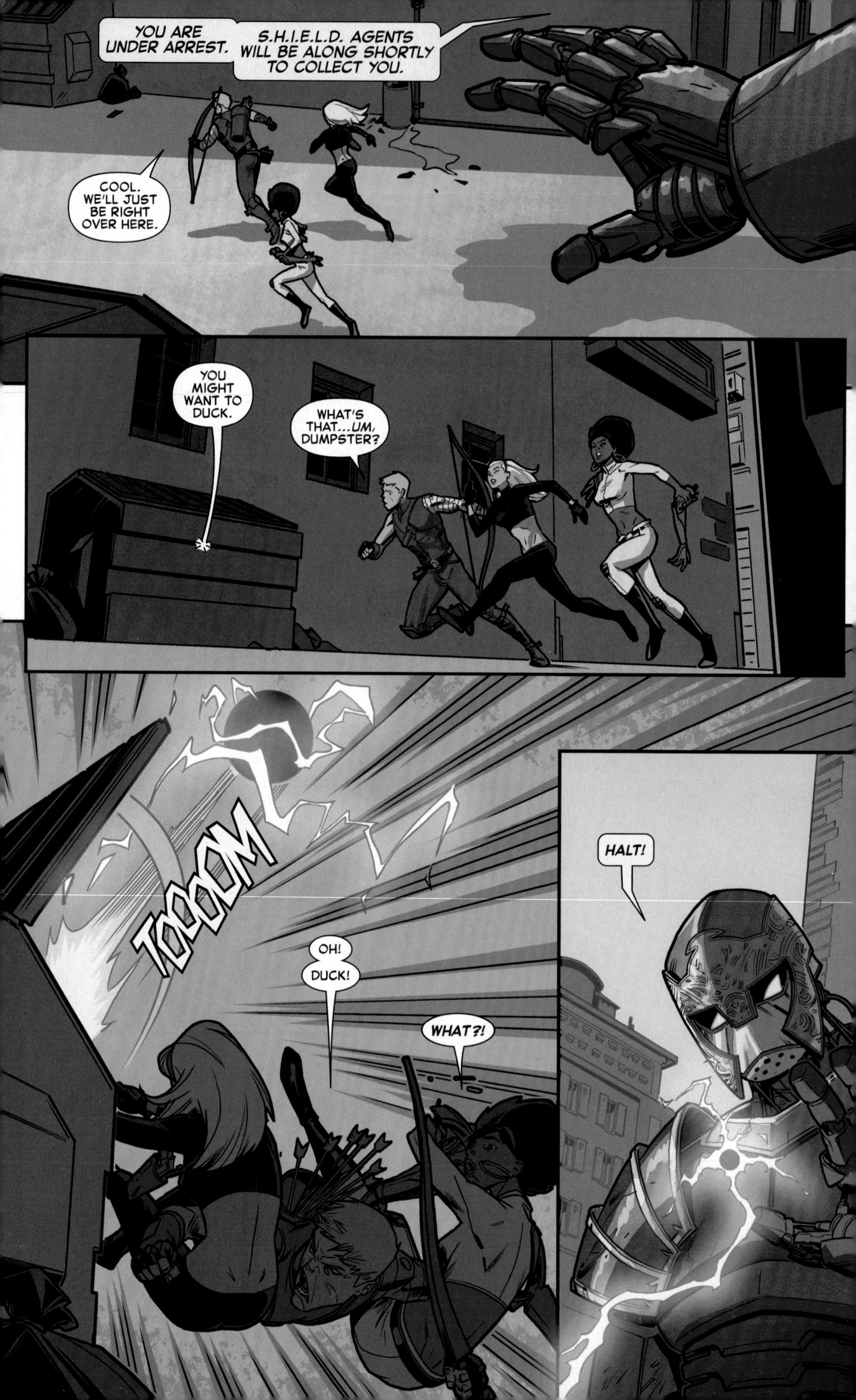
YOU ARE UNDER ARREST.
S.H.I.E.L.D. AGENTS WILL BE ALONG SHORTLY TO COLLECT YOU.
COOL. WE'LL JUST BE RIGHT OVER HERE.
YOU MIGHT WANT TO DUCK.
WHAT'S THAT...*UM,* DUMPSTER?
TOOOOM
OH! DUCK!
WHAT?!
HALT!

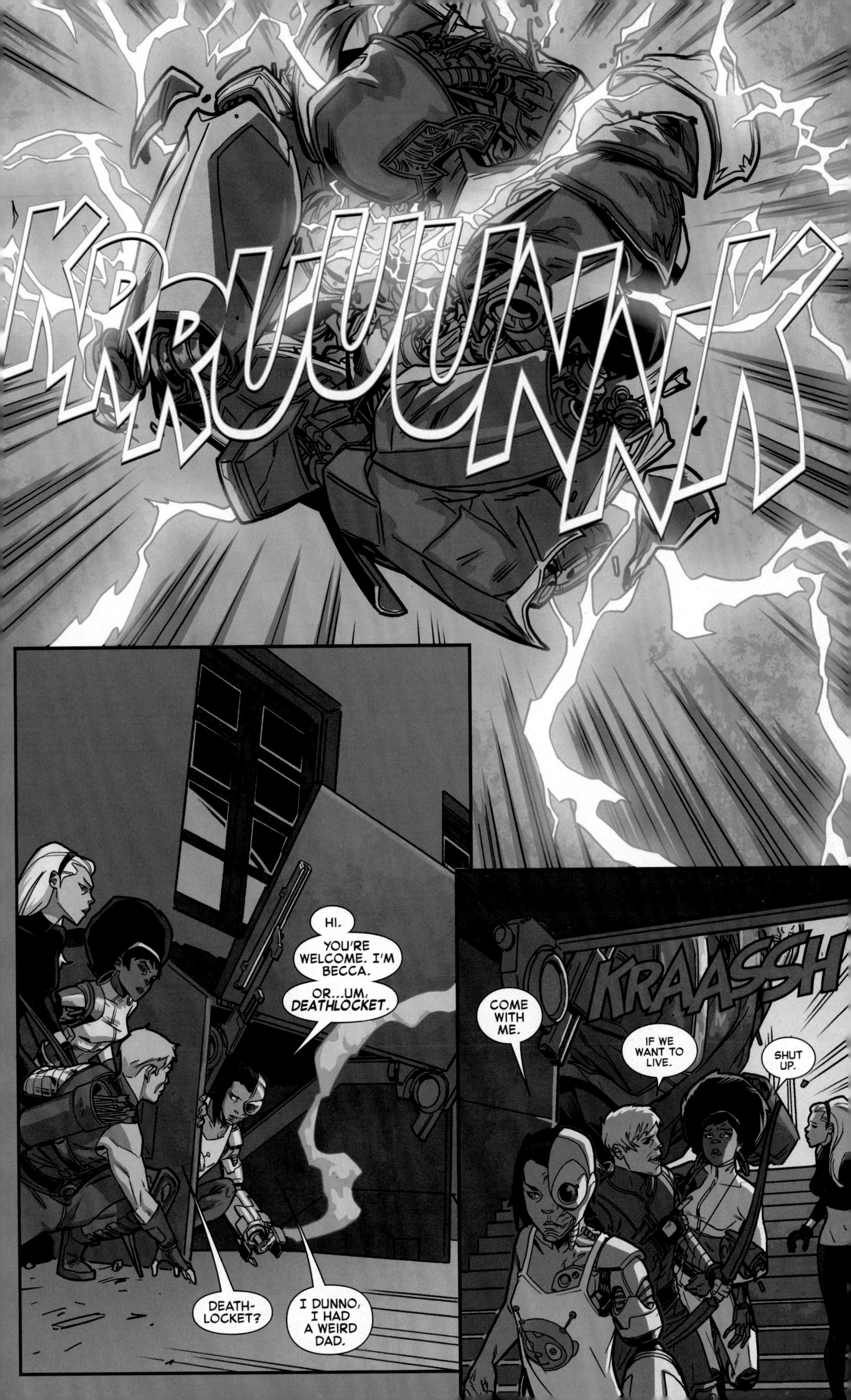
KRRUUUNNK
HI.
YOU'RE WELCOME. I'M BECCA.
OR...UM, DEATHLOCKET.
DEATH-LOCKET?
I DUNNO, I HAD A WEIRD DAD.
KRAASSH
COME WITH ME.
IF WE WANT TO LIVE.
SHUT UP.

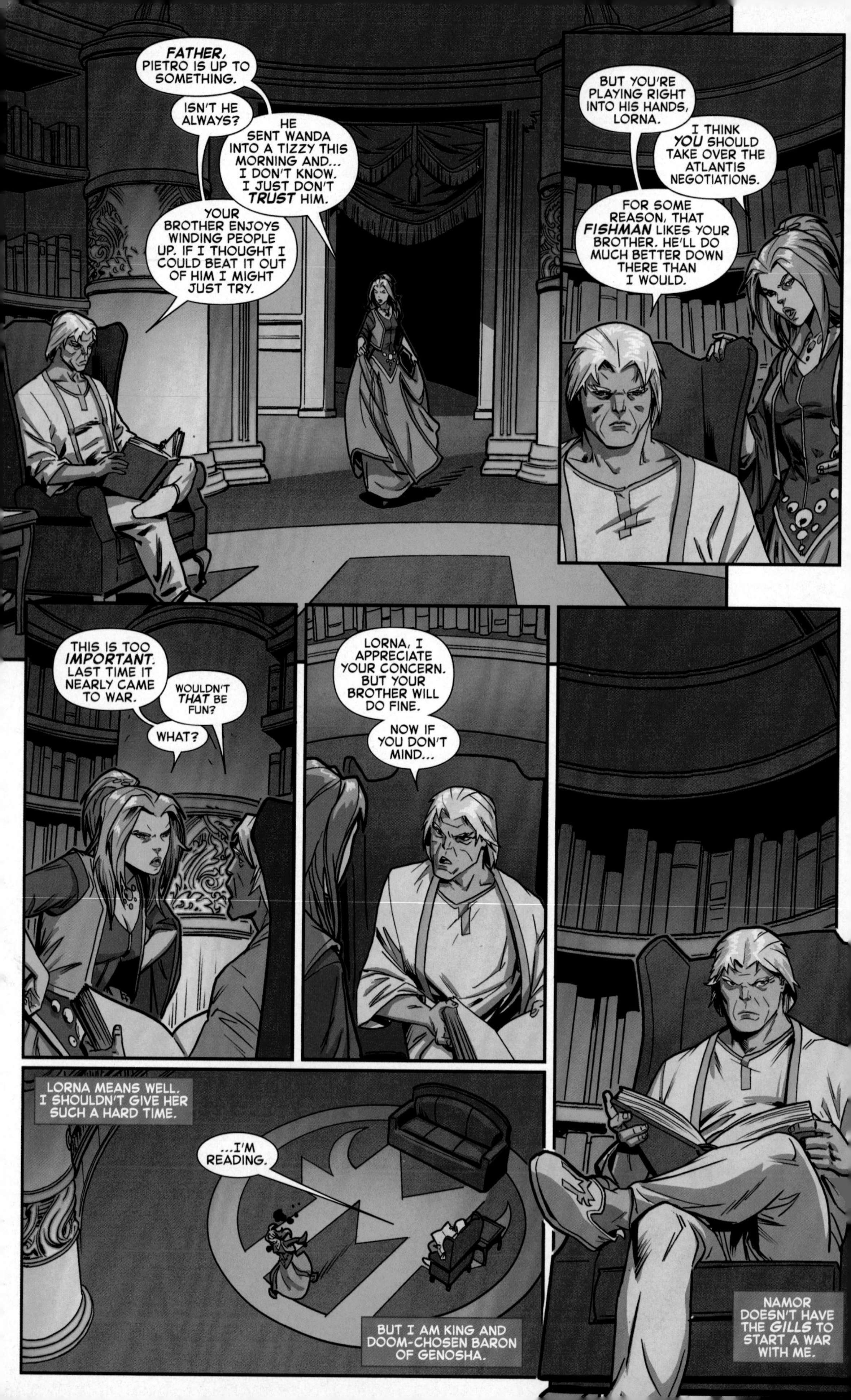
FATHER, PIETRO IS UP TO SOMETHING.
ISN'T HE ALWAYS?
HE SENT WANDA INTO A TIZZY THIS MORNING AND... I DON'T KNOW. I JUST DON'T TRUST HIM.
YOUR BROTHER ENJOYS WINDING PEOPLE UP. IF I THOUGHT I COULD BEAT IT OUT OF HIM I MIGHT JUST TRY.
BUT YOU'RE PLAYING RIGHT INTO HIS HANDS, LORNA.
I THINK YOU SHOULD TAKE OVER THE ATLANTIS NEGOTIATIONS.
FOR SOME REASON, THAT FISHMAN LIKES YOUR BROTHER. HE'LL DO MUCH BETTER DOWN THERE THAN I WOULD.
THIS IS TOO IMPORTANT. LAST TIME IT NEARLY CAME TO WAR.
WOULDN'T THAT BE FUN?
WHAT?
LORNA, I APPRECIATE YOUR CONCERN. BUT YOUR BROTHER WILL DO FINE.
NOW IF YOU DON'T MIND...
LORNA MEANS WELL. I SHOULDN'T GIVE HER SUCH A HARD TIME.
...I'M READING.
BUT I AM KING AND DOOM-CHOSEN BARON OF GENOSHA.
NAMOR DOESN'T HAVE THE GILLS TO START A WAR WITH ME.

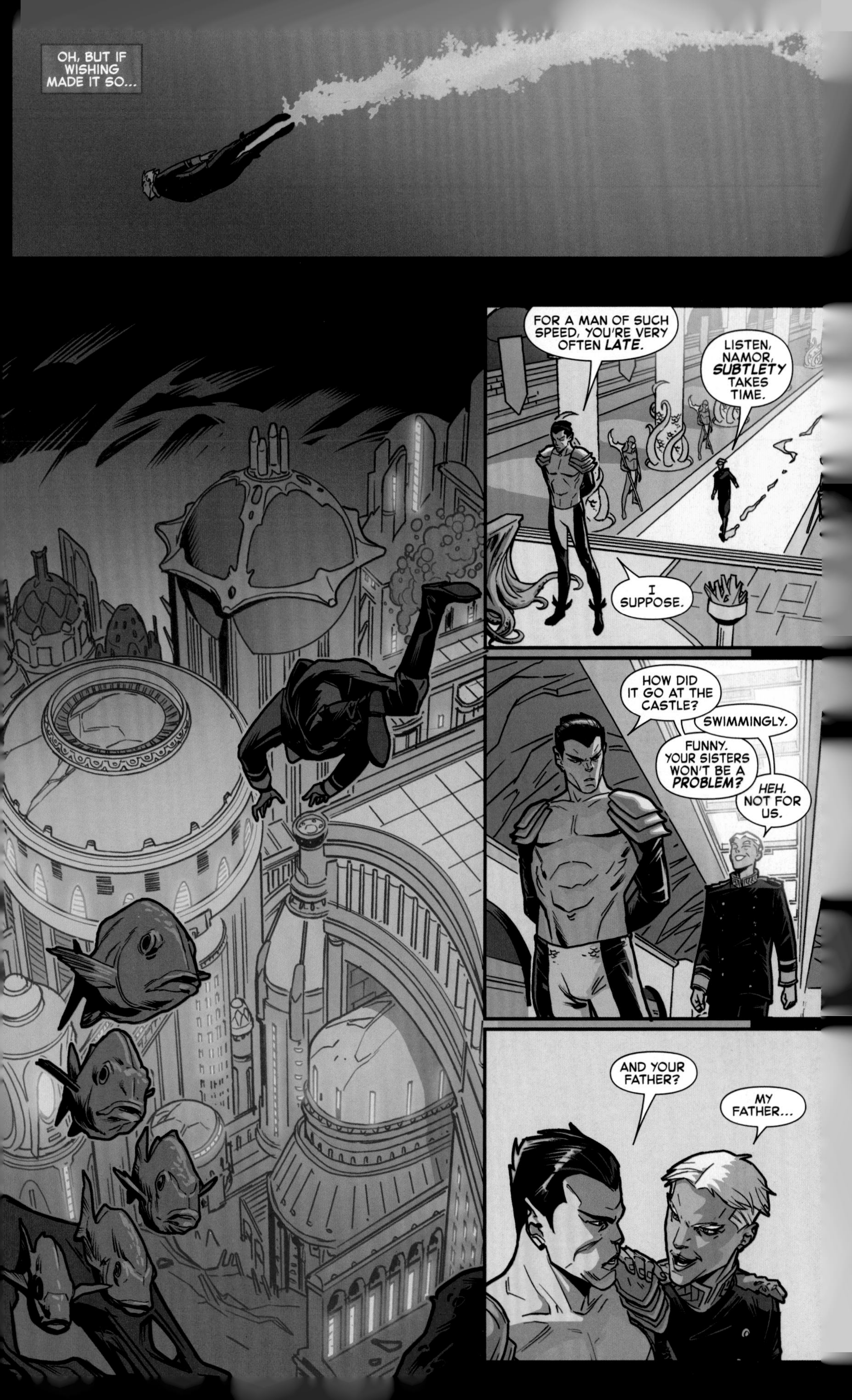
OH, BUT IF WISHING MADE IT SO...
FOR A MAN OF SUCH SPEED, YOU'RE VERY OFTEN LATE.
LISTEN, NAMOR, SUBTLETY TAKES TIME.
I SUPPOSE.
HOW DID IT GO AT THE CASTLE?
SWIMMINGLY.
FUNNY. YOUR SISTERS WON'T BE A PROBLEM?
HEH. NOT FOR US.
AND YOUR FATHER?
MY FATHER...

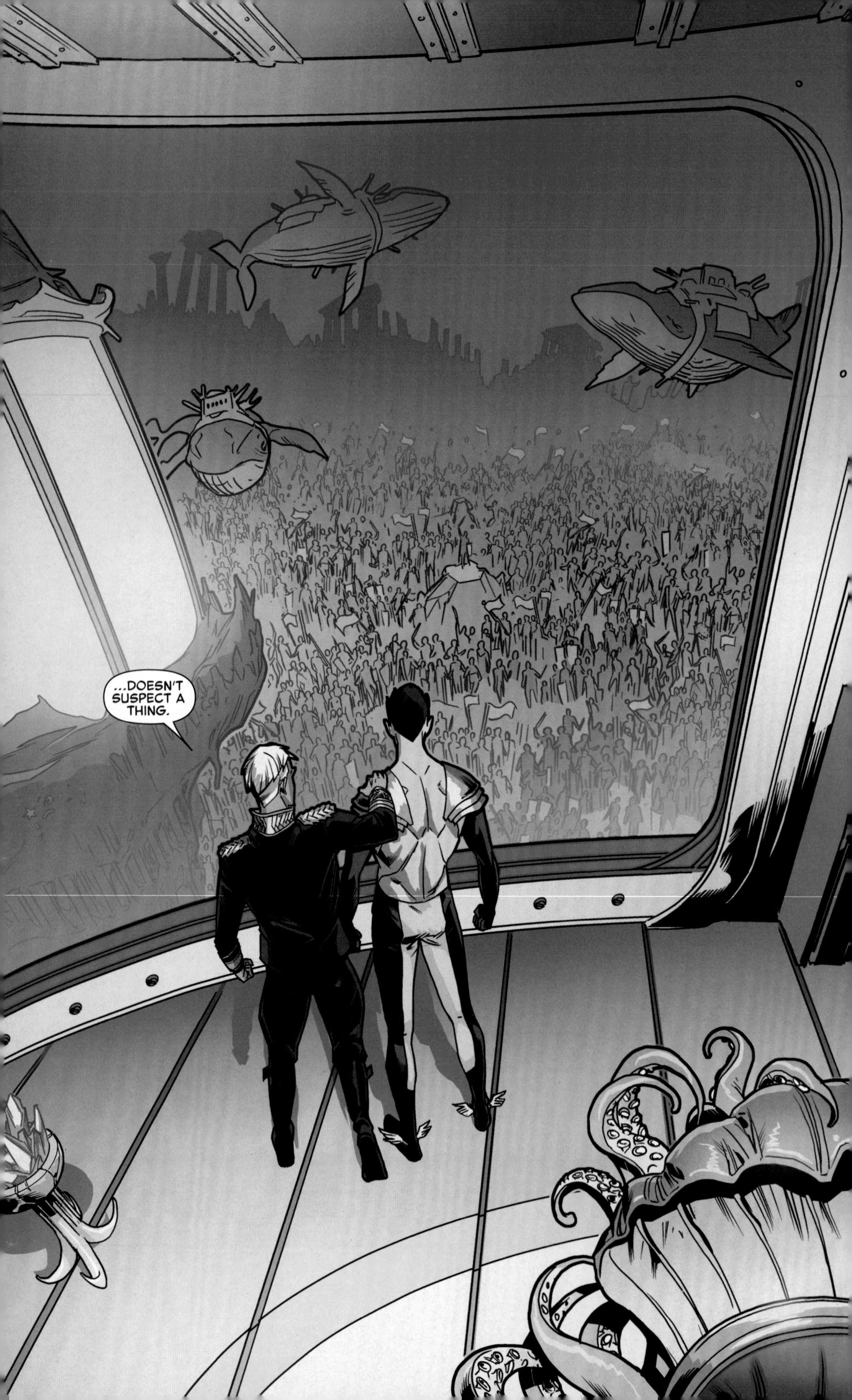
...DOESN'T SUSPECT A THING.

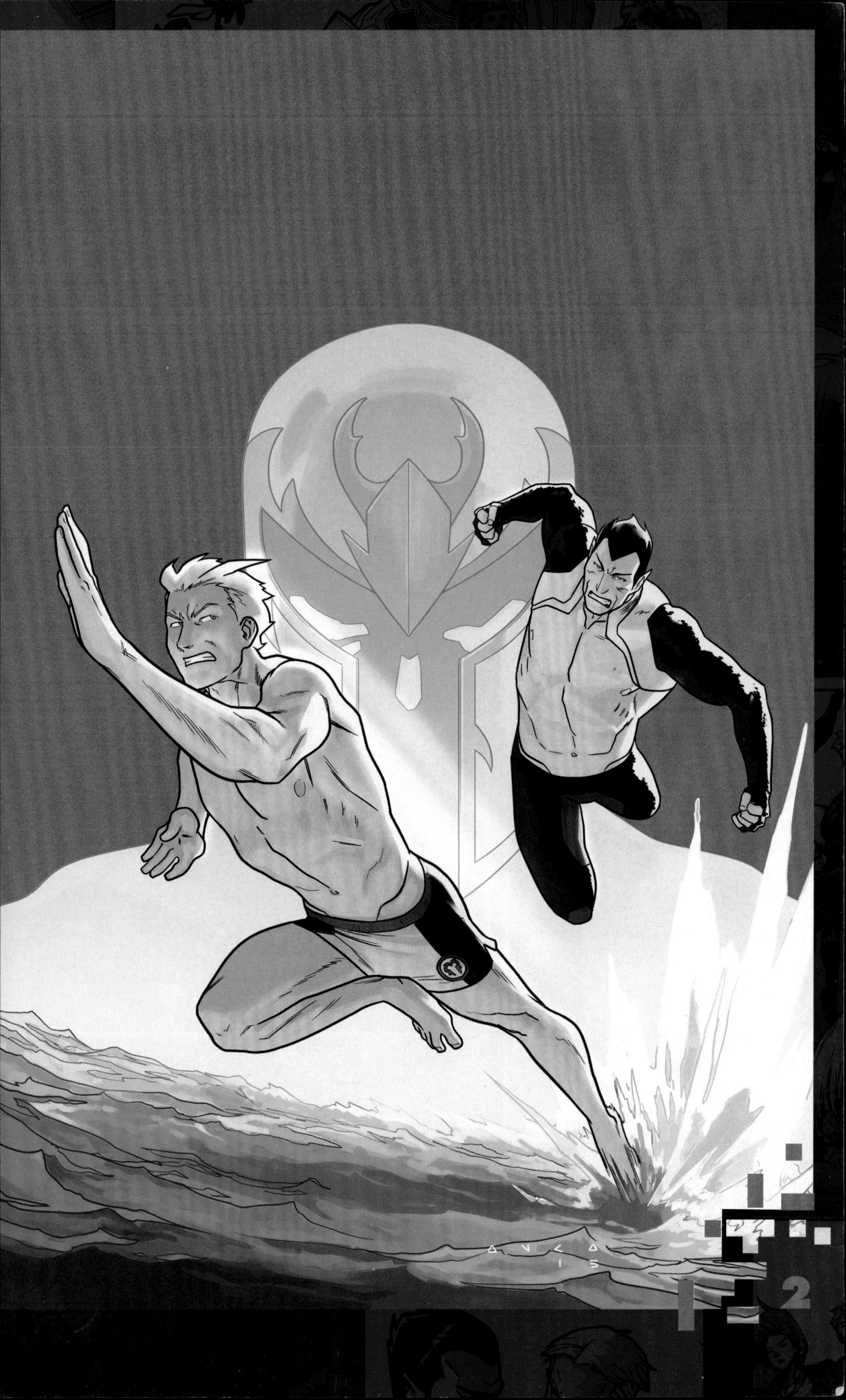
2

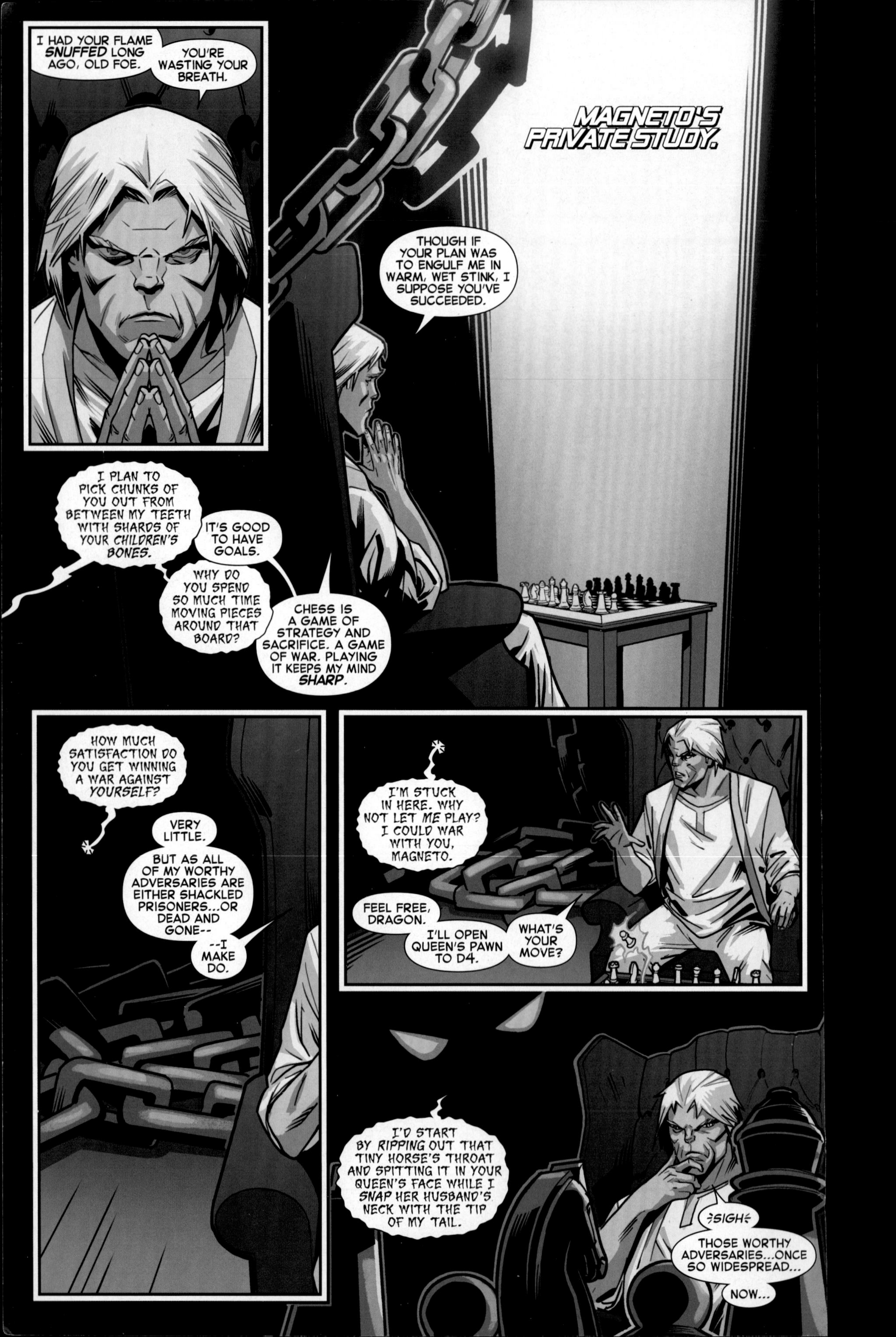
I HAD YOUR FLAME SNUFFED LONG AGO, OLD FOE.
YOU'RE WASTING YOUR BREATH.
MAGNETO'S PRIVATE STUDY.
THOUGH IF YOUR PLAN WAS TO ENGULF ME IN WARM, WET STINK, I SUPPOSE YOU'VE SUCCEEDED.
I PLAN TO PICK CHUNKS OF YOU OUT FROM BETWEEN MY TEETH WITH SHARDS OF YOUR CHILDREN'S BONES.
IT'S GOOD TO HAVE GOALS.
WHY DO YOU SPEND SO MUCH TIME MOVING PIECES AROUND THAT BOARD?
CHESS IS A GAME OF STRATEGY AND SACRIFICE. A GAME OF WAR. PLAYING IT KEEPS MY MIND SHARP.
HOW MUCH SATISFACTION DO YOU GET WINNING A WAR AGAINST YOURSELF?
VERY LITTLE.
BUT AS ALL OF MY WORTHY ADVERSARIES ARE EITHER SHACKLED PRISONERS...OR DEAD AND GONE--
--I MAKE DO.
I'M STUCK IN HERE. WHY NOT LET ME PLAY? I COULD WAR WITH YOU, MAGNETO.
FEEL FREE, DRAGON.
I'LL OPEN QUEEN'S PAWN TO D4.
WHAT'S YOUR MOVE?
I'D START BY RIPPING OUT THAT TINY HORSE'S THROAT AND SPITTING IT IN YOUR QUEEN'S FACE WHILE I SNAP HER HUSBAND'S NECK WITH THE TIP OF MY TAIL.
SIGH
THOSE WORTHY ADVERSARIES...ONCE SO WIDESPREAD...
NOW...

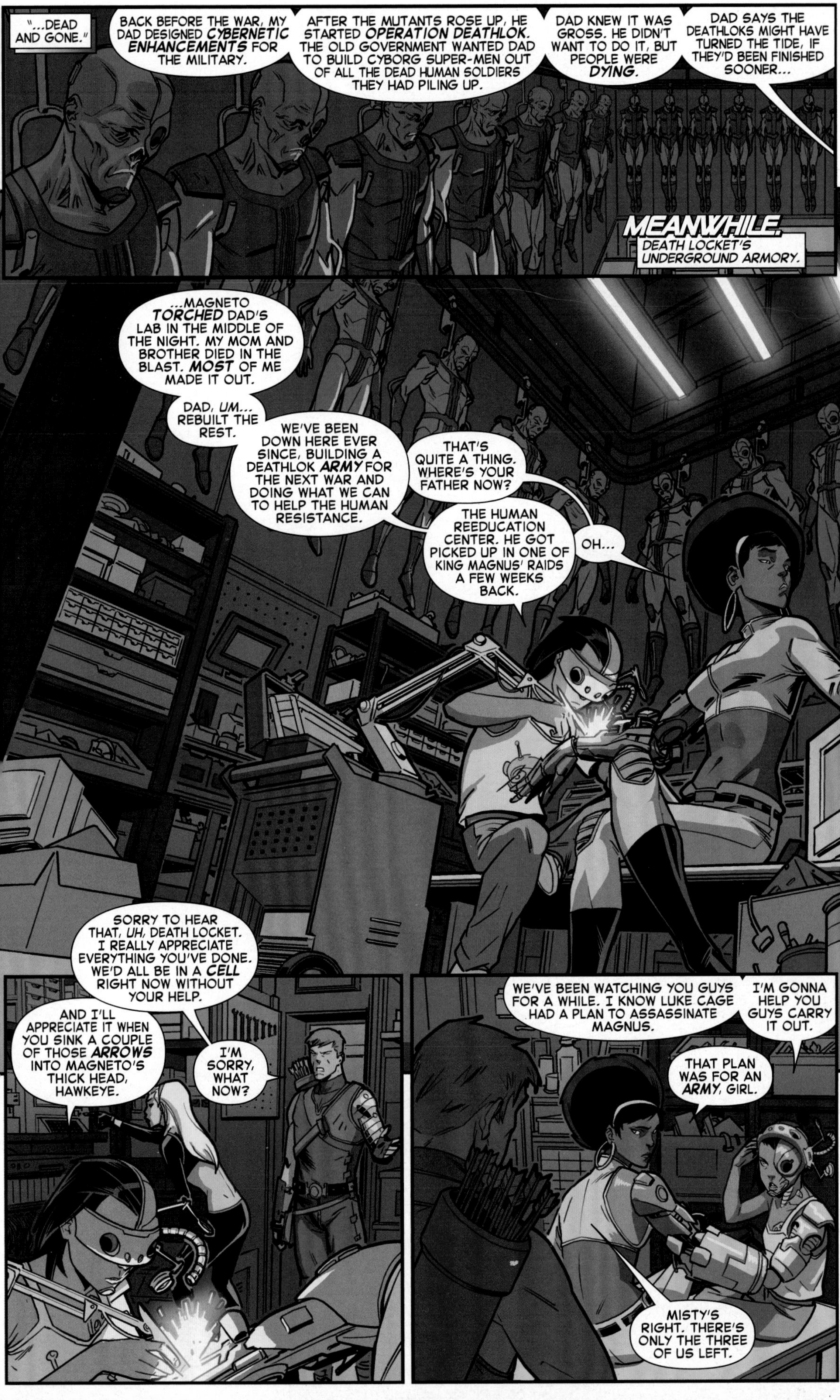
"...DEAD AND GONE."
BACK BEFORE THE WAR, MY DAD DESIGNED CYBERNETIC ENHANCEMENTS FOR THE MILITARY.
AFTER THE MUTANTS ROSE UP, HE STARTED OPERATION DEATHLOK. THE OLD GOVERNMENT WANTED DAD TO BUILD CYBORG SUPER-MEN OUT OF ALL THE DEAD HUMAN SOLDIERS THEY HAD PILING UP.
DAD KNEW IT WAS GROSS. HE DIDN'T WANT TO DO IT, BUT PEOPLE WERE DYING.
DAD SAYS THE DEATHLOKS MIGHT HAVE TURNED THE TIDE, IF THEY'D BEEN FINISHED SOONER...
MEANWHILE.
DEATH LOCKET'S UNDERGROUND ARMORY.
...MAGNETO TORCHED DAD'S LAB IN THE MIDDLE OF THE NIGHT. MY MOM AND BROTHER DIED IN THE BLAST. MOST OF ME MADE IT OUT.
DAD, UM... REBUILT THE REST.
WE'VE BEEN DOWN HERE EVER SINCE, BUILDING A DEATHLOK ARMY FOR THE NEXT WAR AND DOING WHAT WE CAN TO HELP THE HUMAN RESISTANCE.
THAT'S QUITE A THING. WHERE'S YOUR FATHER NOW?
THE HUMAN REEDUCATION CENTER. HE GOT PICKED UP IN ONE OF KING MAGNUS' RAIDS A FEW WEEKS BACK.
OH...
SORRY TO HEAR THAT, UH, DEATH LOCKET. I REALLY APPRECIATE EVERYTHING YOU'VE DONE. WE'D ALL BE IN A CELL RIGHT NOW WITHOUT YOUR HELP.
AND I'LL APPRECIATE IT WHEN YOU SINK A COUPLE OF THOSE ARROWS INTO MAGNETO'S THICK HEAD, HAWKEYE.
I'M SORRY, WHAT NOW?
WE'VE BEEN WATCHING YOU GUYS FOR A WHILE. I KNOW LUKE CAGE HAD A PLAN TO ASSASSINATE MAGNUS.
I'M GONNA HELP YOU GUYS CARRY IT OUT.
THAT PLAN WAS FOR AN ARMY, GIRL.
MISTY'S RIGHT. THERE'S ONLY THE THREE OF US LEFT.

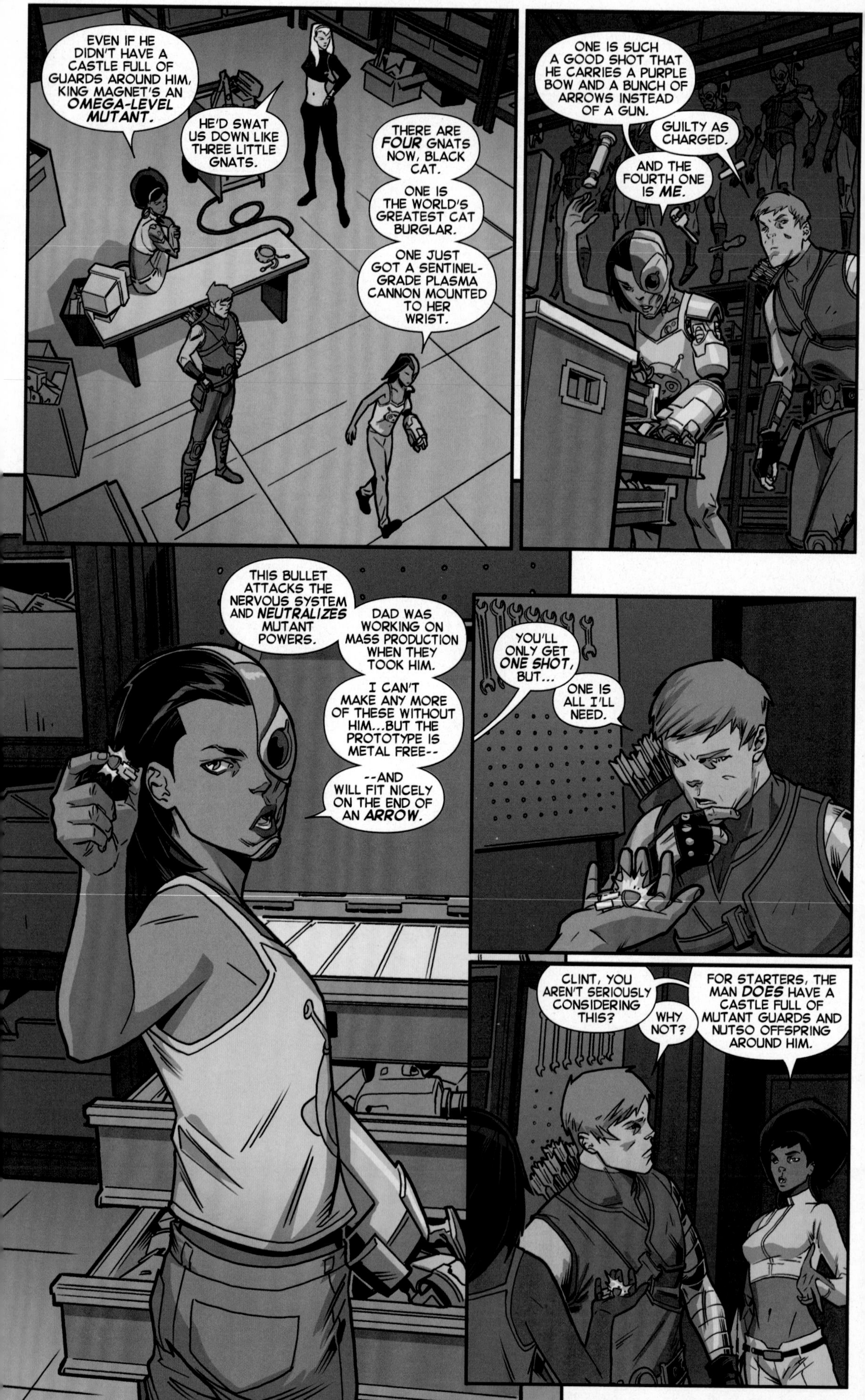
EVEN IF HE DIDN'T HAVE A CASTLE FULL OF GUARDS AROUND HIM, KING MAGNET'S AN *OMEGA-LEVEL MUTANT.*
HE'D SWAT US DOWN LIKE THREE LITTLE GNATS.
THERE ARE *FOUR* GNATS NOW, BLACK CAT.
ONE IS THE WORLD'S GREATEST CAT BURGLAR.
ONE JUST GOT A SENTINEL-GRADE PLASMA CANNON MOUNTED TO HER WRIST.
ONE IS SUCH A GOOD SHOT THAT HE CARRIES A PURPLE BOW AND A BUNCH OF ARROWS INSTEAD OF A GUN.
GUILTY AS CHARGED.
AND THE FOURTH ONE IS *ME.*
THIS BULLET ATTACKS THE NERVOUS SYSTEM AND *NEUTRALIZES* MUTANT POWERS.
DAD WAS WORKING ON MASS PRODUCTION WHEN THEY TOOK HIM.
I CAN'T MAKE ANY MORE OF THESE WITHOUT HIM...BUT THE PROTOTYPE IS METAL FREE--
--AND WILL FIT NICELY ON THE END OF AN *ARROW.*
YOU'LL ONLY GET *ONE SHOT,* BUT...
ONE IS ALL I'LL NEED.
CLINT, YOU AREN'T SERIOUSLY CONSIDERING THIS?
WHY NOT?
FOR STARTERS, THE MAN *DOES* HAVE A CASTLE FULL OF MUTANT GUARDS AND NUTSO OFFSPRING AROUND HIM.

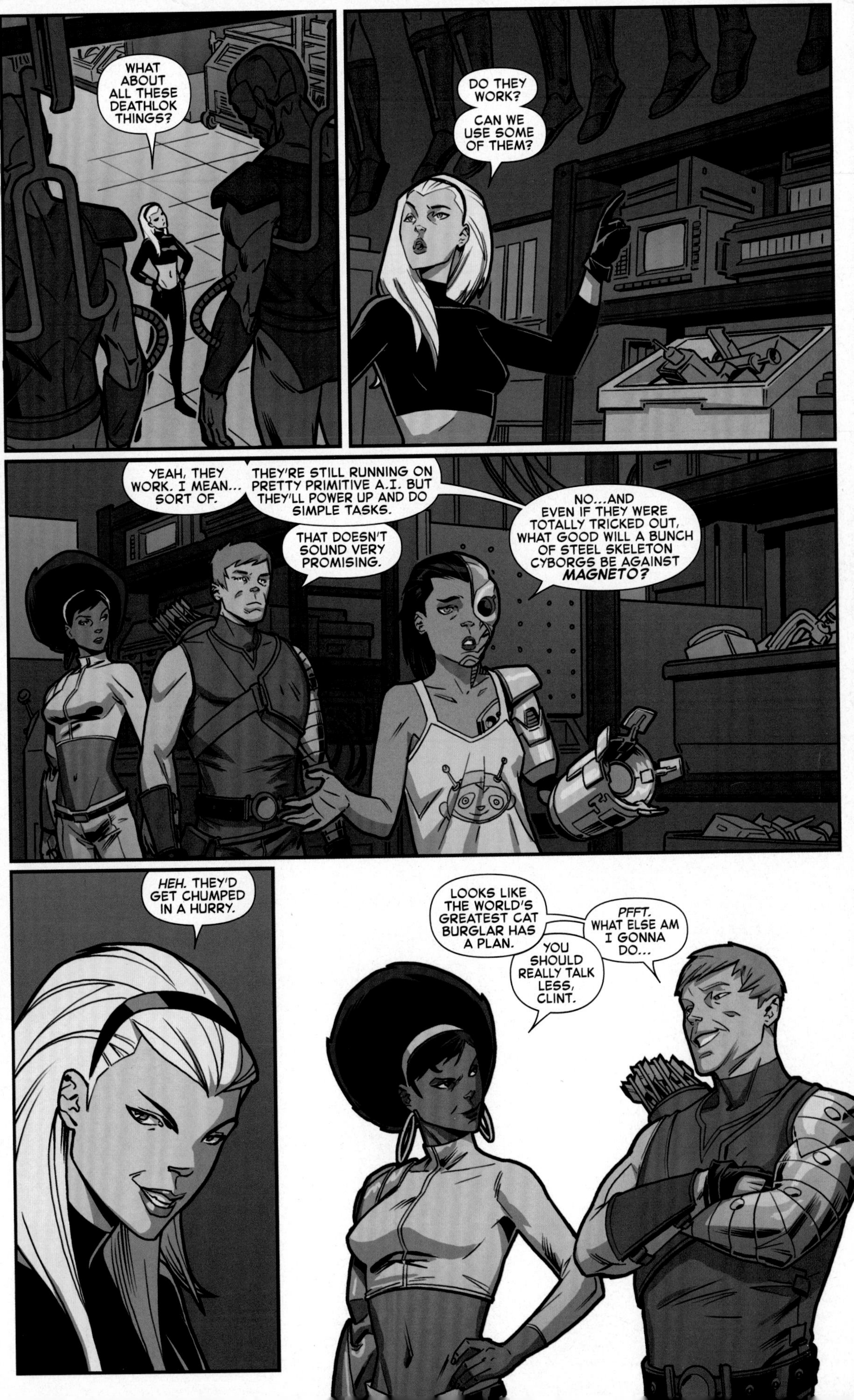
WHAT ABOUT ALL THESE DEATHLOK THINGS?
DO THEY WORK?
CAN WE USE SOME OF THEM?
YEAH, THEY WORK. I MEAN... SORT OF.
THEY'RE STILL RUNNING ON PRETTY PRIMITIVE A.I. BUT THEY'LL POWER UP AND DO SIMPLE TASKS.
THAT DOESN'T SOUND VERY PROMISING.
NO...AND EVEN IF THEY WERE TOTALLY TRICKED OUT, WHAT GOOD WILL A BUNCH OF STEEL SKELETON CYBORGS BE AGAINST MAGNETO?
HEH. THEY'D GET CHUMPED IN A HURRY.
LOOKS LIKE THE WORLD'S GREATEST CAT BURGLAR HAS A PLAN.
PFFT. WHAT ELSE AM I GONNA DO...
YOU SHOULD REALLY TALK LESS, CLINT.

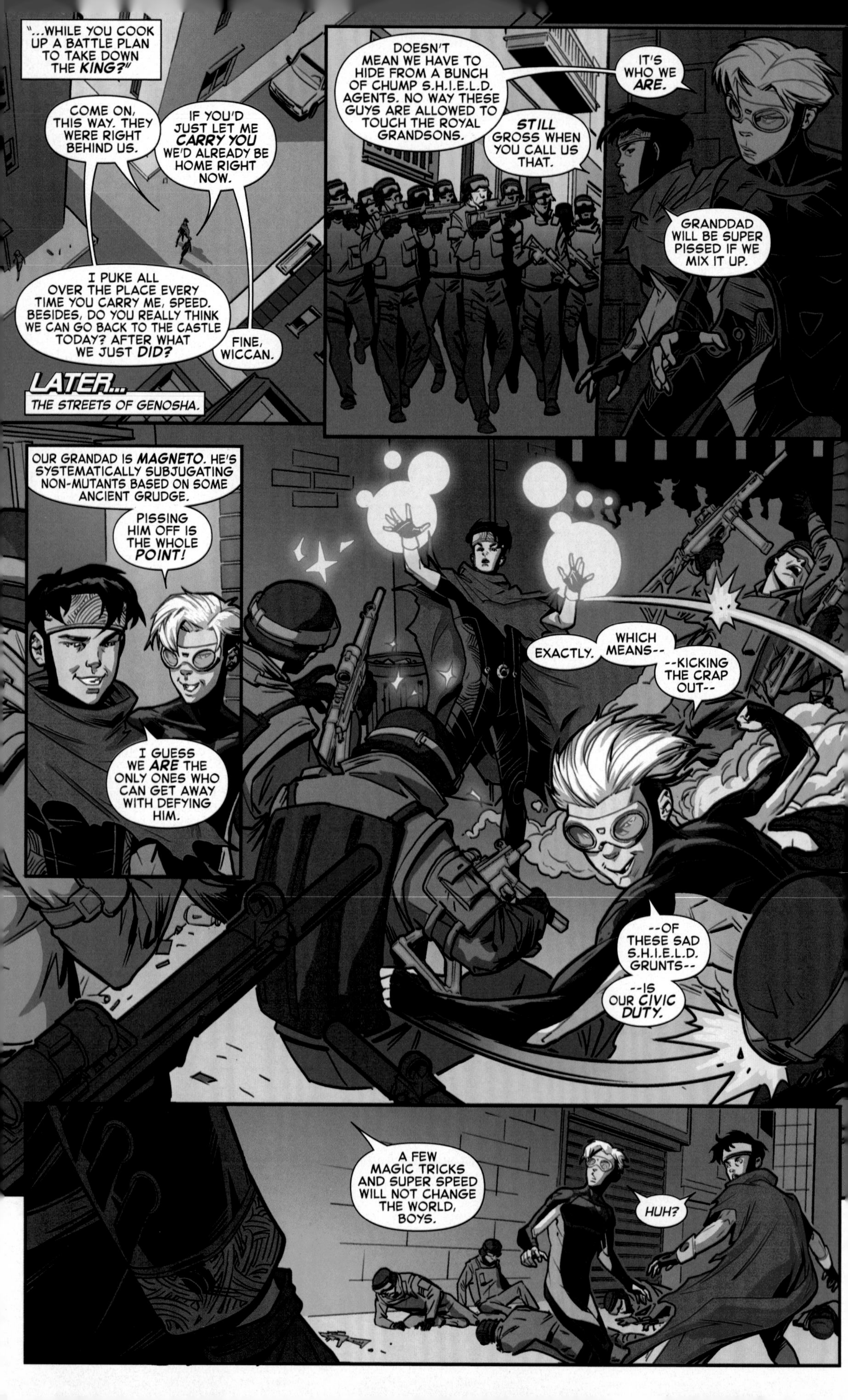
"...WHILE YOU COOK UP A BATTLE PLAN TO TAKE DOWN THE KING?"
COME ON, THIS WAY. THEY WERE RIGHT BEHIND US.
IF YOU'D JUST LET ME CARRY YOU WE'D ALREADY BE HOME RIGHT NOW.
I PUKE ALL OVER THE PLACE EVERY TIME YOU CARRY ME, SPEED. BESIDES, DO YOU REALLY THINK WE CAN GO BACK TO THE CASTLE TODAY? AFTER WHAT WE JUST DID?
FINE, WICCAN.
LATER...
THE STREETS OF GENOSHA.
DOESN'T MEAN WE HAVE TO HIDE FROM A BUNCH OF CHUMP S.H.I.E.L.D. AGENTS. NO WAY THESE GUYS ARE ALLOWED TO TOUCH THE ROYAL GRANDSONS.
IT'S WHO WE ARE.
STILL GROSS WHEN YOU CALL US THAT.
GRANDDAD WILL BE SUPER PISSED IF WE MIX IT UP.
OUR GRANDAD IS MAGNETO. HE'S SYSTEMATICALLY SUBJUGATING NON-MUTANTS BASED ON SOME ANCIENT GRUDGE.
PISSING HIM OFF IS THE WHOLE POINT!
I GUESS WE ARE THE ONLY ONES WHO CAN GET AWAY WITH DEFYING HIM.
EXACTLY.
WHICH MEANS--
--KICKING THE CRAP OUT--
--OF THESE SAD S.H.I.E.L.D. GRUNTS--
--IS OUR CIVIC DUTY.
A FEW MAGIC TRICKS AND SUPER SPEED WILL NOT CHANGE THE WORLD, BOYS.
HUH?

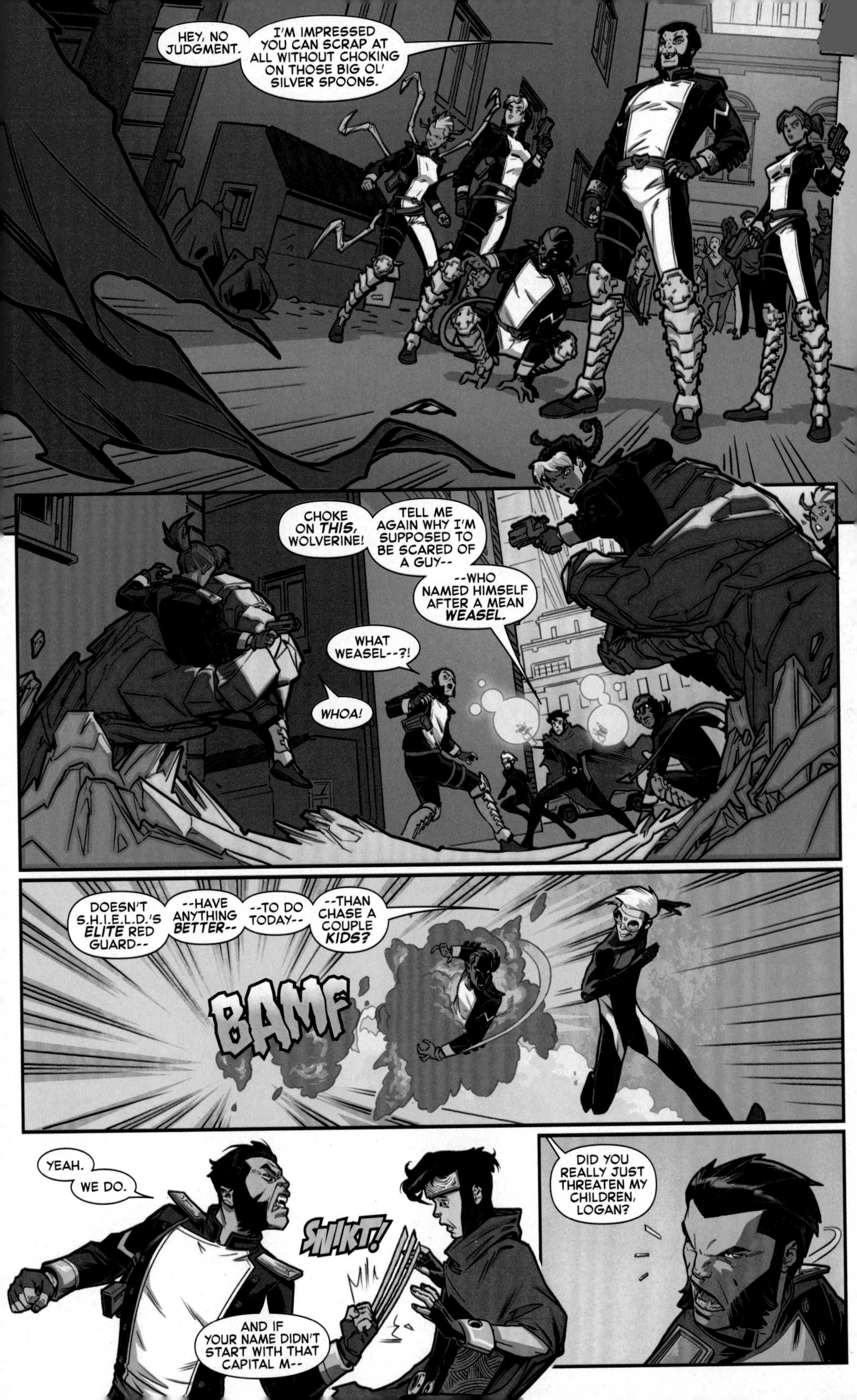
HEY, NO JUDGMENT.
I'M IMPRESSED YOU CAN SCRAP AT ALL WITHOUT CHOKING ON THOSE BIG OL' SILVER SPOONS.
CHOKE ON THIS, WOLVERINE!
TELL ME AGAIN WHY I'M SUPPOSED TO BE SCARED OF A GUY--
--WHO NAMED HIMSELF AFTER A MEAN WEASEL.
WHAT WEASEL--?!
WHOA!
DOESN'T S.H.I.E.L.D.'S ELITE RED GUARD--
--HAVE ANYTHING BETTER--
--TO DO TODAY--
--THAN CHASE A COUPLE KIDS?
BAMF
YEAH.
WE DO.
SNIKT!
AND IF YOUR NAME DIDN'T START WITH THAT CAPITAL M--
DID YOU REALLY JUST THREATEN MY CHILDREN, LOGAN?

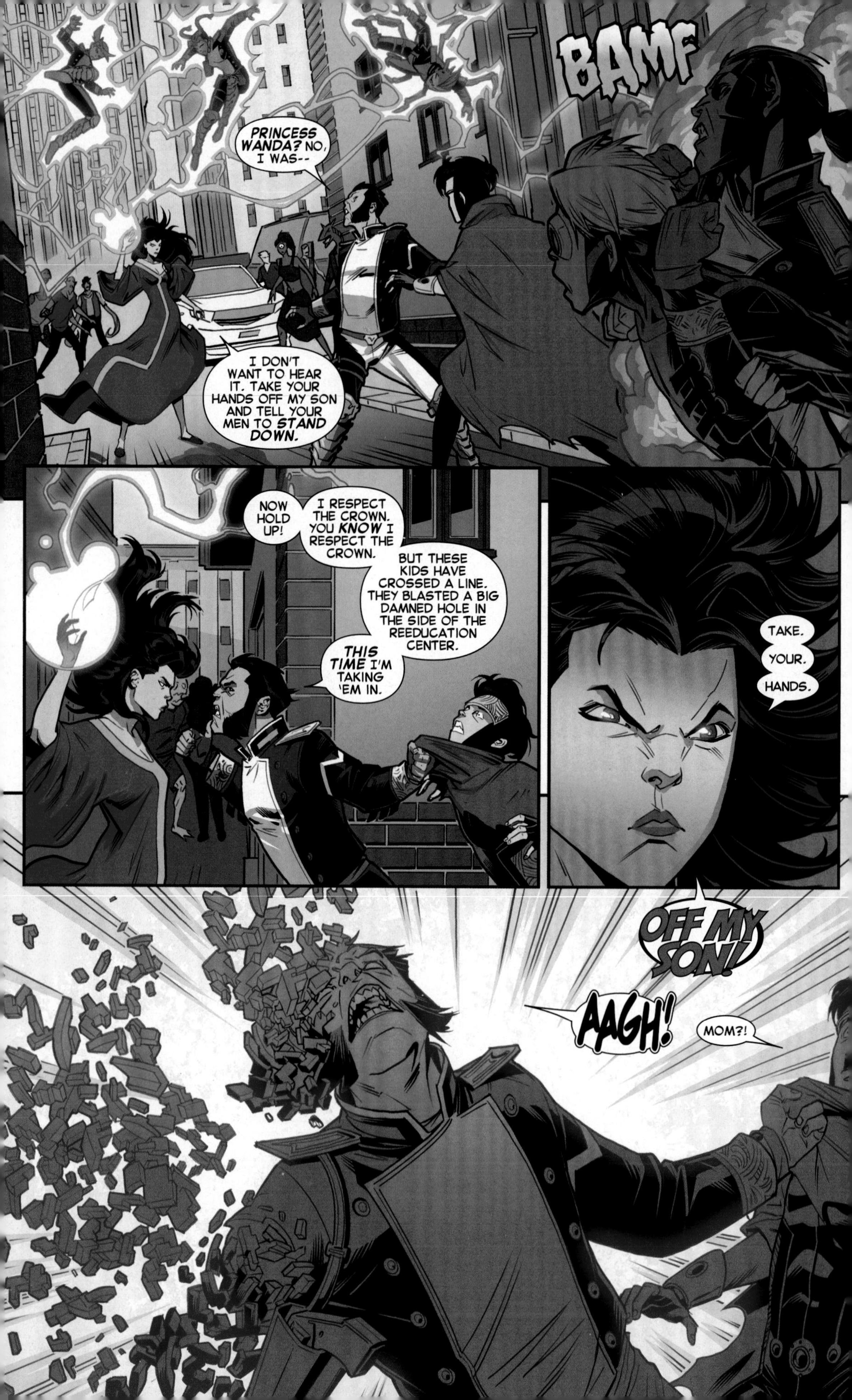
BAMF
PRINCESS WANDA? NO, I WAS--
I DON'T WANT TO HEAR IT. TAKE YOUR HANDS OFF MY SON AND TELL YOUR MEN TO STAND DOWN.
NOW HOLD UP!
I RESPECT THE CROWN. YOU KNOW I RESPECT THE CROWN.
BUT THESE KIDS HAVE CROSSED A LINE. THEY BLASTED A BIG DAMNED HOLE IN THE SIDE OF THE REEDUCATION CENTER.
THIS TIME I'M TAKING 'EM IN.
TAKE.
YOUR.
HANDS.
OFF MY SON!
AAGH!
MOM?!

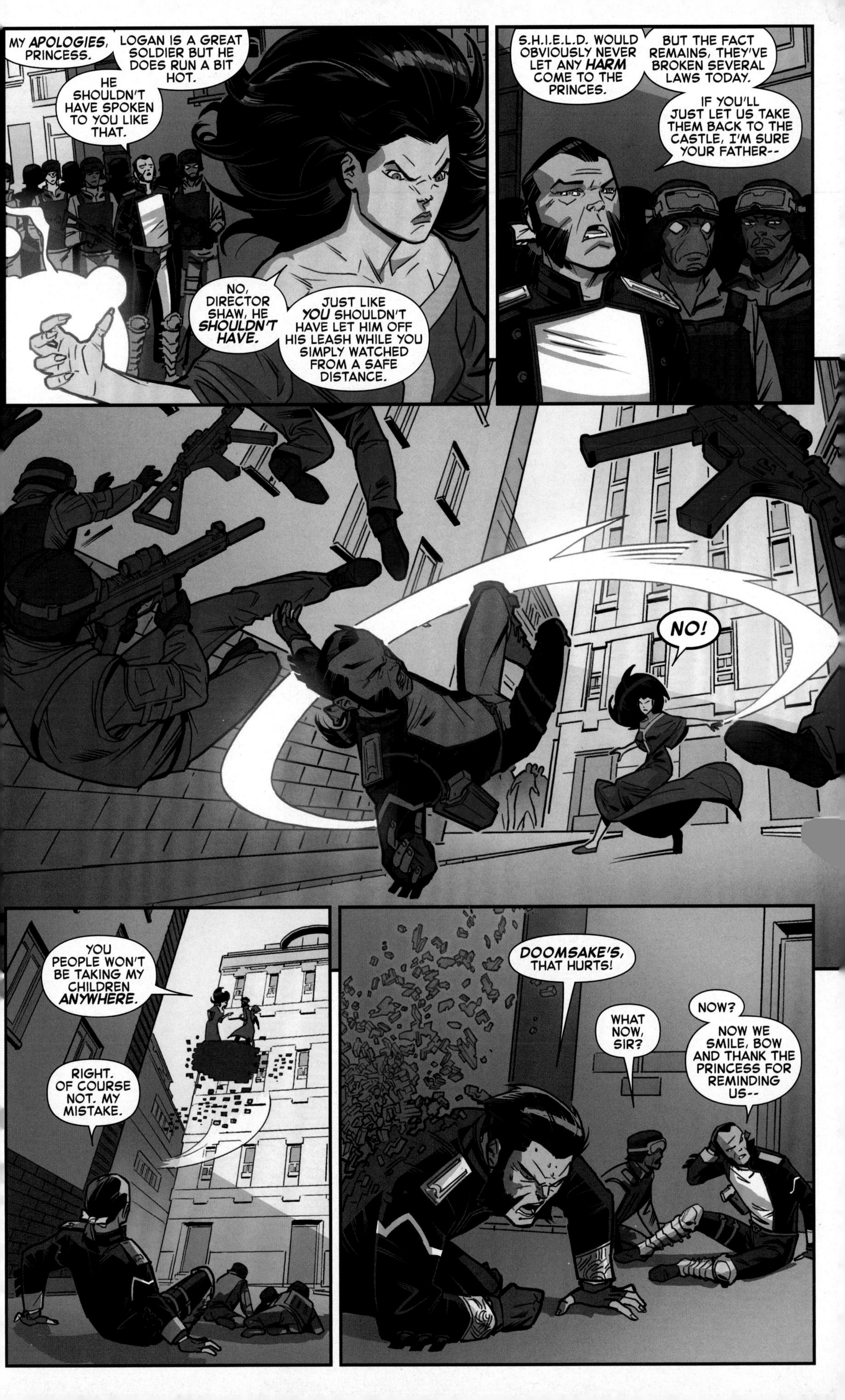
MY APOLOGIES, PRINCESS.
LOGAN IS A GREAT SOLDIER BUT HE DOES RUN A BIT HOT.
HE SHOULDN'T HAVE SPOKEN TO YOU LIKE THAT.
NO, DIRECTOR SHAW, HE SHOULDN'T HAVE.
JUST LIKE YOU SHOULDN'T HAVE LET HIM OFF HIS LEASH WHILE YOU SIMPLY WATCHED FROM A SAFE DISTANCE.
S.H.I.E.L.D. WOULD OBVIOUSLY NEVER LET ANY HARM COME TO THE PRINCES.
BUT THE FACT REMAINS, THEY'VE BROKEN SEVERAL LAWS TODAY.
IF YOU'LL JUST LET US TAKE THEM BACK TO THE CASTLE, I'M SURE YOUR FATHER--
NO!
YOU PEOPLE WON'T BE TAKING MY CHILDREN ANYWHERE.
RIGHT. OF COURSE NOT. MY MISTAKE.
DOOMSAKE'S, THAT HURTS!
WHAT NOW, SIR?
NOW?
NOW WE SMILE, BOW AND THANK THE PRINCESS FOR REMINDING US--

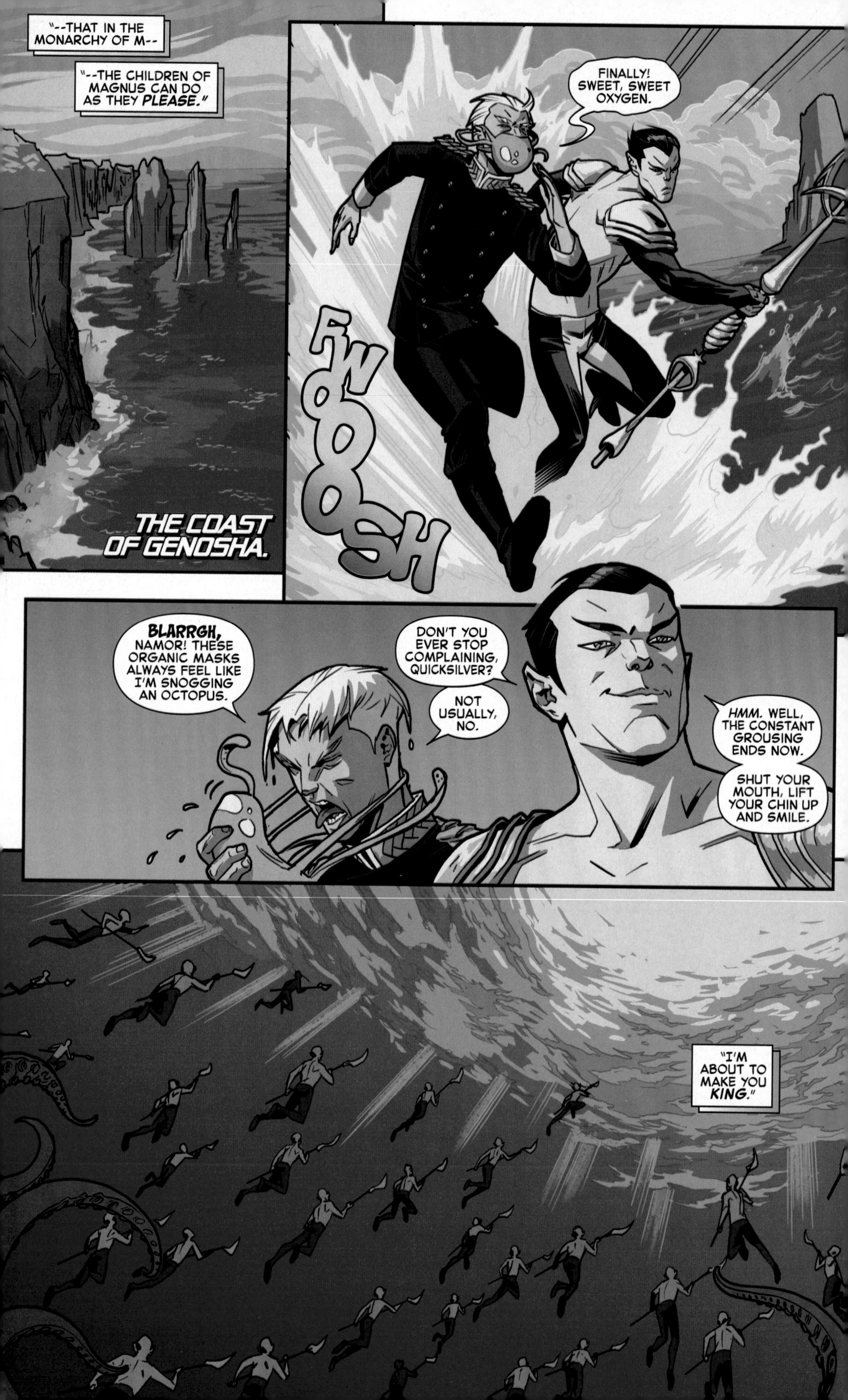
"--THAT IN THE MONARCHY OF M--
"--THE CHILDREN OF MAGNUS CAN DO AS THEY PLEASE."
THE COAST OF GENOSHA.
FINALLY! SWEET, SWEET OXYGEN.
FWOOOSH
BLARRGH, NAMOR! THESE ORGANIC MASKS ALWAYS FEEL LIKE I'M SNOGGING AN OCTOPUS.
DON'T YOU EVER STOP COMPLAINING, QUICKSILVER?
NOT USUALLY, NO.
HMM. WELL, THE CONSTANT GROUSING ENDS NOW.
SHUT YOUR MOUTH, LIFT YOUR CHIN UP AND SMILE.
"I'M ABOUT TO MAKE YOU KING."

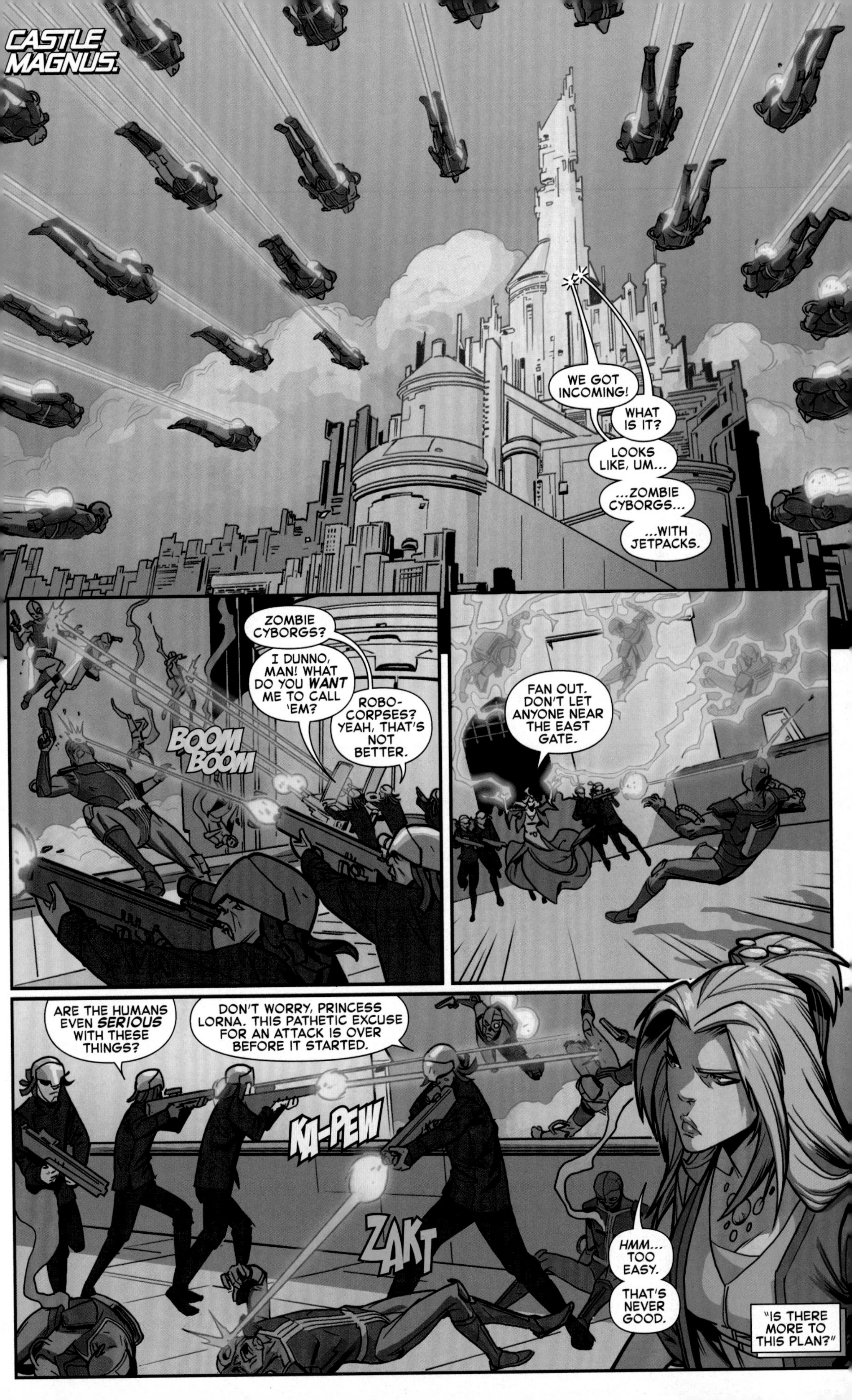
CASTLE MAGNUS.
WE GOT INCOMING!
WHAT IS IT?
LOOKS LIKE, UM...
...ZOMBIE CYBORGS...
...WITH JETPACKS.
ZOMBIE CYBORGS?
I DUNNO, MAN! WHAT DO YOU WANT ME TO CALL 'EM?
ROBO-CORPSES? YEAH, THAT'S NOT BETTER.
BOOM BOOM
FAN OUT. DON'T LET ANYONE NEAR THE EAST GATE.
ARE THE HUMANS EVEN SERIOUS WITH THESE THINGS?
DON'T WORRY, PRINCESS LORNA. THIS PATHETIC EXCUSE FOR AN ATTACK IS OVER BEFORE IT STARTED.
KA-PEW
ZAKT
HMM... TOO EASY.
THAT'S NEVER GOOD.
"IS THERE MORE TO THIS PLAN?"

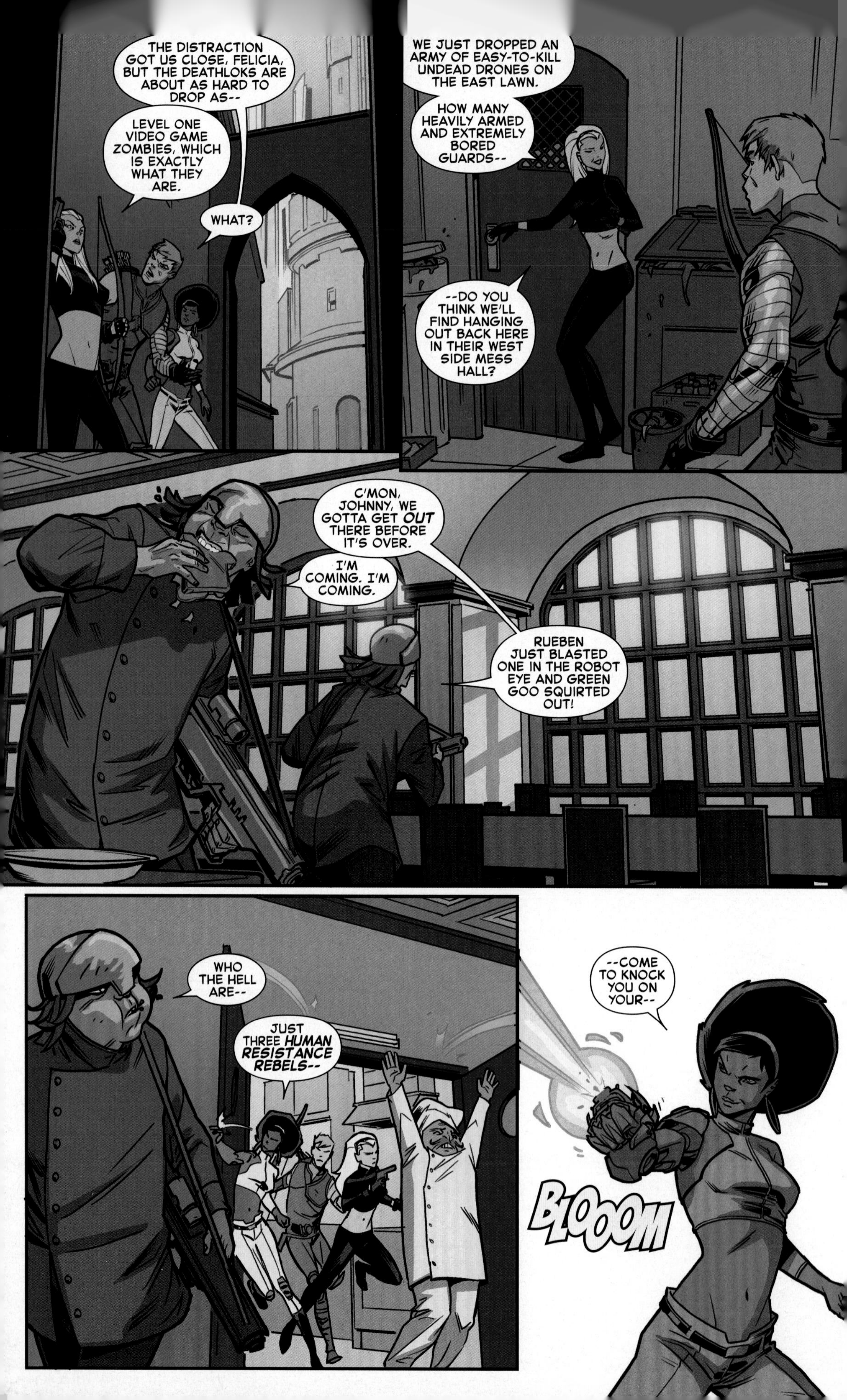
THE DISTRACTION GOT US CLOSE, FELICIA, BUT THE DEATHLOKS ARE ABOUT AS HARD TO DROP AS--
LEVEL ONE VIDEO GAME ZOMBIES, WHICH IS EXACTLY WHAT THEY ARE.
WHAT?
WE JUST DROPPED AN ARMY OF EASY-TO-KILL UNDEAD DRONES ON THE EAST LAWN.
HOW MANY HEAVILY ARMED AND EXTREMELY BORED GUARDS--
--DO YOU THINK WE'LL FIND HANGING OUT BACK HERE IN THEIR WEST SIDE MESS HALL?
C'MON, JOHNNY, WE GOTTA GET *OUT* THERE BEFORE IT'S OVER.
I'M COMING. I'M COMING.
RUEBEN JUST BLASTED ONE IN THE ROBOT EYE AND GREEN GOO SQUIRTED OUT!
WHO THE HELL ARE--
JUST THREE *HUMAN RESISTANCE REBELS--*
--COME TO KNOCK YOU ON YOUR--
BLOOOM

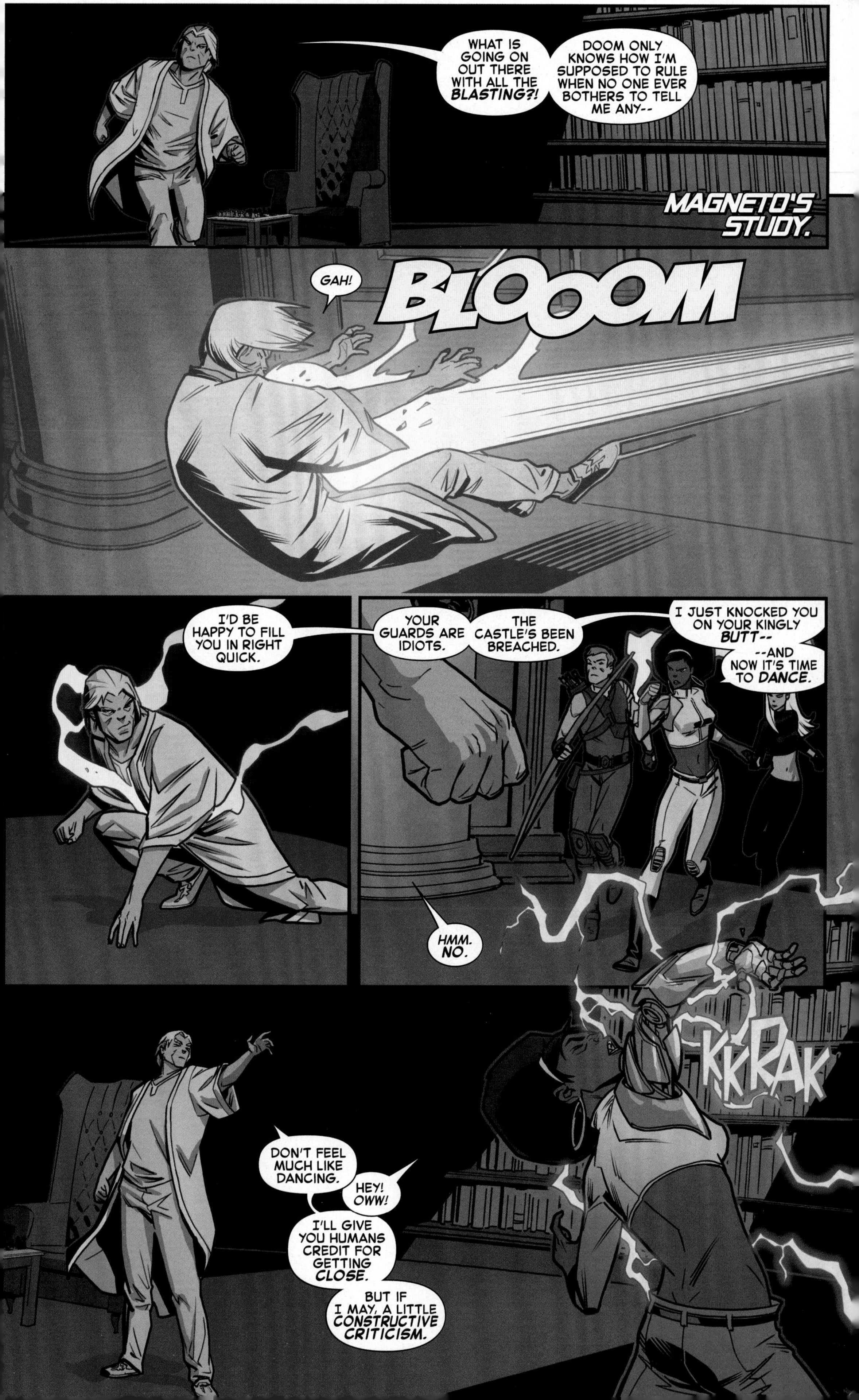
WHAT IS GOING ON OUT THERE WITH ALL THE BLASTING?!
DOOM ONLY KNOWS HOW I'M SUPPOSED TO RULE WHEN NO ONE EVER BOTHERS TO TELL ME ANY--
MAGNETO'S STUDY.
GAH!
BLOOOM
I'D BE HAPPY TO FILL YOU IN RIGHT QUICK.
YOUR GUARDS ARE IDIOTS.
THE CASTLE'S BEEN BREACHED.
I JUST KNOCKED YOU ON YOUR KINGLY BUTT--
--AND NOW IT'S TIME TO DANCE.
HMM. NO.
KKRAK
DON'T FEEL MUCH LIKE DANCING.
HEY! OWW!
I'LL GIVE YOU HUMANS CREDIT FOR GETTING CLOSE.
BUT IF I MAY, A LITTLE CONSTRUCTIVE CRITICISM.

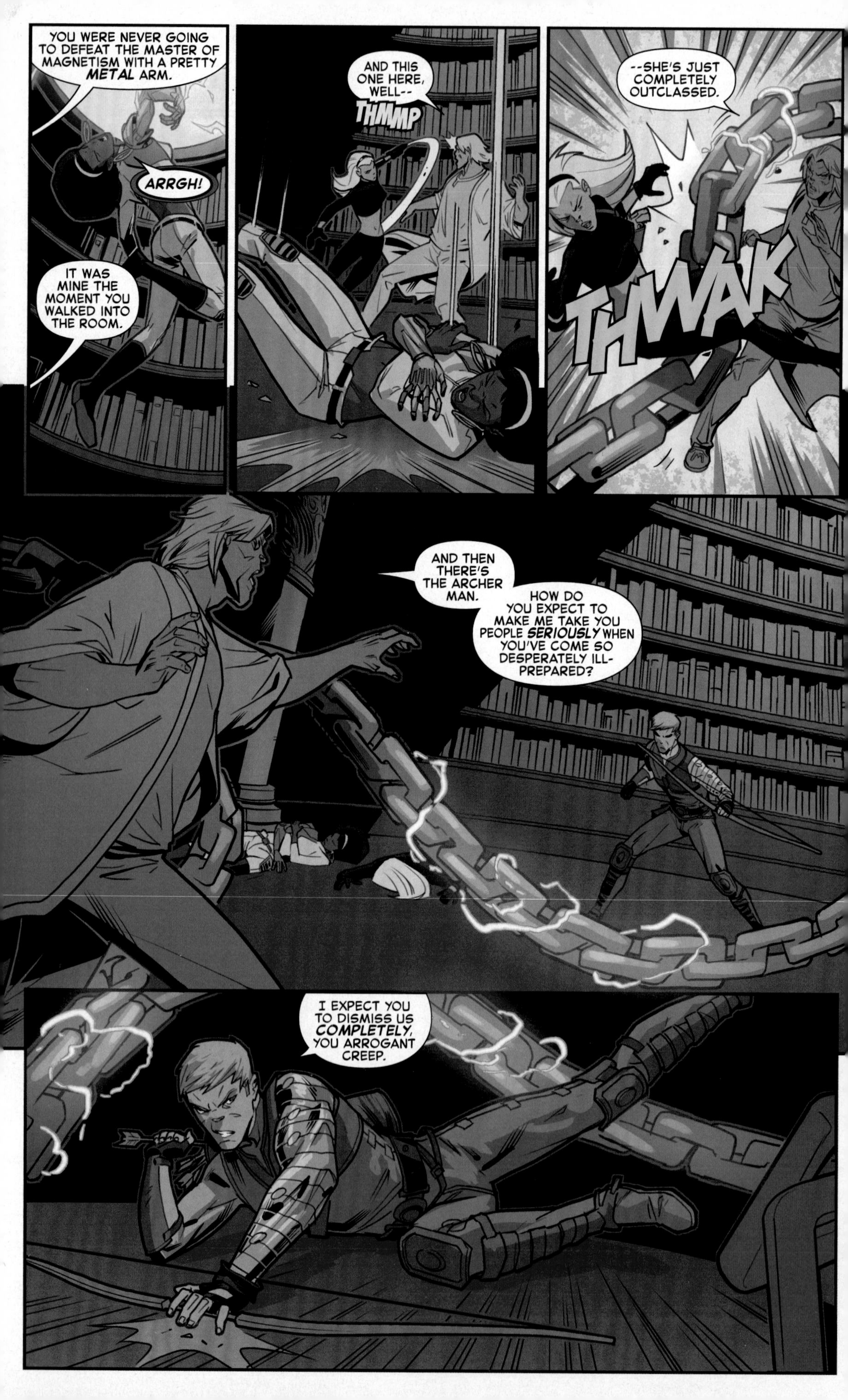

YOU WERE NEVER GOING TO DEFEAT THE MASTER OF MAGNETISM WITH A PRETTY *METAL* ARM.
ARRGH!
IT WAS MINE THE MOMENT YOU WALKED INTO THE ROOM.
AND THIS ONE HERE, WELL--
THMMP
--SHE'S JUST COMPLETELY OUTCLASSED.
THWAK
AND THEN THERE'S THE ARCHER MAN.
HOW DO YOU EXPECT TO MAKE ME TAKE YOU PEOPLE *SERIOUSLY* WHEN YOU'VE COME SO DESPERATELY ILL-PREPARED?
I EXPECT YOU TO DISMISS US *COMPLETELY*, YOU ARROGANT CREEP.

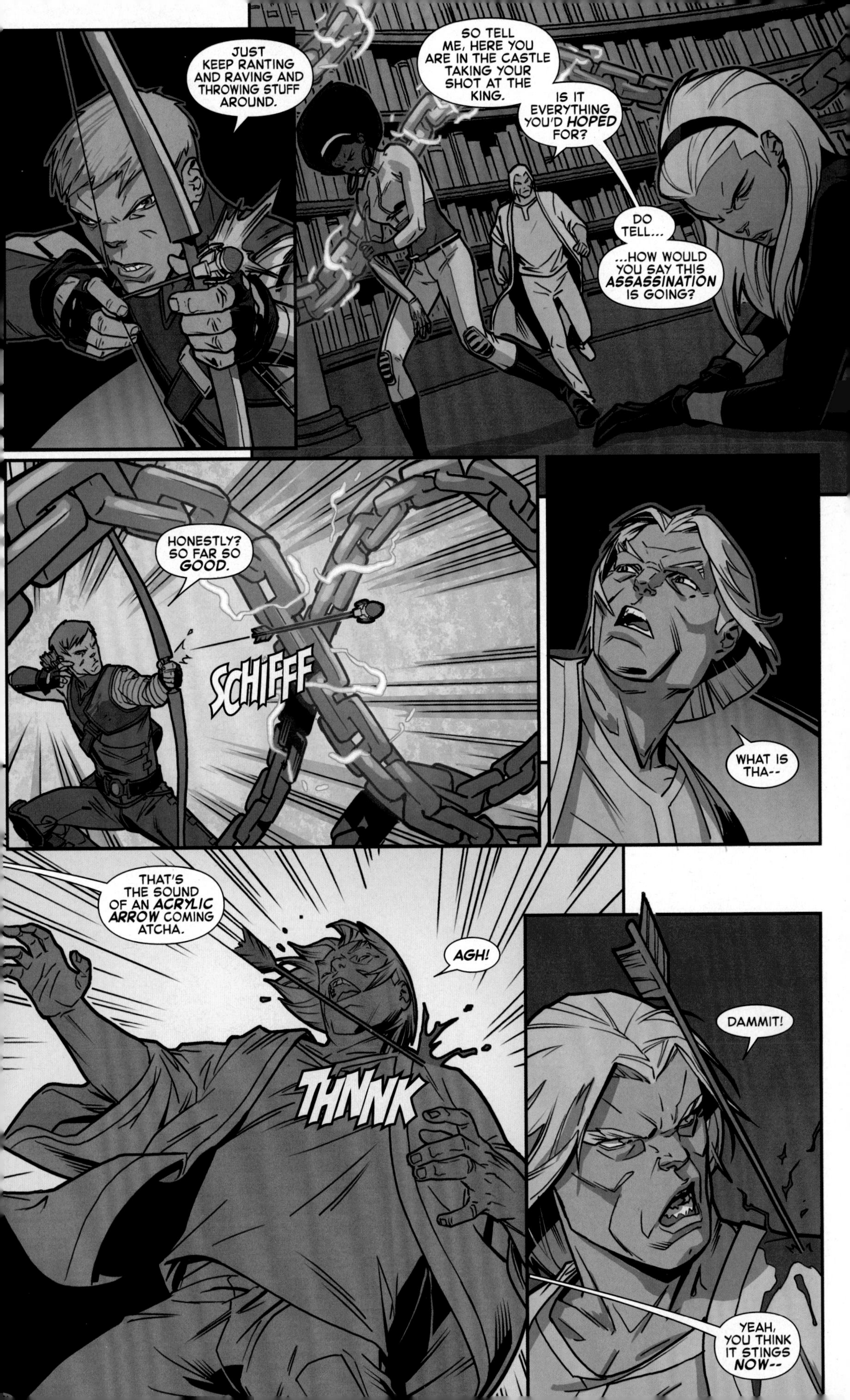
JUST KEEP RANTING AND RAVING AND THROWING STUFF AROUND.
SO TELL ME, HERE YOU ARE IN THE CASTLE TAKING YOUR SHOT AT THE KING.
IS IT EVERYTHING YOU'D HOPED FOR?
DO TELL...
...HOW WOULD YOU SAY THIS ASSASSINATION IS GOING?
HONESTLY? SO FAR SO GOOD.
SCHIFFF
WHAT IS THA--
THAT'S THE SOUND OF AN ACRYLIC ARROW COMING ATCHA.
AGH!
THNNK
DAMMIT!
YEAH, YOU THINK IT STINGS NOW--

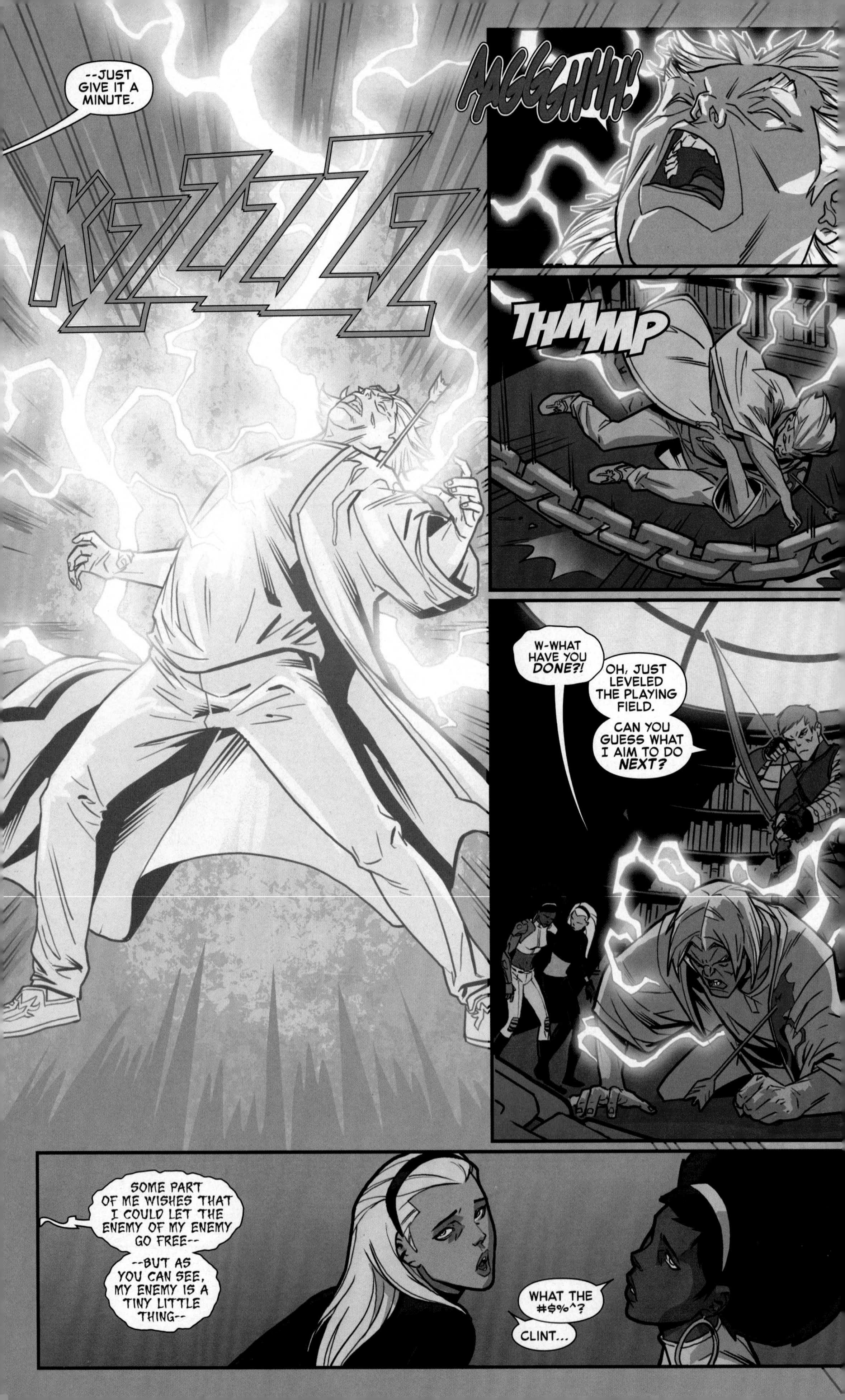
--JUST GIVE IT A MINUTE.
KZZZZZ
AAGGGHHH!
THMMMP
W-WHAT HAVE YOU DONE?!
OH, JUST LEVELED THE PLAYING FIELD.
CAN YOU GUESS WHAT I AIM TO DO NEXT?
SOME PART OF ME WISHES THAT I COULD LET THE ENEMY OF MY ENEMY GO FREE--
--BUT AS YOU CAN SEE, MY ENEMY IS A TINY LITTLE THING--
WHAT THE #$%^?
CLINT...

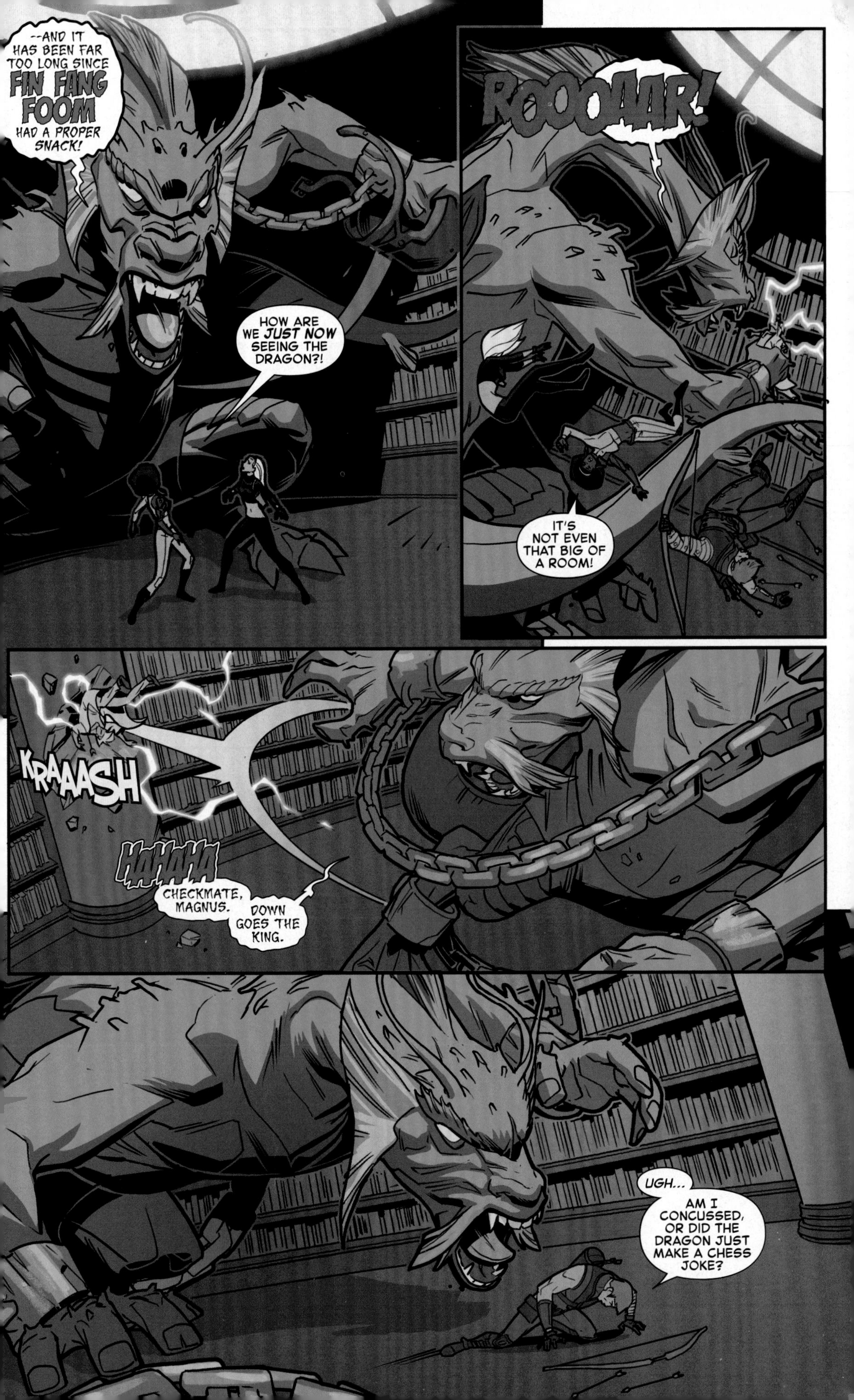

--AND IT HAS BEEN FAR TOO LONG SINCE FIN FANG FOOM HAD A PROPER SNACK!
HOW ARE WE JUST NOW SEEING THE DRAGON?!
ROOOAAR!
IT'S NOT EVEN THAT BIG OF A ROOM!
KRAAASH
HAHAHA
CHECKMATE, MAGNUS.
DOWN GOES THE KING.
UGH...
AM I CONCUSSED, OR DID THE DRAGON JUST MAKE A CHESS JOKE?

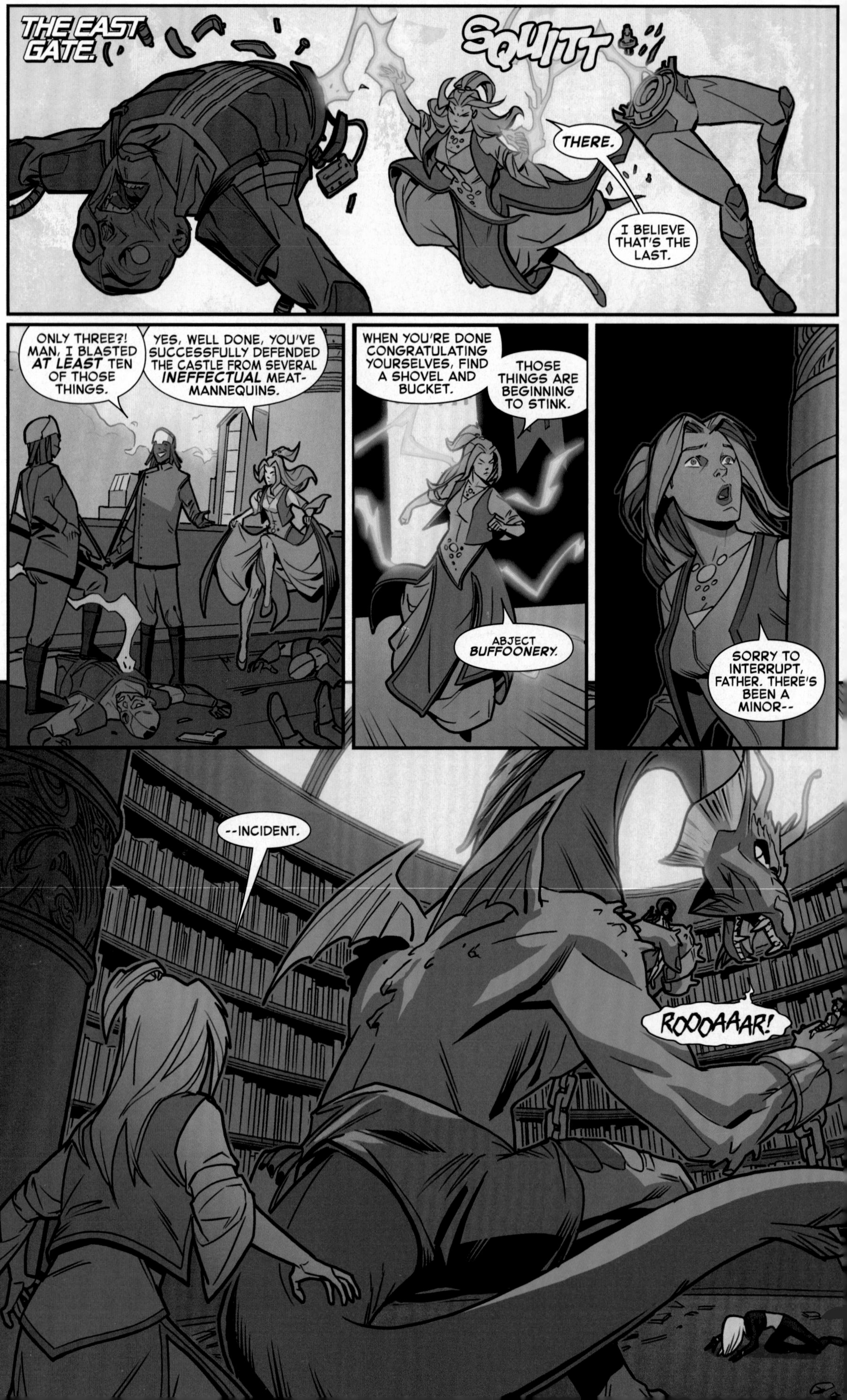
THE EAST GATE.
SQUITT
THERE.
I BELIEVE THAT'S THE LAST.
ONLY THREE?! MAN, I BLASTED AT LEAST TEN OF THOSE THINGS.
YES, WELL DONE, YOU'VE SUCCESSFULLY DEFENDED THE CASTLE FROM SEVERAL INEFFECTUAL MEAT-MANNEQUINS.
WHEN YOU'RE DONE CONGRATULATING YOURSELVES, FIND A SHOVEL AND BUCKET.
THOSE THINGS ARE BEGINNING TO STINK.
ABJECT BUFFOONERY.
SORRY TO INTERRUPT, FATHER. THERE'S BEEN A MINOR--
--INCIDENT.
ROOOAAAR!

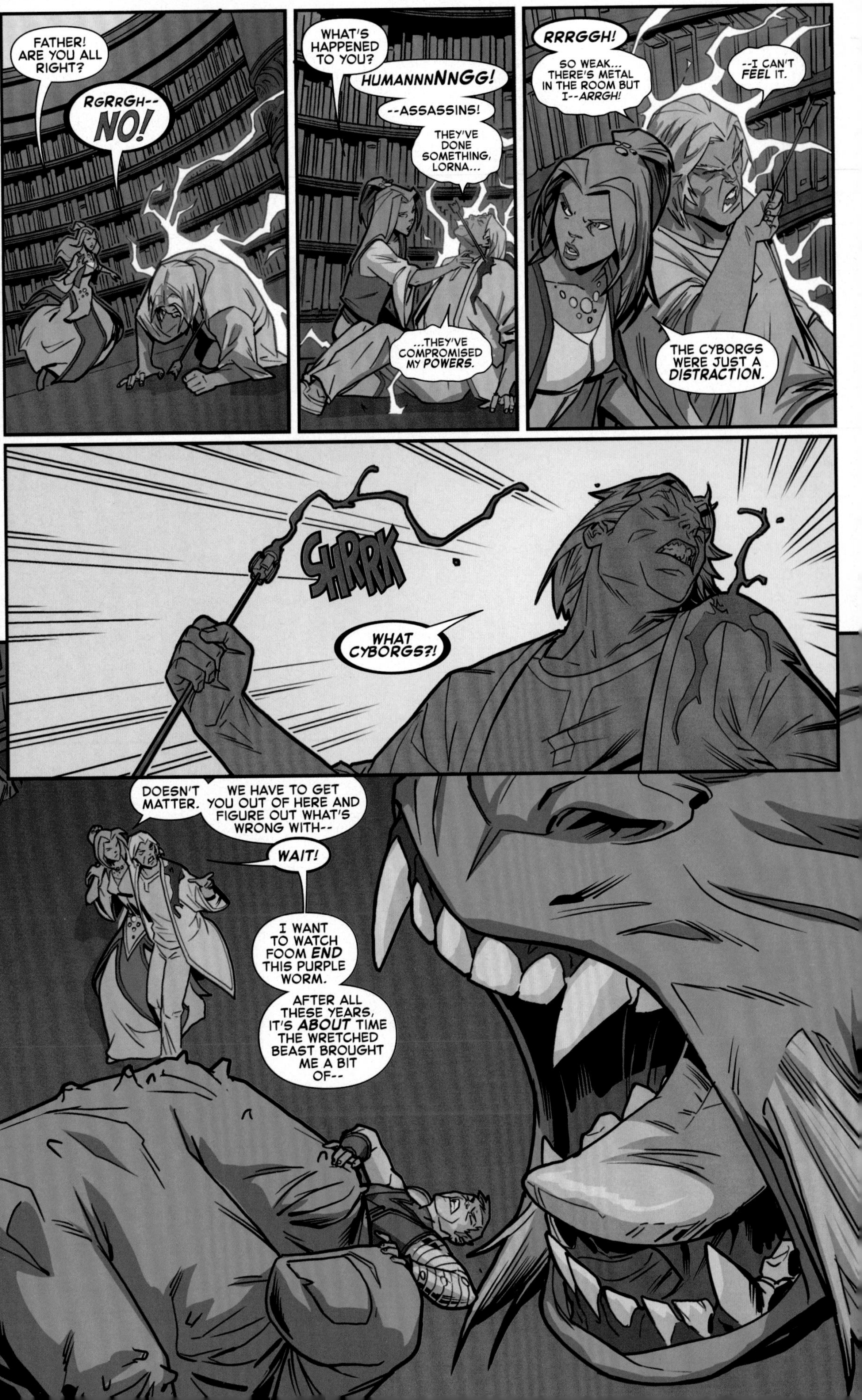
FATHER! ARE YOU ALL RIGHT?
RGRRGH-- NO!
WHAT'S HAPPENED TO YOU?
HUMANNNNNGG!
--ASSASSINS!
THEY'VE DONE SOMETHING, LORNA...
...THEY'VE COMPROMISED MY POWERS.
RRRGGH!
SO WEAK... THERE'S METAL IN THE ROOM BUT I--ARRGH!
--I CAN'T FEEL IT.
THE CYBORGS WERE JUST A DISTRACTION.
SHRRK
WHAT CYBORGS?!
DOESN'T MATTER.
WE HAVE TO GET YOU OUT OF HERE AND FIGURE OUT WHAT'S WRONG WITH--
WAIT!
I WANT TO WATCH FOOM END THIS PURPLE WORM.
AFTER ALL THESE YEARS, IT'S ABOUT TIME THE WRETCHED BEAST BROUGHT ME A BIT OF--

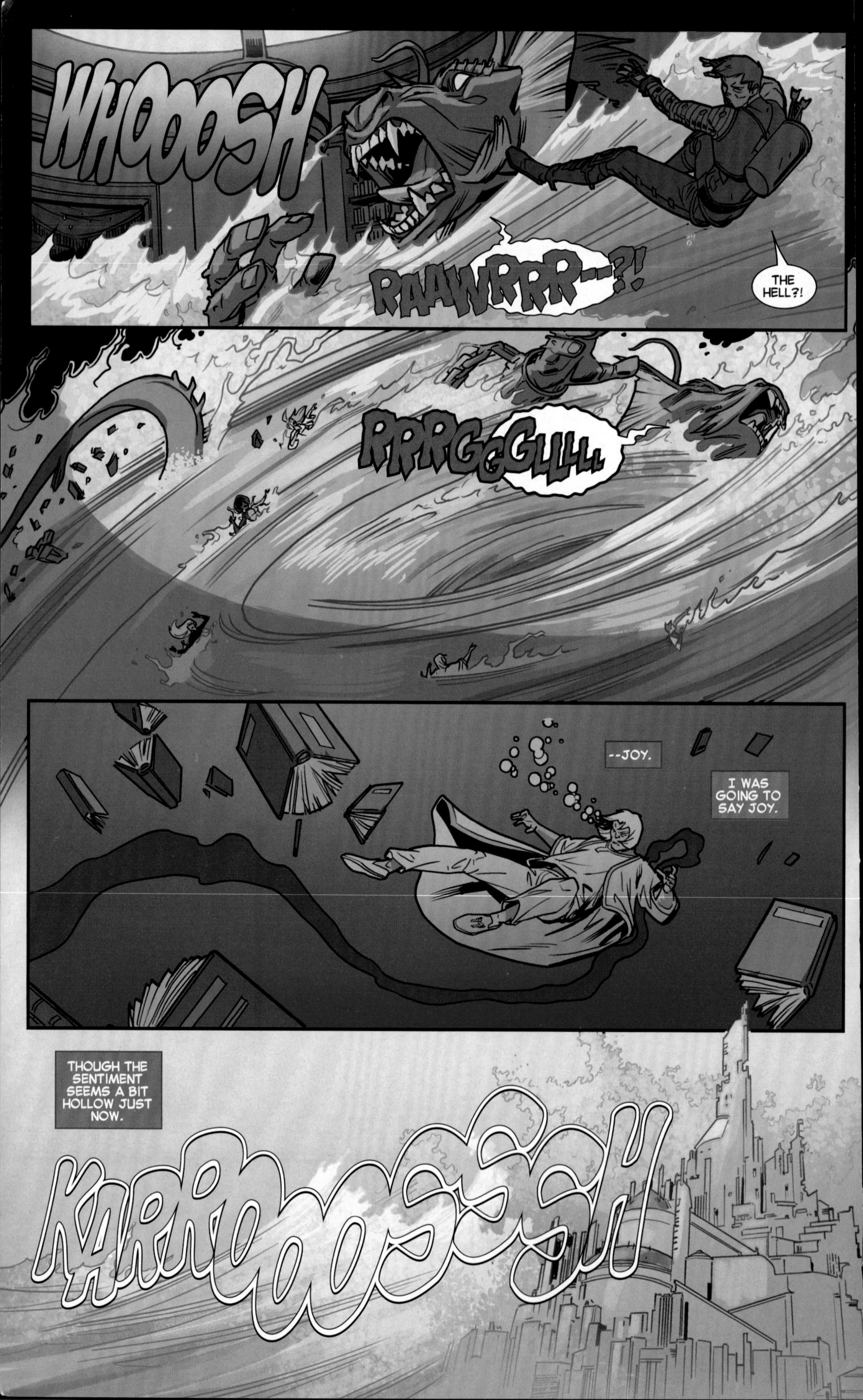
WHOOOSH
RAAWRRR--?!
THE HELL?!
RRRGGGLLLL
--JOY.
I WAS GOING TO SAY JOY.
THOUGH THE SENTIMENT SEEMS A BIT HOLLOW JUST NOW.
KARRROOOSSSH

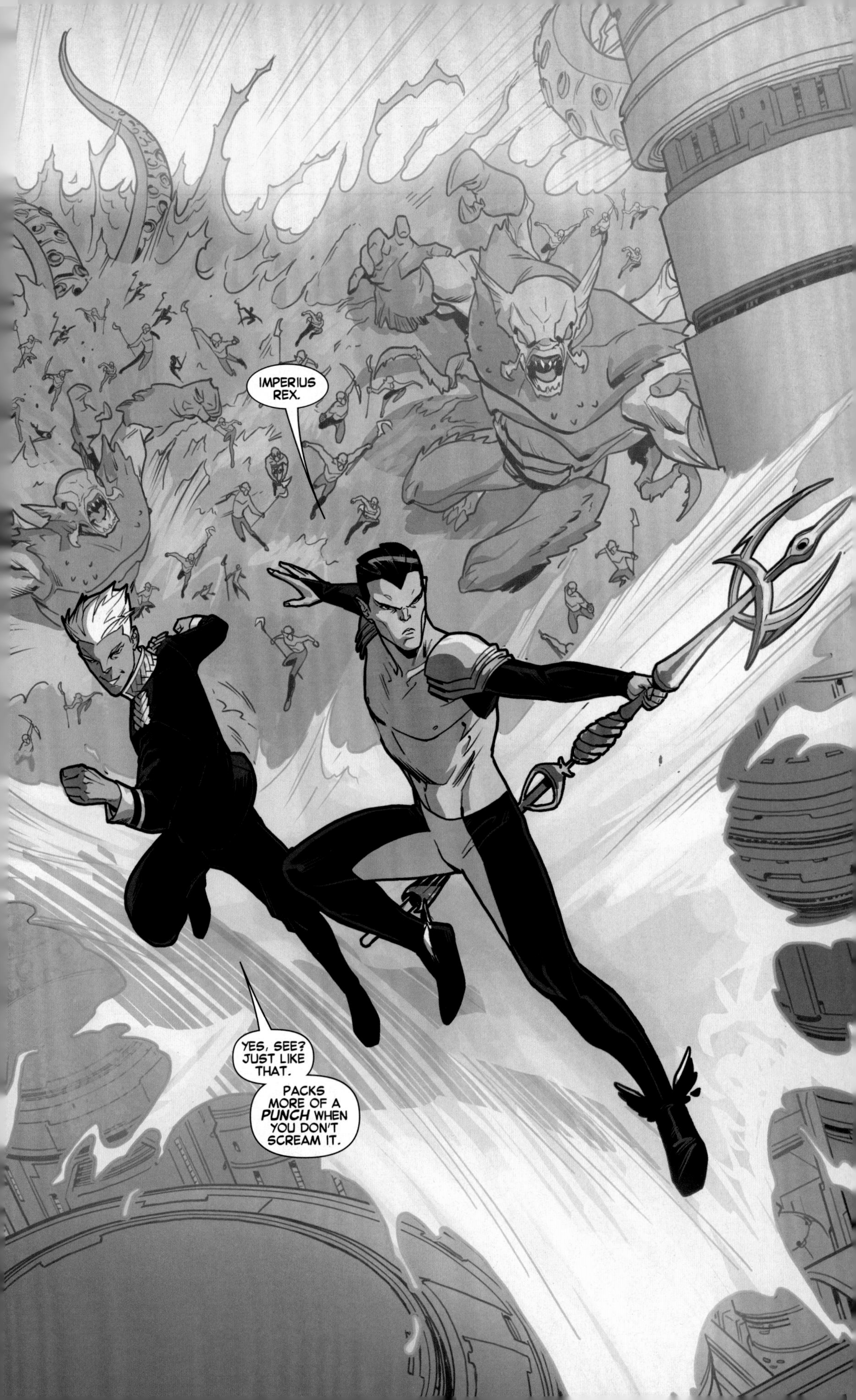
IMPERIUS REX.
YES, SEE? JUST LIKE THAT.
PACKS MORE OF A *PUNCH* WHEN YOU DON'T SCREAM IT.

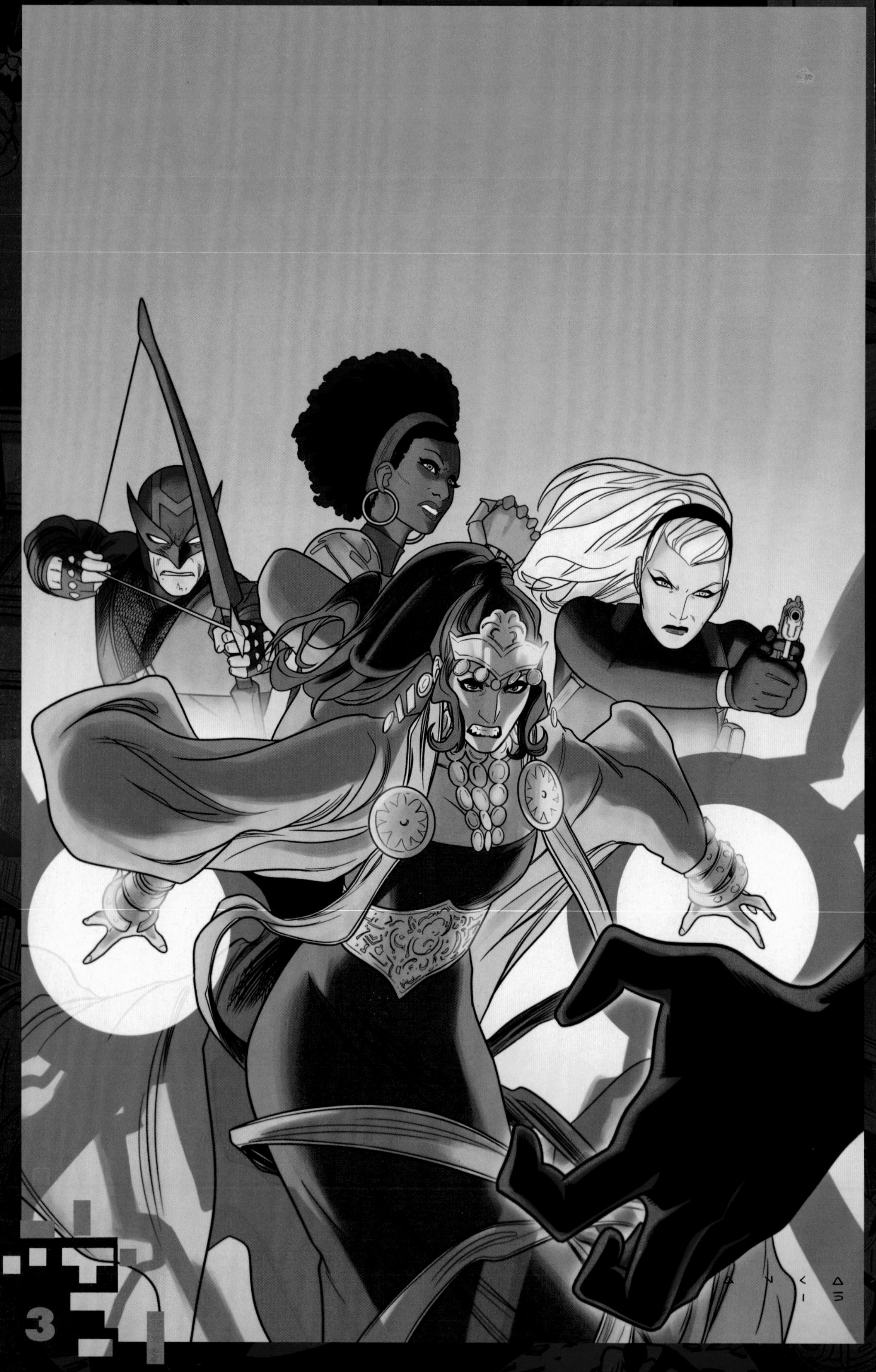
3

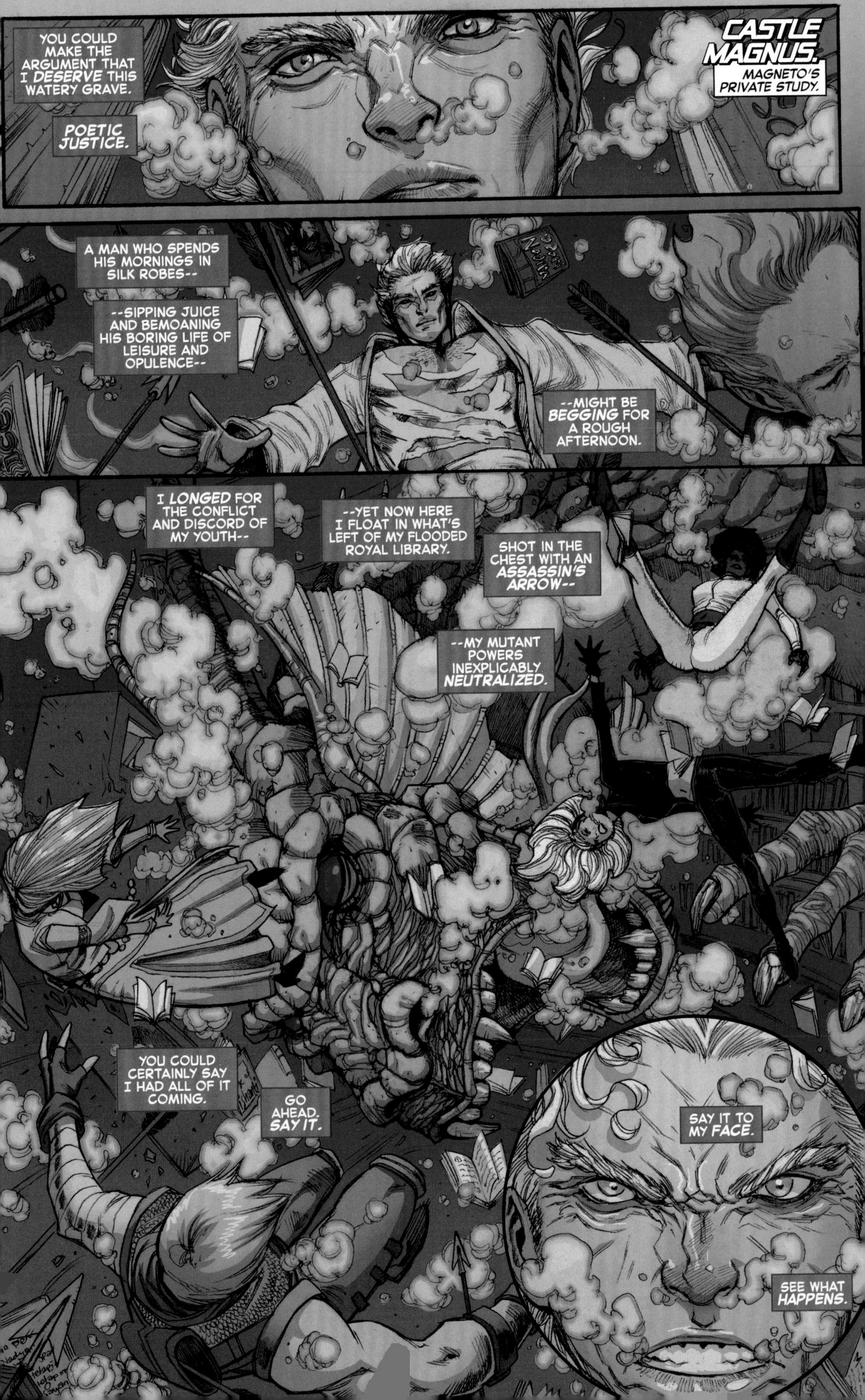
CASTLE MAGNUS.
MAGNETO'S PRIVATE STUDY.
YOU COULD MAKE THE ARGUMENT THAT I DESERVE THIS WATERY GRAVE.
POETIC JUSTICE.
A MAN WHO SPENDS HIS MORNINGS IN SILK ROBES--
--SIPPING JUICE AND BEMOANING HIS BORING LIFE OF LEISURE AND OPULENCE--
--MIGHT BE BEGGING FOR A ROUGH AFTERNOON.
I LONGED FOR THE CONFLICT AND DISCORD OF MY YOUTH--
--YET NOW HERE I FLOAT IN WHAT'S LEFT OF MY FLOODED ROYAL LIBRARY.
SHOT IN THE CHEST WITH AN ASSASSIN'S ARROW--
--MY MUTANT POWERS INEXPLICABLY NEUTRALIZED.
YOU COULD CERTAINLY SAY I HAD ALL OF IT COMING.
GO AHEAD. SAY IT.
SAY IT TO MY FACE.
SEE WHAT HAPPENS.

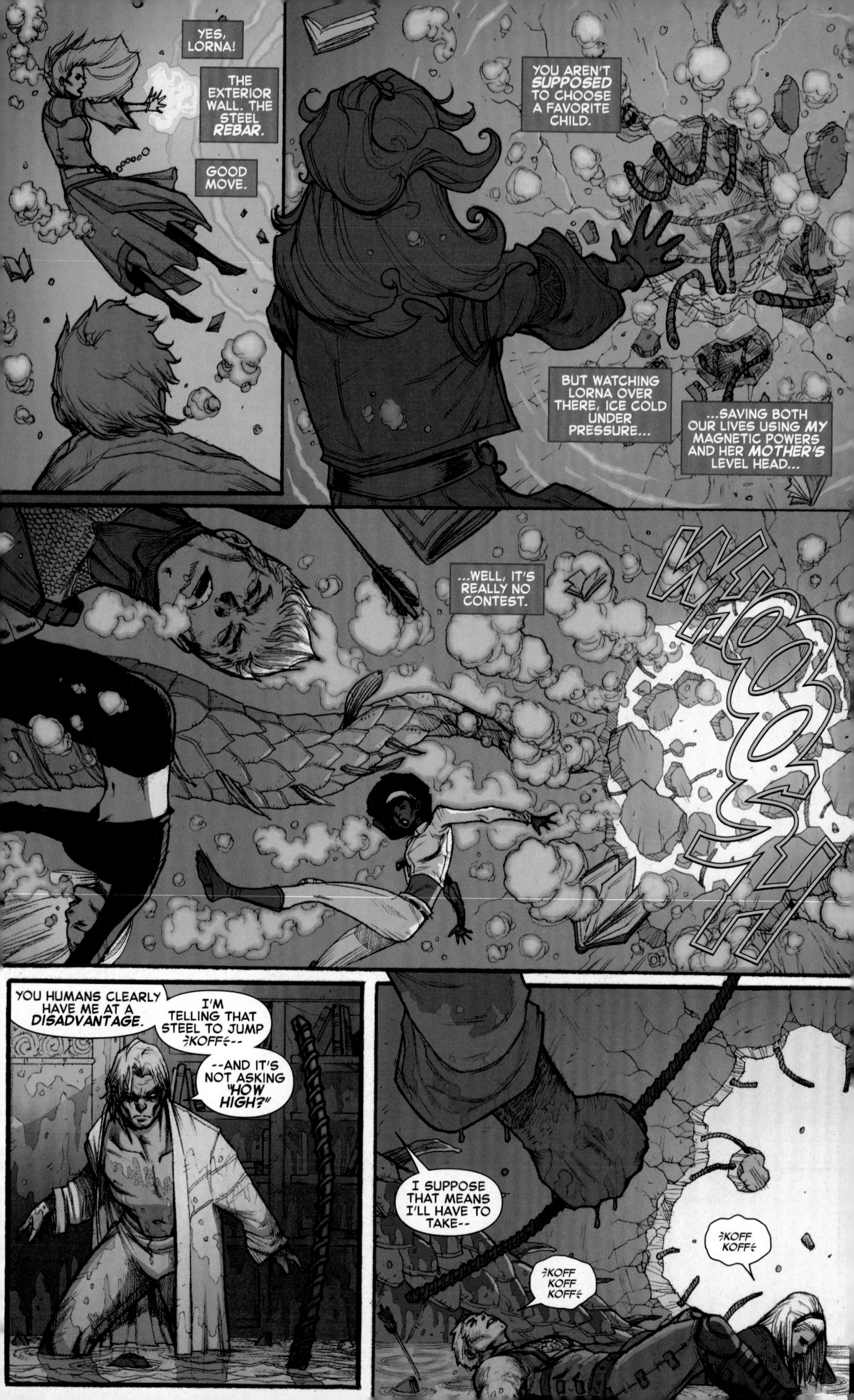
YES, LORNA!
THE EXTERIOR WALL. THE STEEL REBAR.
GOOD MOVE.
YOU AREN'T SUPPOSED TO CHOOSE A FAVORITE CHILD.
BUT WATCHING LORNA OVER THERE, ICE COLD UNDER PRESSURE...
...SAVING BOTH OUR LIVES USING MY MAGNETIC POWERS AND HER MOTHER'S LEVEL HEAD...
...WELL, IT'S REALLY NO CONTEST.
WHOOOOSH
YOU HUMANS CLEARLY HAVE ME AT A DISADVANTAGE.
I'M TELLING THAT STEEL TO JUMP ⇒KOFF⇐--
--AND IT'S NOT ASKING "HOW HIGH?"
I SUPPOSE THAT MEANS I'LL HAVE TO TAKE--
⇒KOFF KOFF⇐
⇒KOFF KOFF KOFF⇐

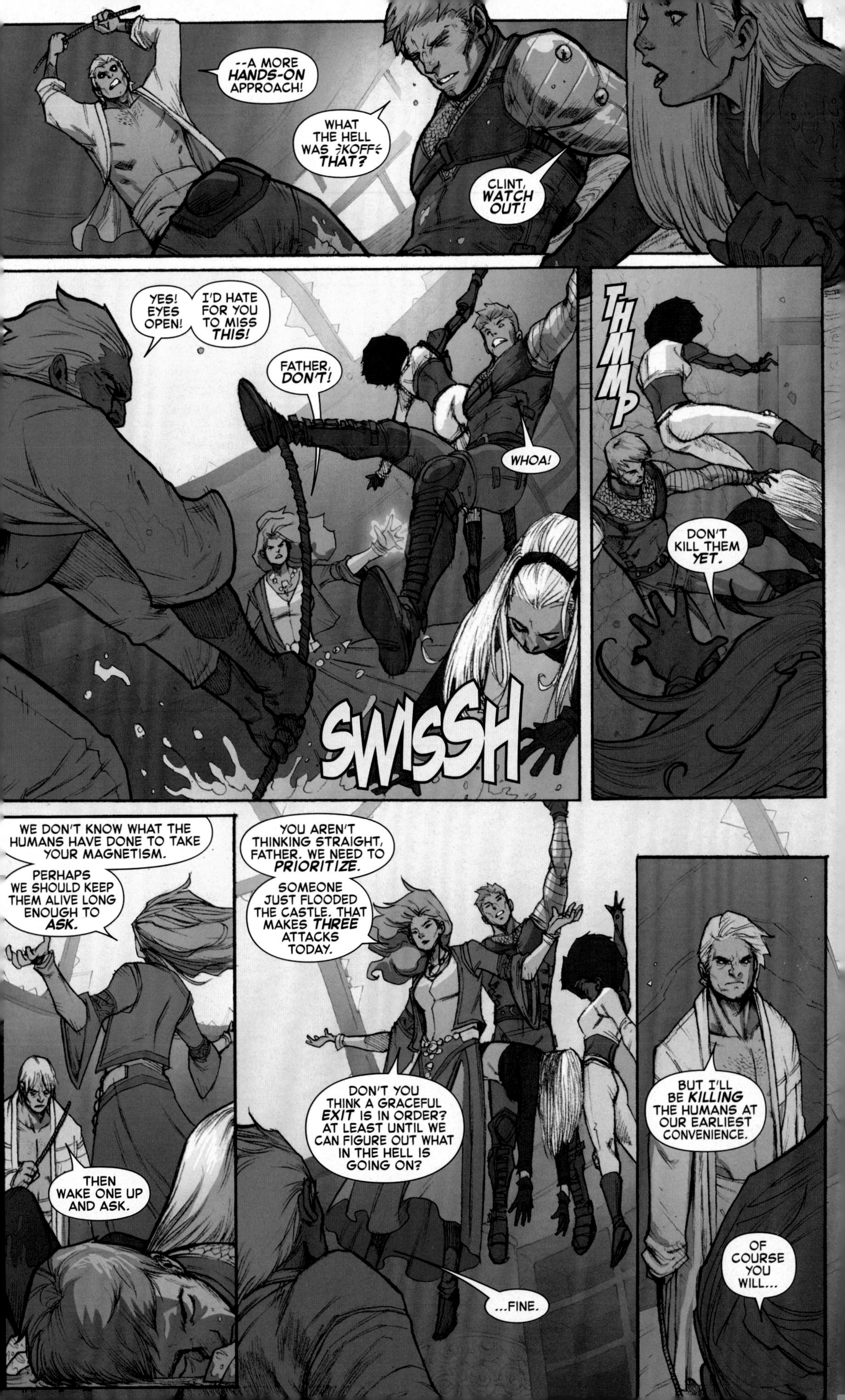
--A MORE HANDS-ON APPROACH!
WHAT THE HELL WAS ⺘KOFF⺘ THAT?
CLINT, WATCH OUT!
YES! EYES OPEN!
I'D HATE FOR YOU TO MISS THIS!
FATHER, DON'T!
WHOA!
SWISSH
THMMP
DON'T KILL THEM YET.
WE DON'T KNOW WHAT THE HUMANS HAVE DONE TO TAKE YOUR MAGNETISM.
PERHAPS WE SHOULD KEEP THEM ALIVE LONG ENOUGH TO ASK.
THEN WAKE ONE UP AND ASK.
YOU AREN'T THINKING STRAIGHT, FATHER. WE NEED TO PRIORITIZE.
SOMEONE JUST FLOODED THE CASTLE. THAT MAKES THREE ATTACKS TODAY.
DON'T YOU THINK A GRACEFUL EXIT IS IN ORDER? AT LEAST UNTIL WE CAN FIGURE OUT WHAT IN THE HELL IS GOING ON?
...FINE.
BUT I'LL BE KILLING THE HUMANS AT OUR EARLIEST CONVENIENCE.
OF COURSE YOU WILL...

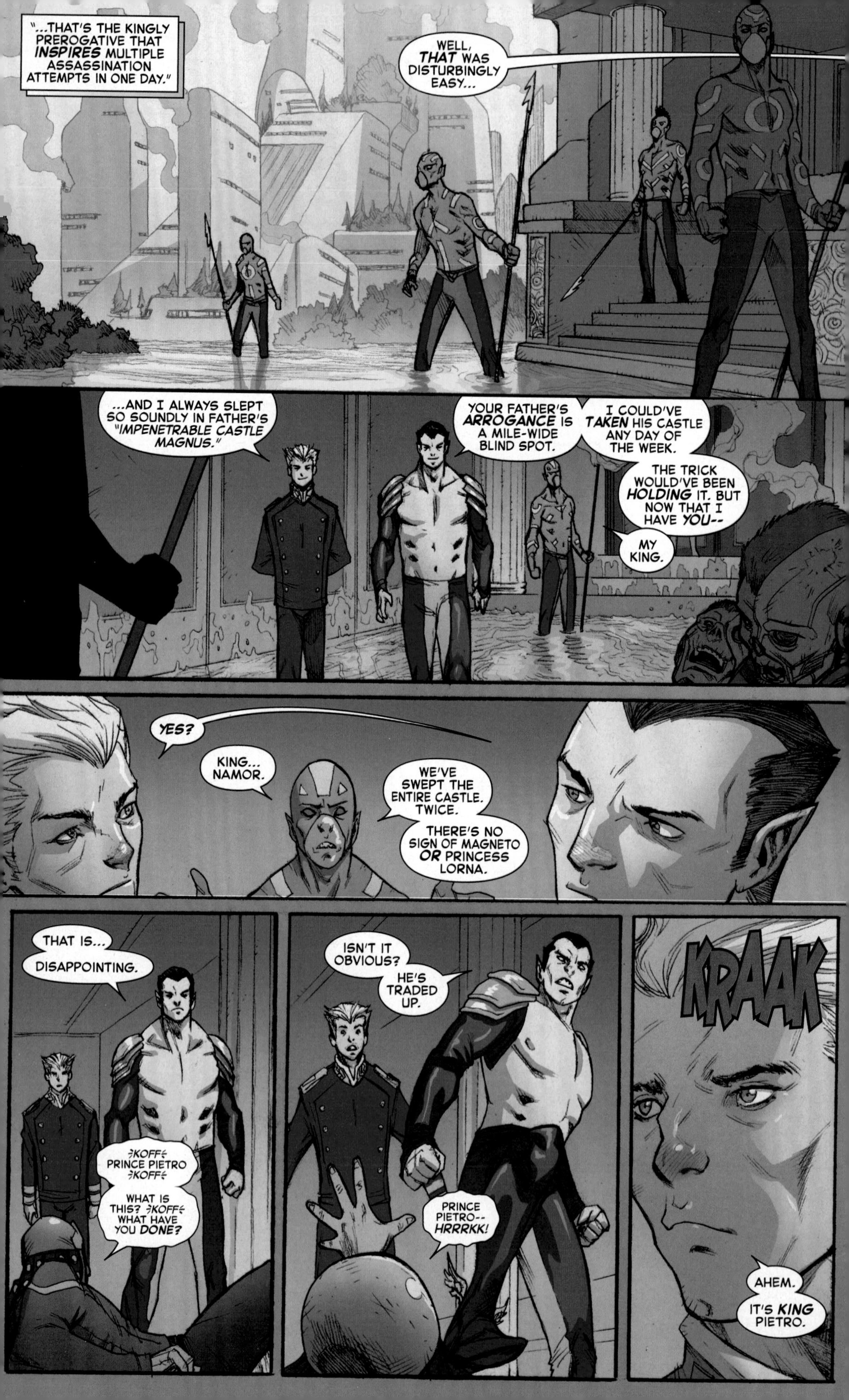
"...THAT'S THE KINGLY PREROGATIVE THAT INSPIRES MULTIPLE ASSASSINATION ATTEMPTS IN ONE DAY."
WELL, THAT WAS DISTURBINGLY EASY...
...AND I ALWAYS SLEPT SO SOUNDLY IN FATHER'S "IMPENETRABLE CASTLE MAGNUS."
YOUR FATHER'S ARROGANCE IS A MILE-WIDE BLIND SPOT.
I COULD'VE TAKEN HIS CASTLE ANY DAY OF THE WEEK.
THE TRICK WOULD'VE BEEN HOLDING IT. BUT NOW THAT I HAVE YOU--
MY KING.
YES?
KING... NAMOR.
WE'VE SWEPT THE ENTIRE CASTLE. TWICE.
THERE'S NO SIGN OF MAGNETO OR PRINCESS LORNA.
THAT IS...
DISAPPOINTING.
KOFF PRINCE PIETRO KOFF
WHAT IS THIS? KOFF WHAT HAVE YOU DONE?
ISN'T IT OBVIOUS?
HE'S TRADED UP.
PRINCE PIETRO-- HRRRKK!
KRAAK
AHEM.
IT'S KING PIETRO.

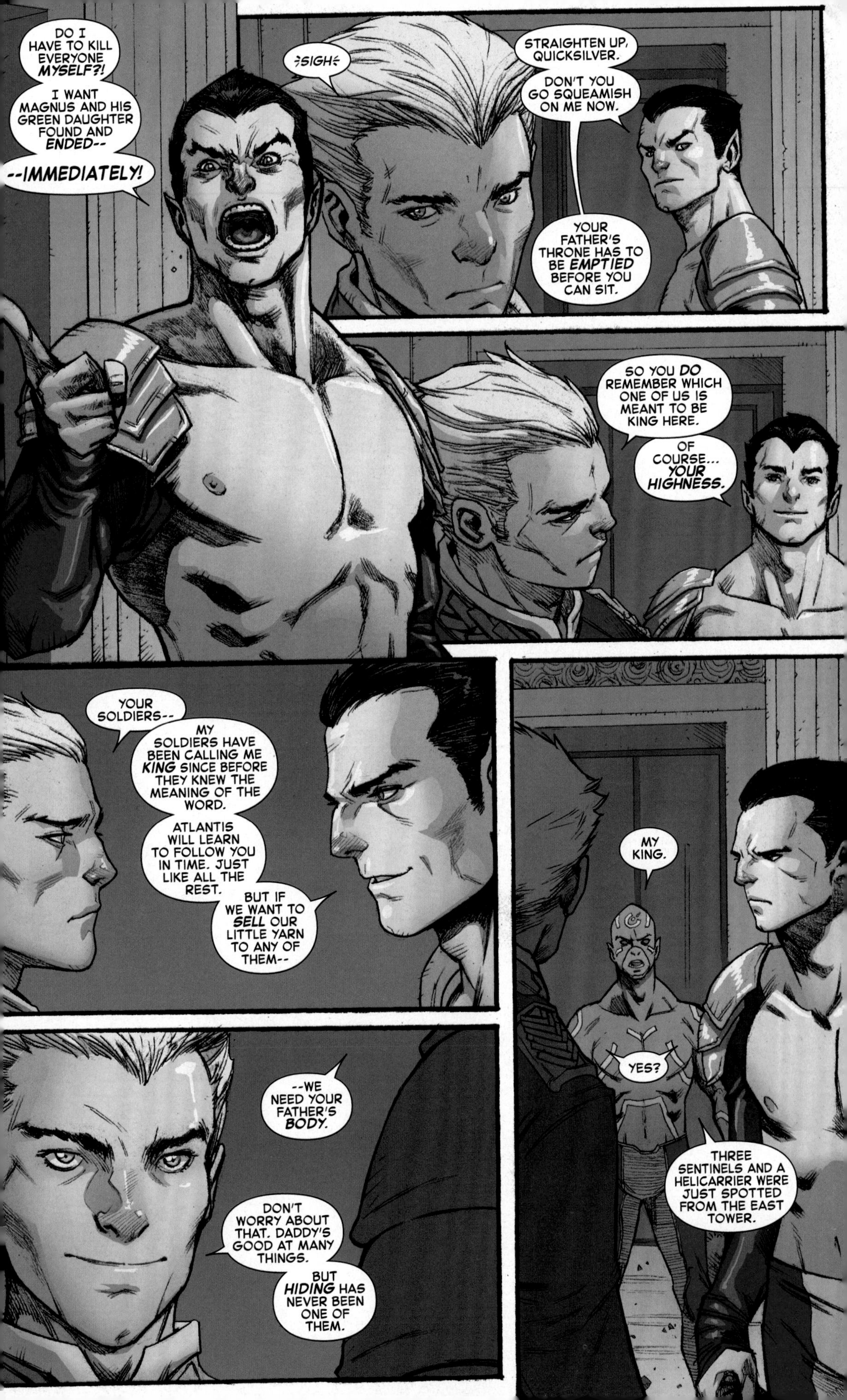
DO I HAVE TO KILL EVERYONE *MYSELF?!*
I WANT MAGNUS AND HIS GREEN DAUGHTER FOUND AND *ENDED--*
--IMMEDIATELY!
SIGH
STRAIGHTEN UP, QUICKSILVER.
DON'T YOU GO SQUEAMISH ON ME NOW.
YOUR FATHER'S THRONE HAS TO BE *EMPTIED* BEFORE YOU CAN SIT.
SO YOU *DO* REMEMBER WHICH ONE OF US IS MEANT TO BE KING HERE.
OF COURSE... *YOUR HIGHNESS.*
YOUR SOLDIERS--
MY SOLDIERS HAVE BEEN CALLING ME *KING* SINCE BEFORE THEY KNEW THE MEANING OF THE WORD.
ATLANTIS WILL LEARN TO FOLLOW YOU IN TIME. JUST LIKE ALL THE REST.
BUT IF WE WANT TO *SELL* OUR LITTLE YARN TO ANY OF THEM--
--WE NEED YOUR FATHER'S *BODY*.
DON'T WORRY ABOUT THAT. DADDY'S GOOD AT MANY THINGS.
BUT *HIDING* HAS NEVER BEEN ONE OF THEM.
MY KING.
YES?
THREE SENTINELS AND A HELICARRIER WERE JUST SPOTTED FROM THE EAST TOWER.

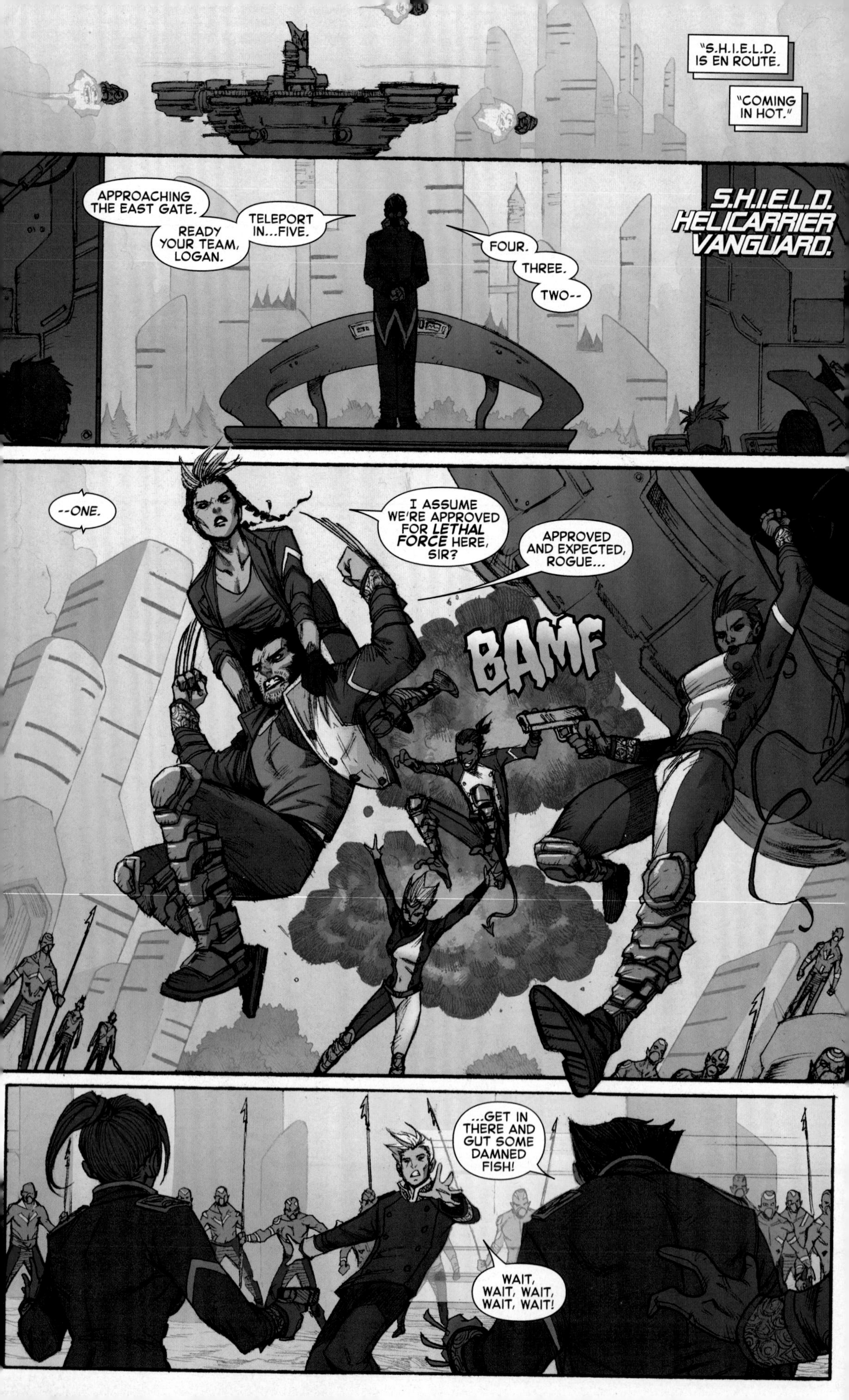
"S.H.I.E.L.D. IS EN ROUTE.
"COMING IN HOT."
APPROACHING THE EAST GATE.
READY YOUR TEAM, LOGAN.
TELEPORT IN...FIVE.
S.H.I.E.L.D. HELICARRIER VANGUARD.
FOUR.
THREE.
TWO--
--ONE.
I ASSUME WE'RE APPROVED FOR LETHAL FORCE HERE, SIR?
APPROVED AND EXPECTED, ROGUE...
BAMF
...GET IN THERE AND GUT SOME DAMNED FISH!
WAIT, WAIT, WAIT, WAIT, WAIT!

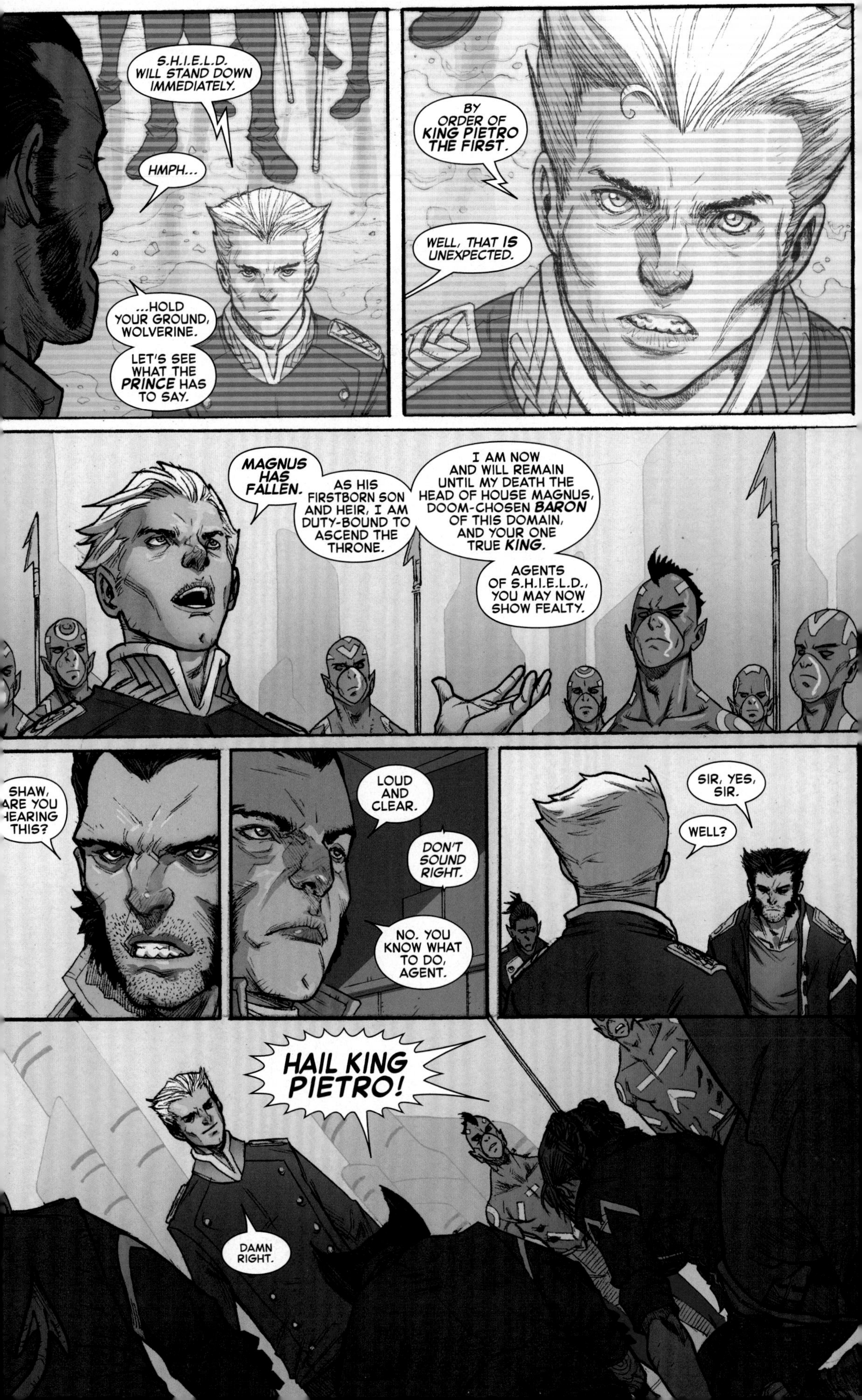
S.H.I.E.L.D. WILL STAND DOWN IMMEDIATELY.
HMPH...
...HOLD YOUR GROUND, WOLVERINE.
LET'S SEE WHAT THE PRINCE HAS TO SAY.
BY ORDER OF KING PIETRO THE FIRST.
WELL, THAT IS UNEXPECTED.
MAGNUS HAS FALLEN.
AS HIS FIRSTBORN SON AND HEIR, I AM DUTY-BOUND TO ASCEND THE THRONE.
I AM NOW AND WILL REMAIN UNTIL MY DEATH THE HEAD OF HOUSE MAGNUS, DOOM-CHOSEN BARON OF THIS DOMAIN, AND YOUR ONE TRUE KING.
AGENTS OF S.H.I.E.L.D., YOU MAY NOW SHOW FEALTY.
SHAW, ARE YOU HEARING THIS?
LOUD AND CLEAR.
DON'T SOUND RIGHT.
NO. YOU KNOW WHAT TO DO, AGENT.
WELL?
SIR, YES, SIR.
HAIL KING PIETRO!
DAMN RIGHT.

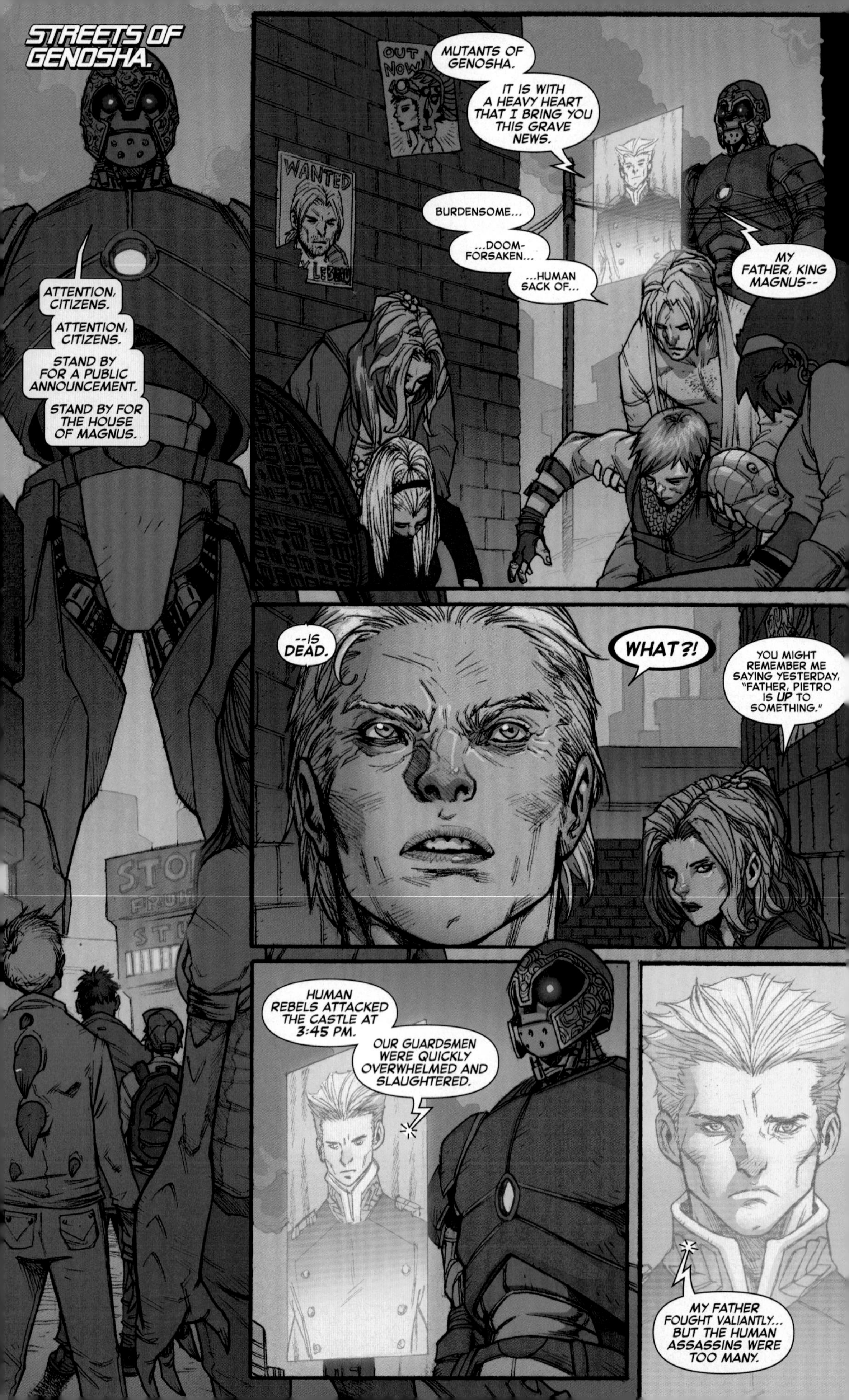

STREETS OF GENOSHA.
ATTENTION, CITIZENS.
ATTENTION, CITIZENS.
STAND BY FOR A PUBLIC ANNOUNCEMENT.
STAND BY FOR THE HOUSE OF MAGNUS.
OUT NOW
WANTED
MUTANTS OF GENOSHA.
IT IS WITH A HEAVY HEART THAT I BRING YOU THIS GRAVE NEWS.
BURDENSOME...
...DOOM-FORSAKEN...
...HUMAN SACK OF...
MY FATHER, KING MAGNUS--
--IS DEAD.
WHAT?!
YOU MIGHT REMEMBER ME SAYING YESTERDAY, "FATHER, PIETRO IS UP TO SOMETHING."
HUMAN REBELS ATTACKED THE CASTLE AT 3:45 PM.
OUR GUARDSMEN WERE QUICKLY OVERWHELMED AND SLAUGHTERED.
MY FATHER FOUGHT VALIANTLY... BUT THE HUMAN ASSASSINS WERE TOO MANY.

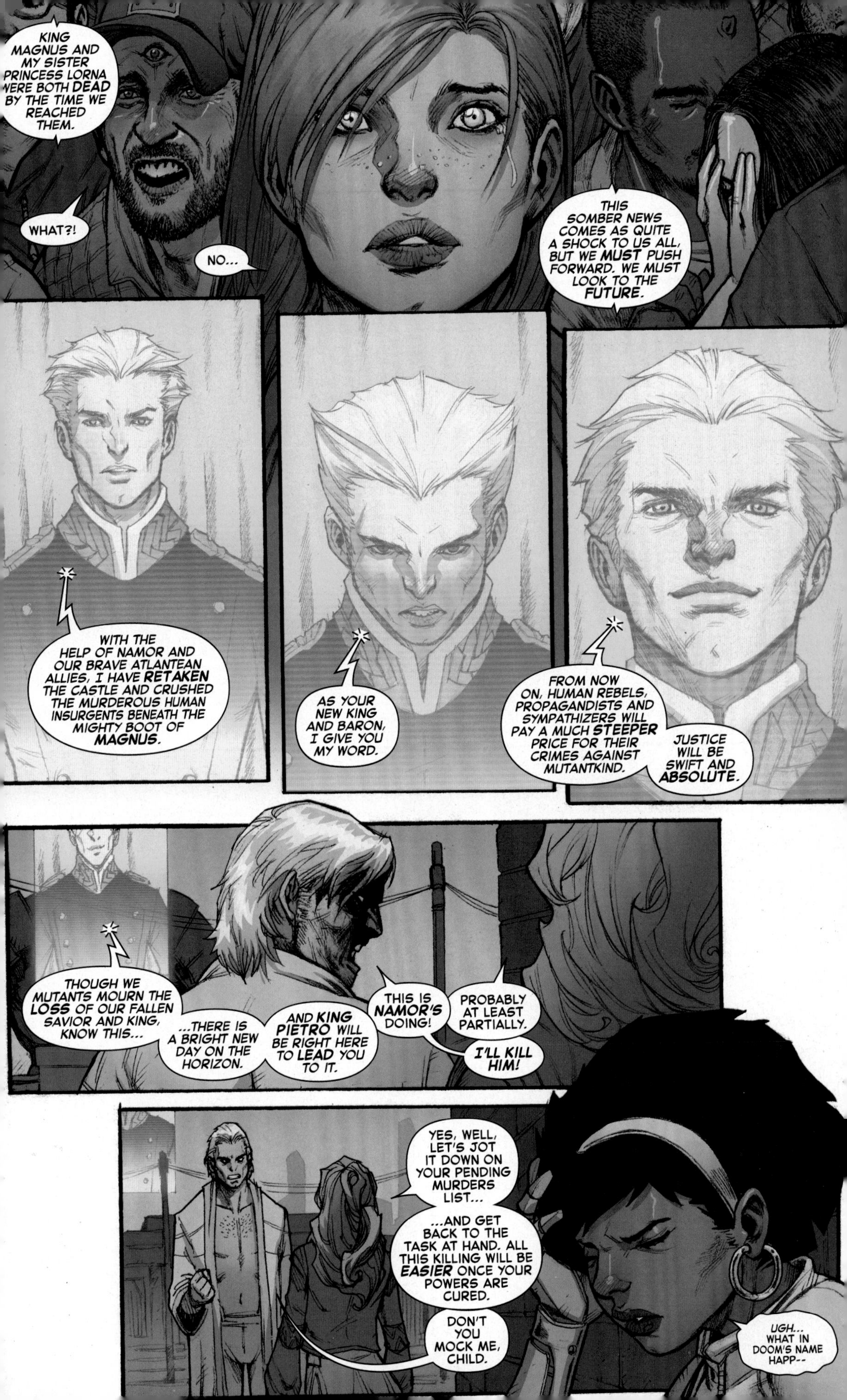

KING MAGNUS AND MY SISTER PRINCESS LORNA WERE BOTH DEAD BY THE TIME WE REACHED THEM.
WHAT?!
NO...
THIS SOMBER NEWS COMES AS QUITE A SHOCK TO US ALL, BUT WE MUST PUSH FORWARD. WE MUST LOOK TO THE FUTURE.
WITH THE HELP OF NAMOR AND OUR BRAVE ATLANTEAN ALLIES, I HAVE RETAKEN THE CASTLE AND CRUSHED THE MURDEROUS HUMAN INSURGENTS BENEATH THE MIGHTY BOOT OF MAGNUS.
AS YOUR NEW KING AND BARON, I GIVE YOU MY WORD.
FROM NOW ON, HUMAN REBELS, PROPAGANDISTS AND SYMPATHIZERS WILL PAY A MUCH STEEPER PRICE FOR THEIR CRIMES AGAINST MUTANTKIND.
JUSTICE WILL BE SWIFT AND ABSOLUTE.
THOUGH WE MUTANTS MOURN THE LOSS OF OUR FALLEN SAVIOR AND KING, KNOW THIS...
...THERE IS A BRIGHT NEW DAY ON THE HORIZON.
AND KING PIETRO WILL BE RIGHT HERE TO LEAD YOU TO IT.
THIS IS NAMOR'S DOING!
I'LL KILL HIM!
PROBABLY AT LEAST PARTIALLY.
YES, WELL, LET'S JOT IT DOWN ON YOUR PENDING MURDERS LIST...
...AND GET BACK TO THE TASK AT HAND. ALL THIS KILLING WILL BE EASIER ONCE YOUR POWERS ARE CURED.
DON'T YOU MOCK ME, CHILD.
UGH... WHAT IN DOOM'S NAME HAPP--

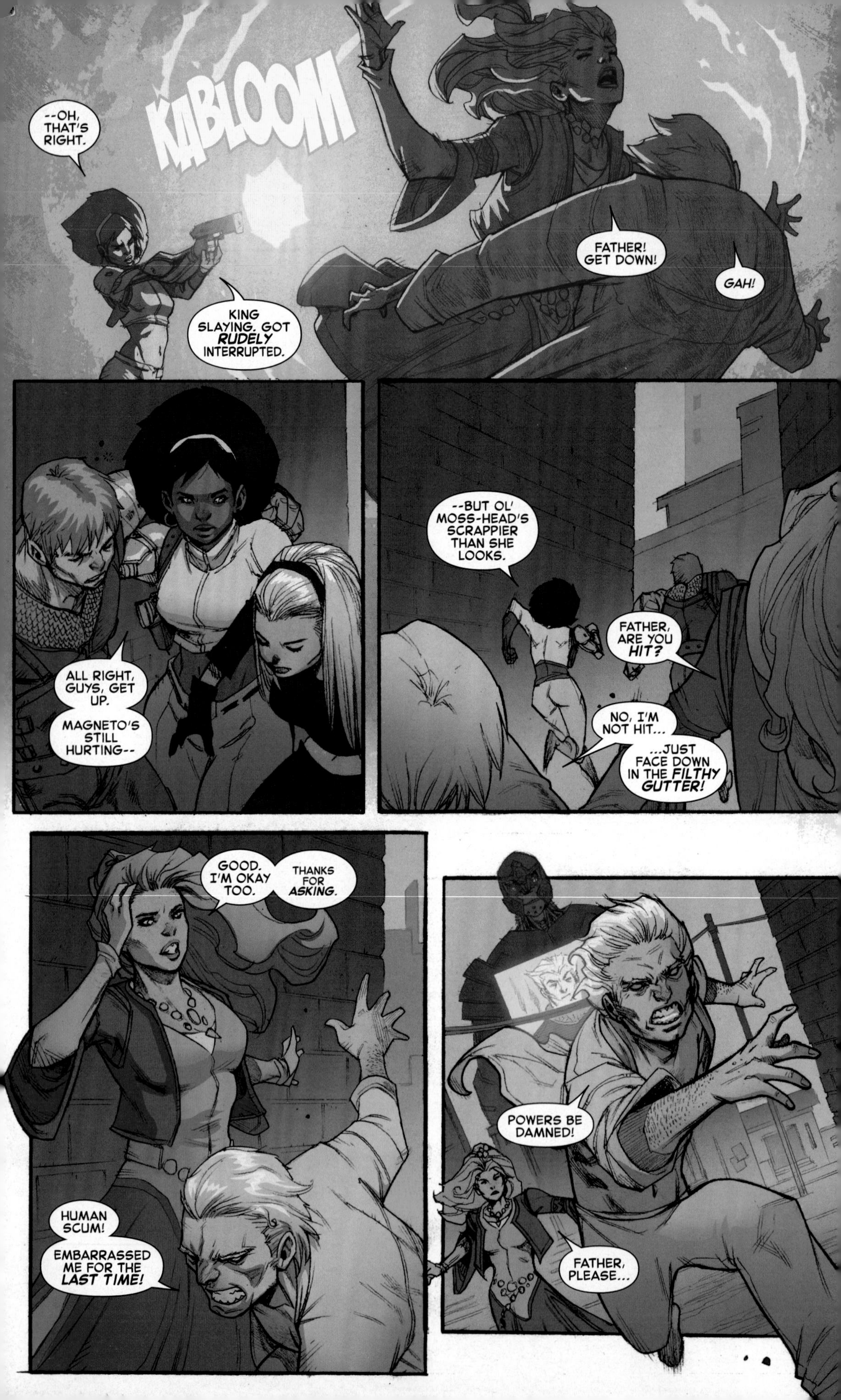

--OH, THAT'S RIGHT.
KABLOOM
KING SLAYING. GOT RUDELY INTERRUPTED.
FATHER! GET DOWN!
GAH!
ALL RIGHT, GUYS, GET UP.
MAGNETO'S STILL HURTING--
--BUT OL' MOSS-HEAD'S SCRAPPIER THAN SHE LOOKS.
FATHER, ARE YOU HIT?
NO, I'M NOT HIT...
...JUST FACE DOWN IN THE FILTHY GUTTER!
GOOD. I'M OKAY TOO.
THANKS FOR ASKING.
HUMAN SCUM!
EMBARRASSED ME FOR THE LAST TIME!
POWERS BE DAMNED!
FATHER, PLEASE...

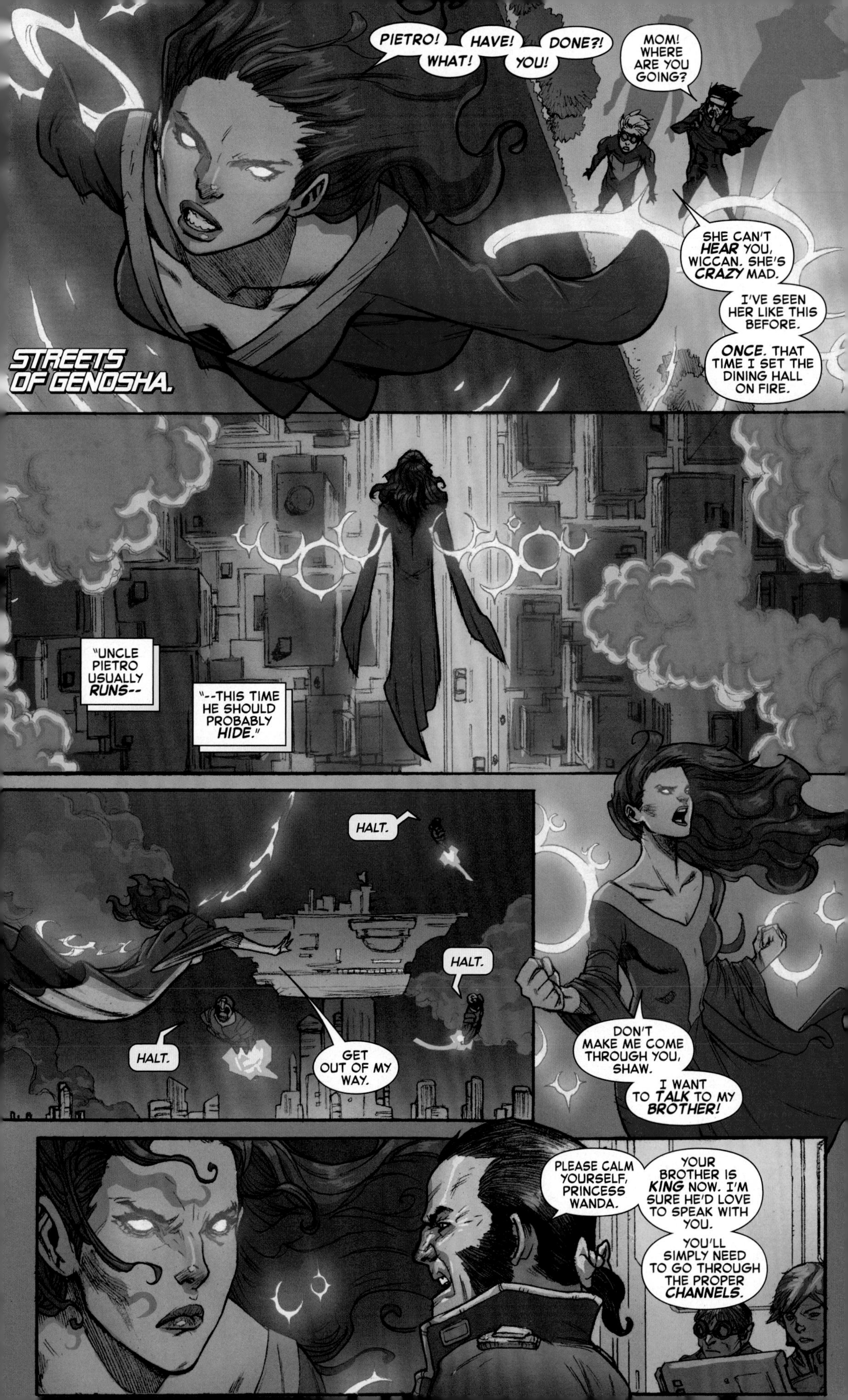
PIETRO! WHAT! HAVE! YOU! DONE?!
MOM! WHERE ARE YOU GOING?
SHE CAN'T HEAR YOU, WICCAN. SHE'S CRAZY MAD.
I'VE SEEN HER LIKE THIS BEFORE.
ONCE. THAT TIME I SET THE DINING HALL ON FIRE.
STREETS OF GENOSHA.
"UNCLE PIETRO USUALLY RUNS--
"--THIS TIME HE SHOULD PROBABLY HIDE."
HALT.
HALT.
HALT.
GET OUT OF MY WAY.
DON'T MAKE ME COME THROUGH YOU, SHAW.
I WANT TO TALK TO MY BROTHER!
PLEASE CALM YOURSELF, PRINCESS WANDA.
YOUR BROTHER IS KING NOW. I'M SURE HE'D LOVE TO SPEAK WITH YOU.
YOU'LL SIMPLY NEED TO GO THROUGH THE PROPER CHANNELS.

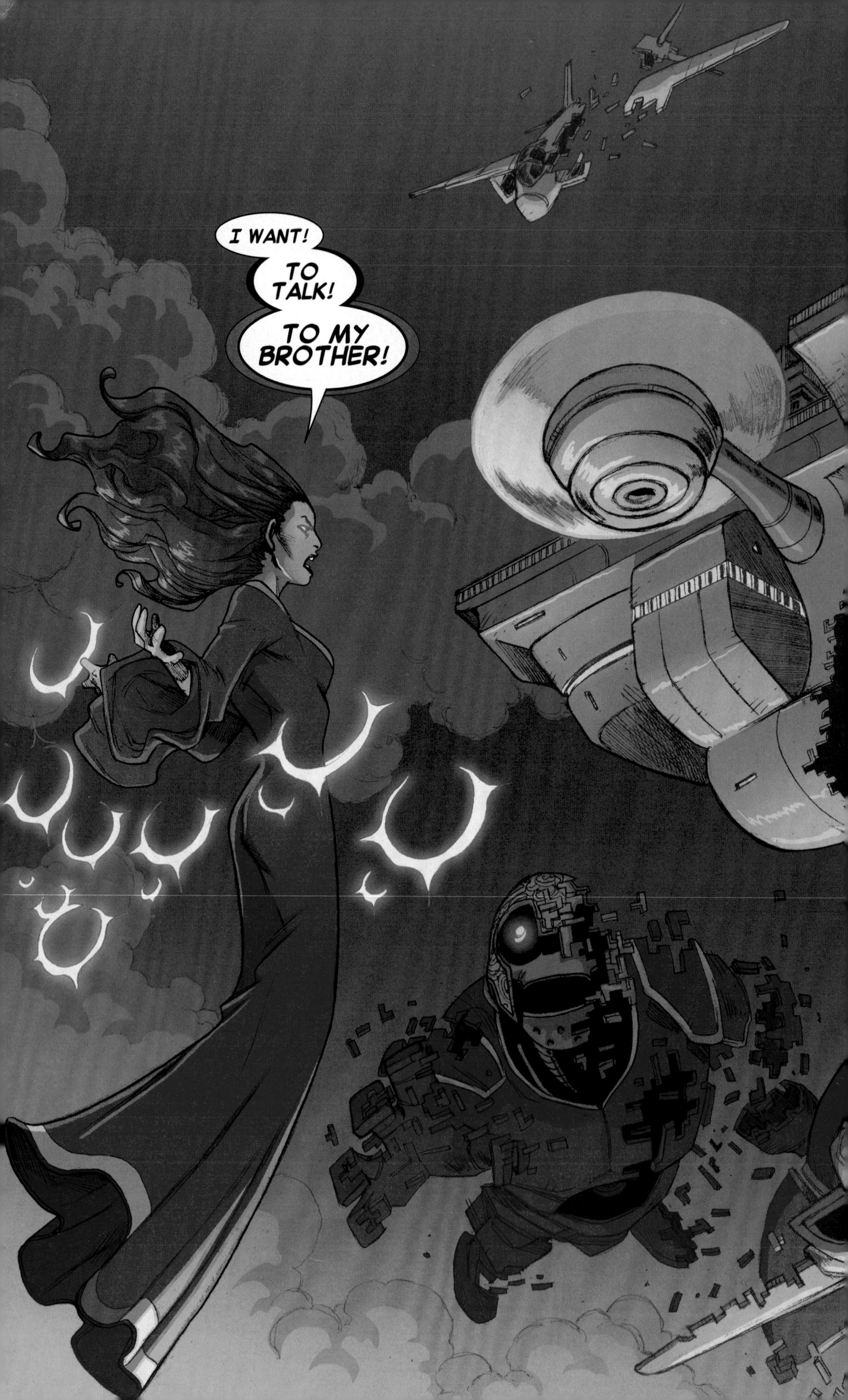
I WANT!
TO TALK!
TO MY BROTHER!

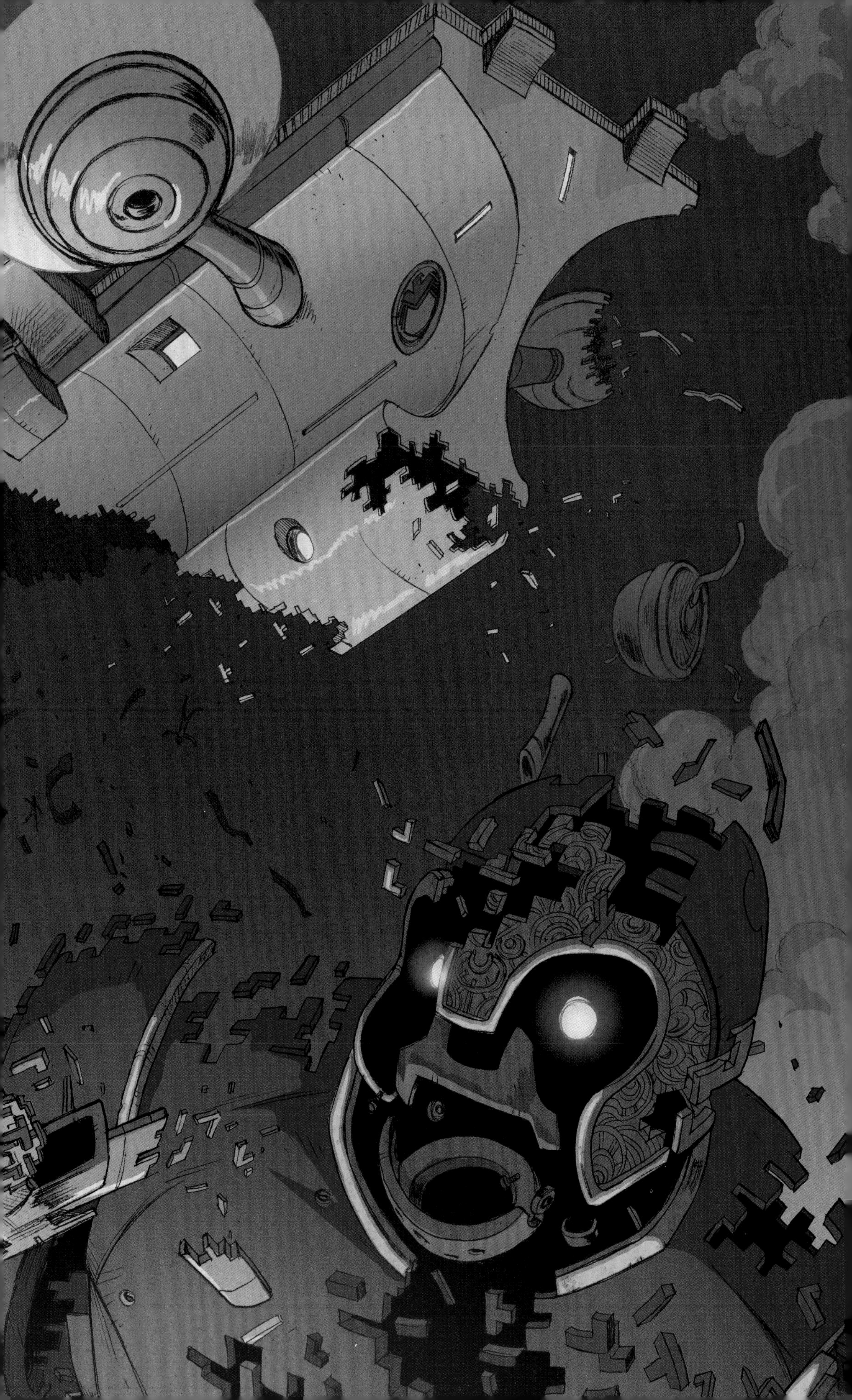

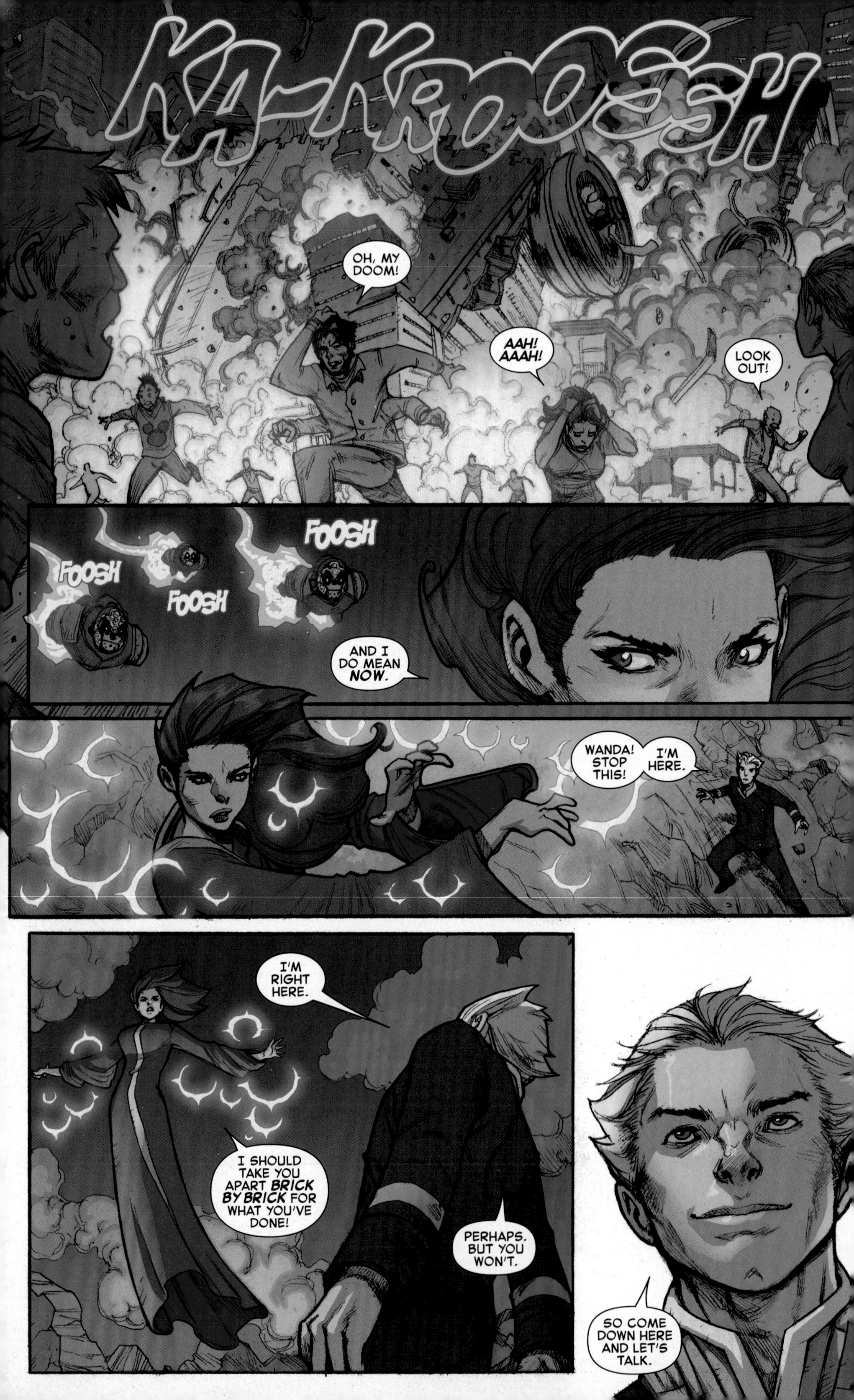
KA-KROOSH
OH, MY DOOM!
AAH! AAAH!
LOOK OUT!
FOOSH
FOOSH
FOOSH
AND I DO MEAN NOW.
WANDA! STOP THIS!
I'M HERE.
I'M RIGHT HERE.
I SHOULD TAKE YOU APART BRICK BY BRICK FOR WHAT YOU'VE DONE!
PERHAPS. BUT YOU WON'T.
SO COME DOWN HERE AND LET'S TALK.

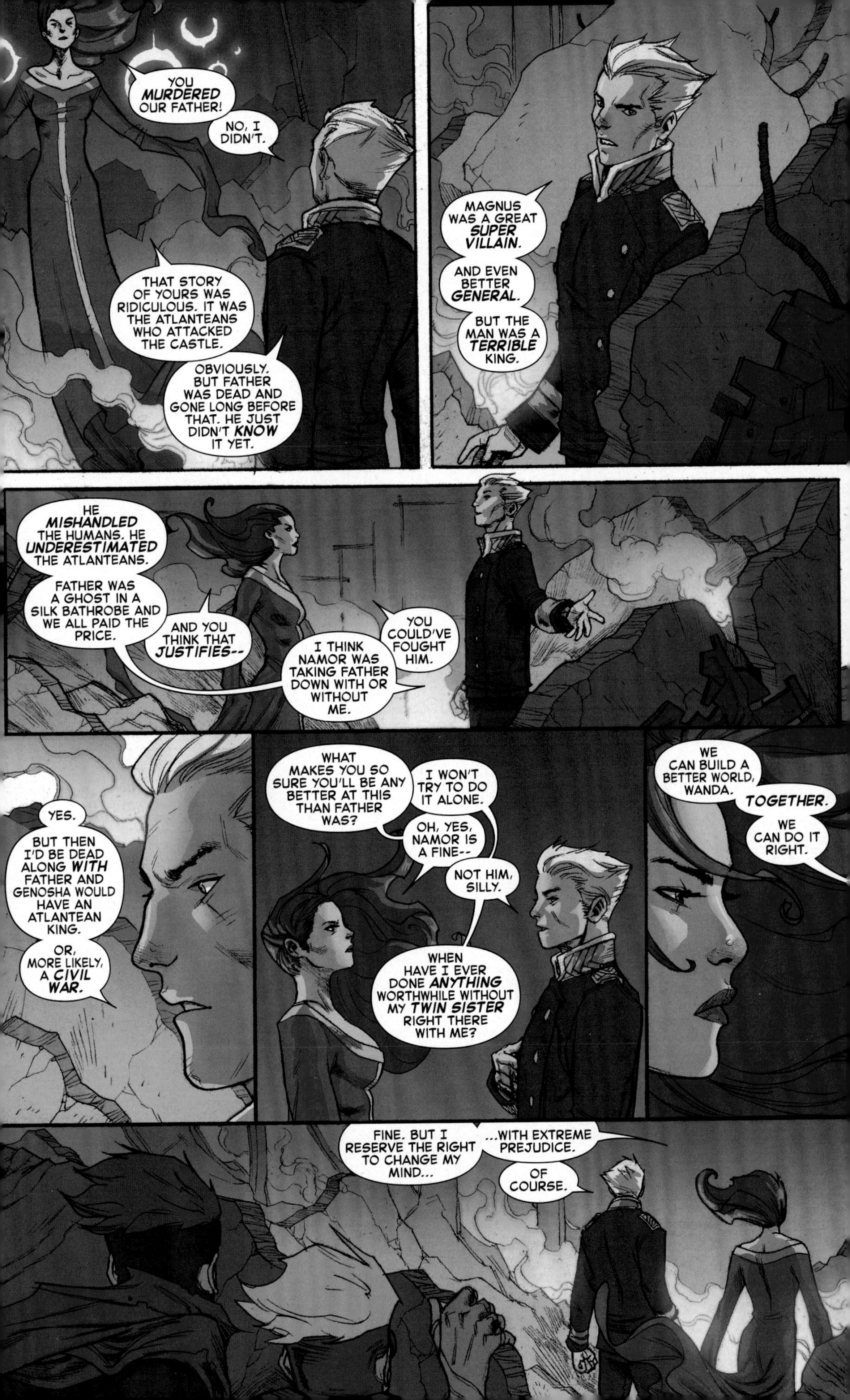

YOU *MURDERED* OUR FATHER!
NO, I DIDN'T.
THAT STORY OF YOURS WAS RIDICULOUS. IT WAS THE ATLANTEANS WHO ATTACKED THE CASTLE.
OBVIOUSLY. BUT FATHER WAS DEAD AND GONE LONG BEFORE THAT. HE JUST DIDN'T *KNOW* IT YET.
MAGNUS WAS A GREAT *SUPER VILLAIN.*
AND EVEN BETTER *GENERAL.*
BUT THE MAN WAS A *TERRIBLE* KING.
HE *MISHANDLED* THE HUMANS. HE *UNDERESTIMATED* THE ATLANTEANS.
FATHER WAS A GHOST IN A SILK BATHROBE AND WE ALL PAID THE PRICE.
AND YOU THINK THAT *JUSTIFIES--*
I THINK NAMOR WAS TAKING FATHER DOWN WITH OR WITHOUT ME.
YOU COULD'VE FOUGHT HIM.
YES.
BUT THEN I'D BE DEAD ALONG *WITH* FATHER AND GENOSHA WOULD HAVE AN ATLANTEAN KING.
OR, MORE LIKELY, A *CIVIL WAR.*
WHAT MAKES YOU SO SURE YOU'LL BE ANY BETTER AT THIS THAN FATHER WAS?
I WON'T TRY TO DO IT ALONE.
OH, YES, NAMOR IS A FINE--
NOT HIM, SILLY.
WHEN HAVE I EVER DONE *ANYTHING* WORTHWHILE WITHOUT MY *TWIN SISTER* RIGHT THERE WITH ME?
WE CAN BUILD A BETTER WORLD, WANDA.
TOGETHER.
WE CAN DO IT RIGHT.
FINE. BUT I RESERVE THE RIGHT TO CHANGE MY MIND...
...WITH EXTREME PREJUDICE.
OF COURSE.

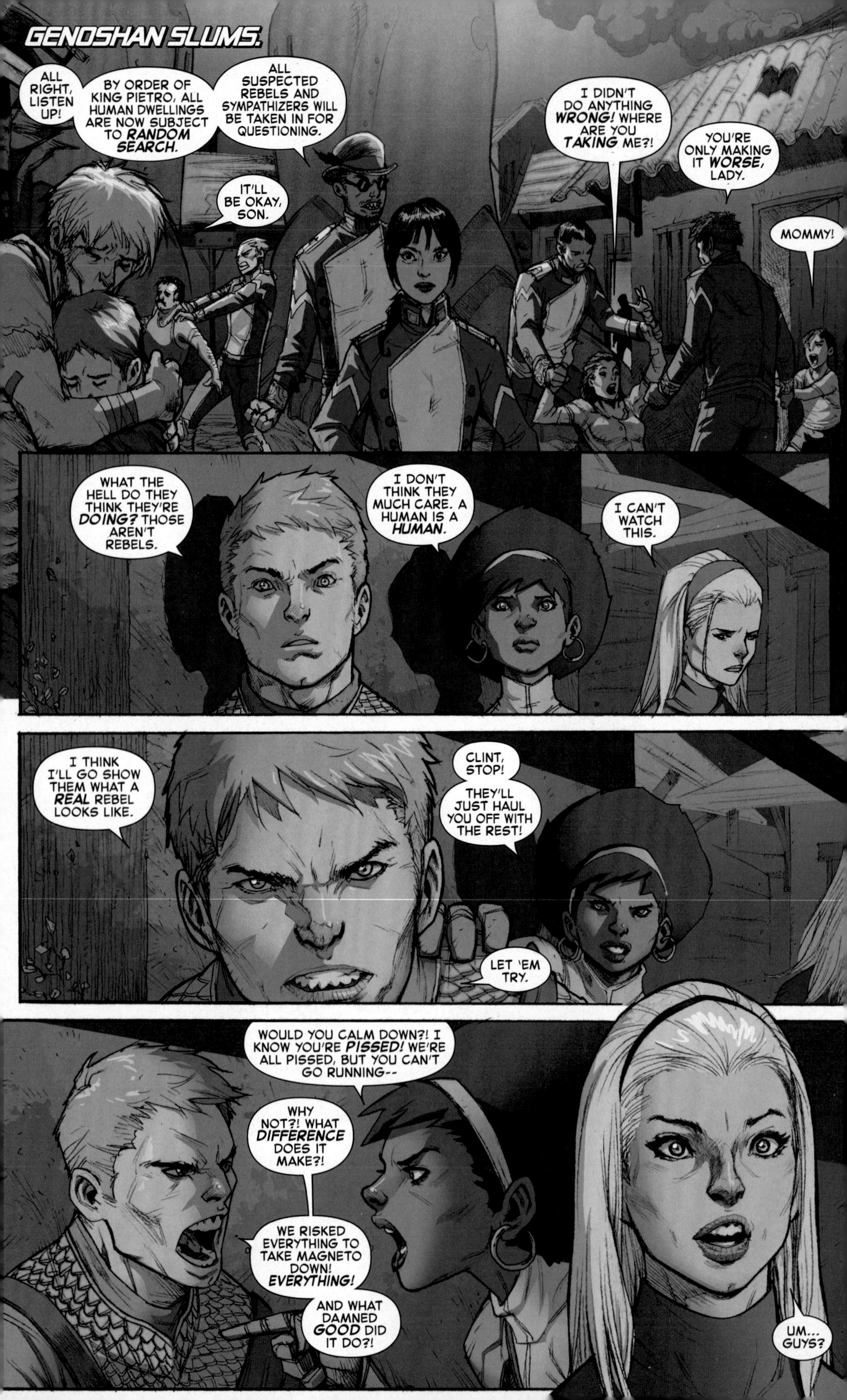

GENOSHAN SLUMS.
ALL RIGHT, LISTEN UP!
BY ORDER OF KING PIETRO, ALL HUMAN DWELLINGS ARE NOW SUBJECT TO RANDOM SEARCH.
ALL SUSPECTED REBELS AND SYMPATHIZERS WILL BE TAKEN IN FOR QUESTIONING.
IT'LL BE OKAY, SON.
I DIDN'T DO ANYTHING WRONG! WHERE ARE YOU TAKING ME?!
YOU'RE ONLY MAKING IT WORSE, LADY.
MOMMY!
WHAT THE HELL DO THEY THINK THEY'RE DOING? THOSE AREN'T REBELS.
I DON'T THINK THEY MUCH CARE. A HUMAN IS A HUMAN.
I CAN'T WATCH THIS.
I THINK I'LL GO SHOW THEM WHAT A REAL REBEL LOOKS LIKE.
CLINT, STOP!
THEY'LL JUST HAUL YOU OFF WITH THE REST!
LET 'EM TRY.
WOULD YOU CALM DOWN?! I KNOW YOU'RE PISSED! WE'RE ALL PISSED, BUT YOU CAN'T GO RUNNING--
WHY NOT?! WHAT DIFFERENCE DOES IT MAKE?!
WE RISKED EVERYTHING TO TAKE MAGNETO DOWN! EVERYTHING!
AND WHAT DAMNED GOOD DID IT DO?!
UM... GUYS?

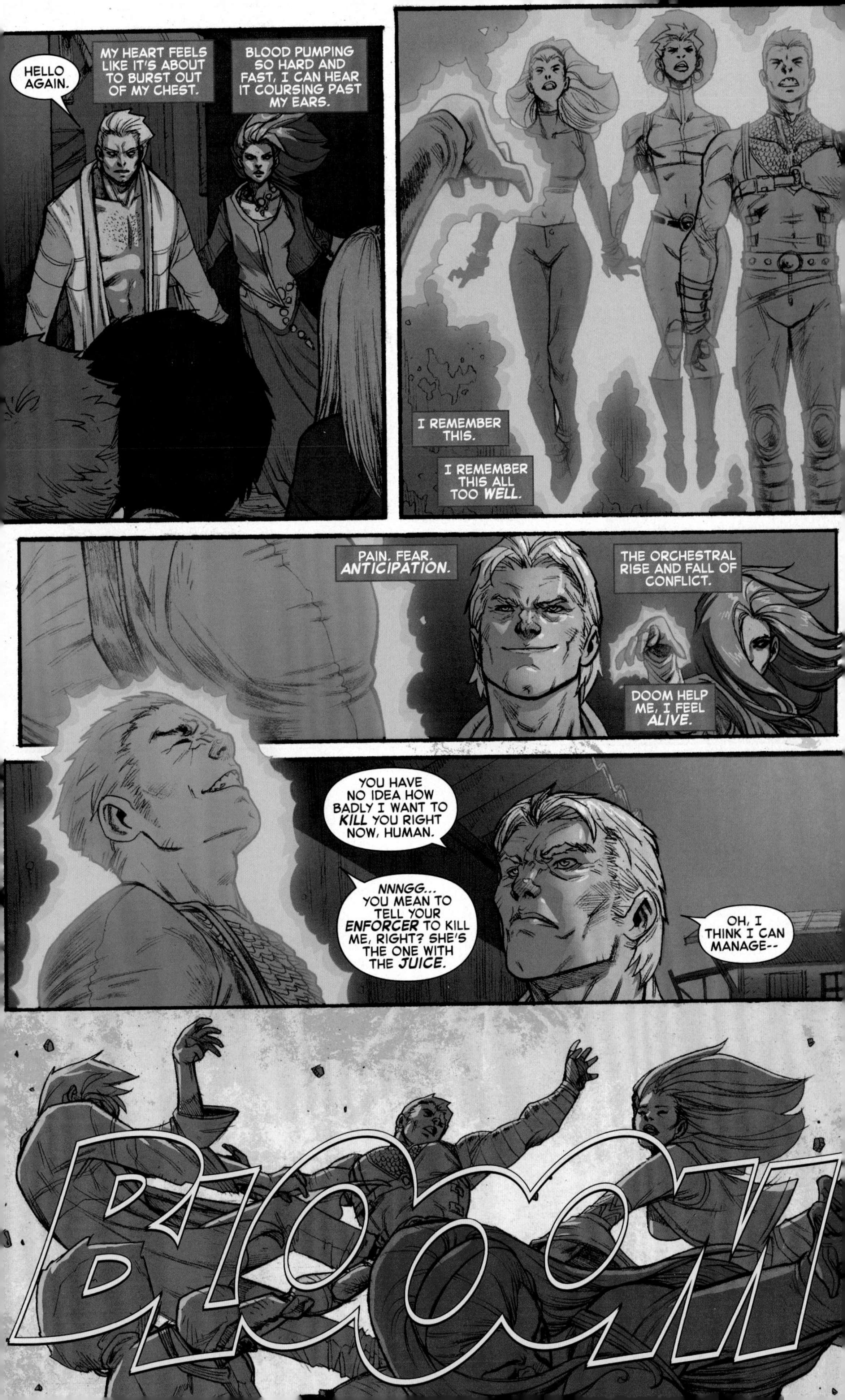
HELLO AGAIN.
MY HEART FEELS LIKE IT'S ABOUT TO BURST OUT OF MY CHEST.
BLOOD PUMPING SO HARD AND FAST, I CAN HEAR IT COURSING PAST MY EARS.
I REMEMBER THIS.
I REMEMBER THIS ALL TOO WELL.
PAIN. FEAR. ANTICIPATION.
THE ORCHESTRAL RISE AND FALL OF CONFLICT.
DOOM HELP ME, I FEEL ALIVE.
YOU HAVE NO IDEA HOW BADLY I WANT TO KILL YOU RIGHT NOW, HUMAN.
NNNGG... YOU MEAN TO TELL YOUR ENFORCER TO KILL ME, RIGHT? SHE'S THE ONE WITH THE JUICE.
OH, I THINK I CAN MANAGE--
BLOOM

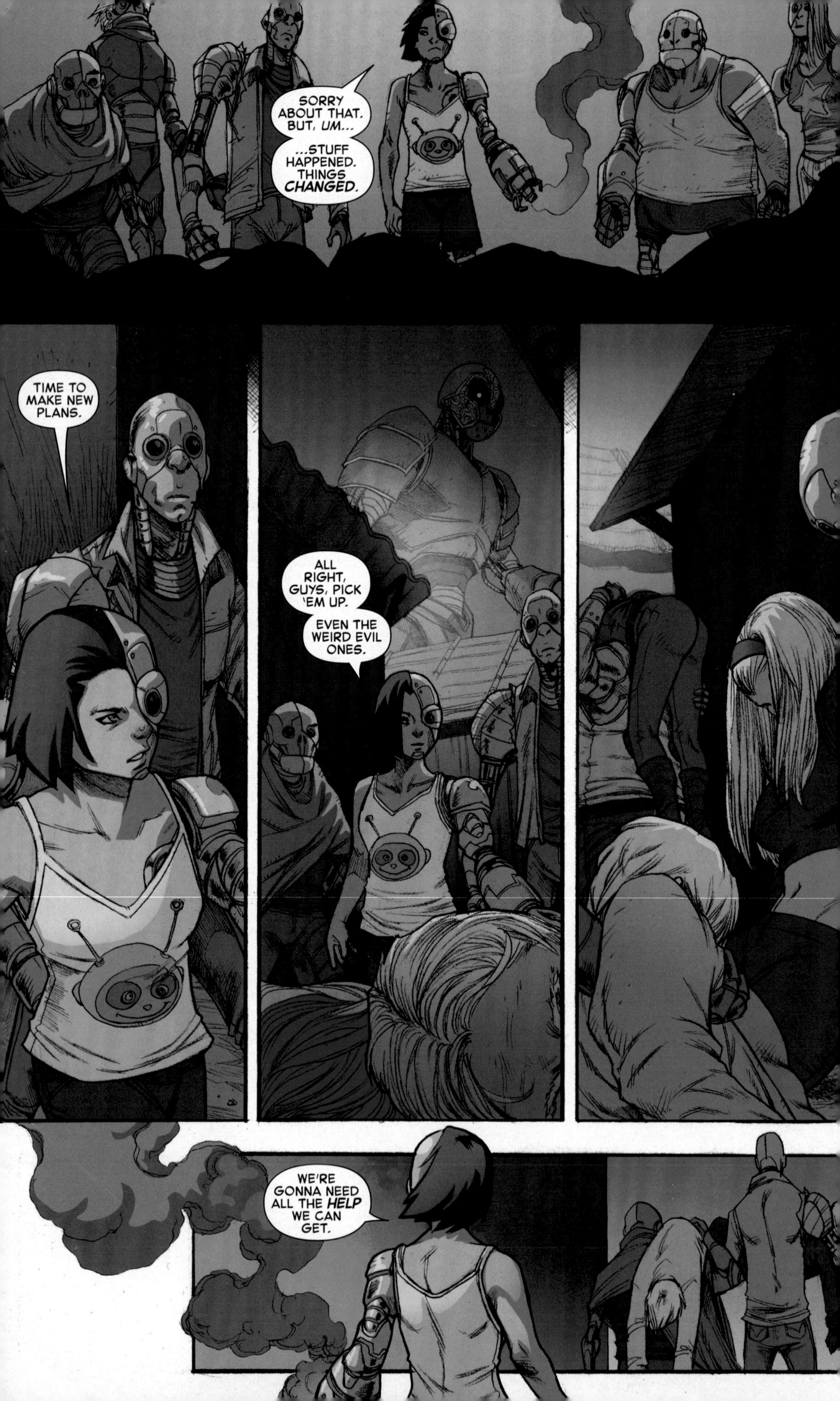
SORRY ABOUT THAT. BUT, UM...
...STUFF HAPPENED. THINGS CHANGED.
TIME TO MAKE NEW PLANS.
ALL RIGHT, GUYS, PICK 'EM UP.
EVEN THE WEIRD EVIL ONES.
WE'RE GONNA NEED ALL THE HELP WE CAN GET.

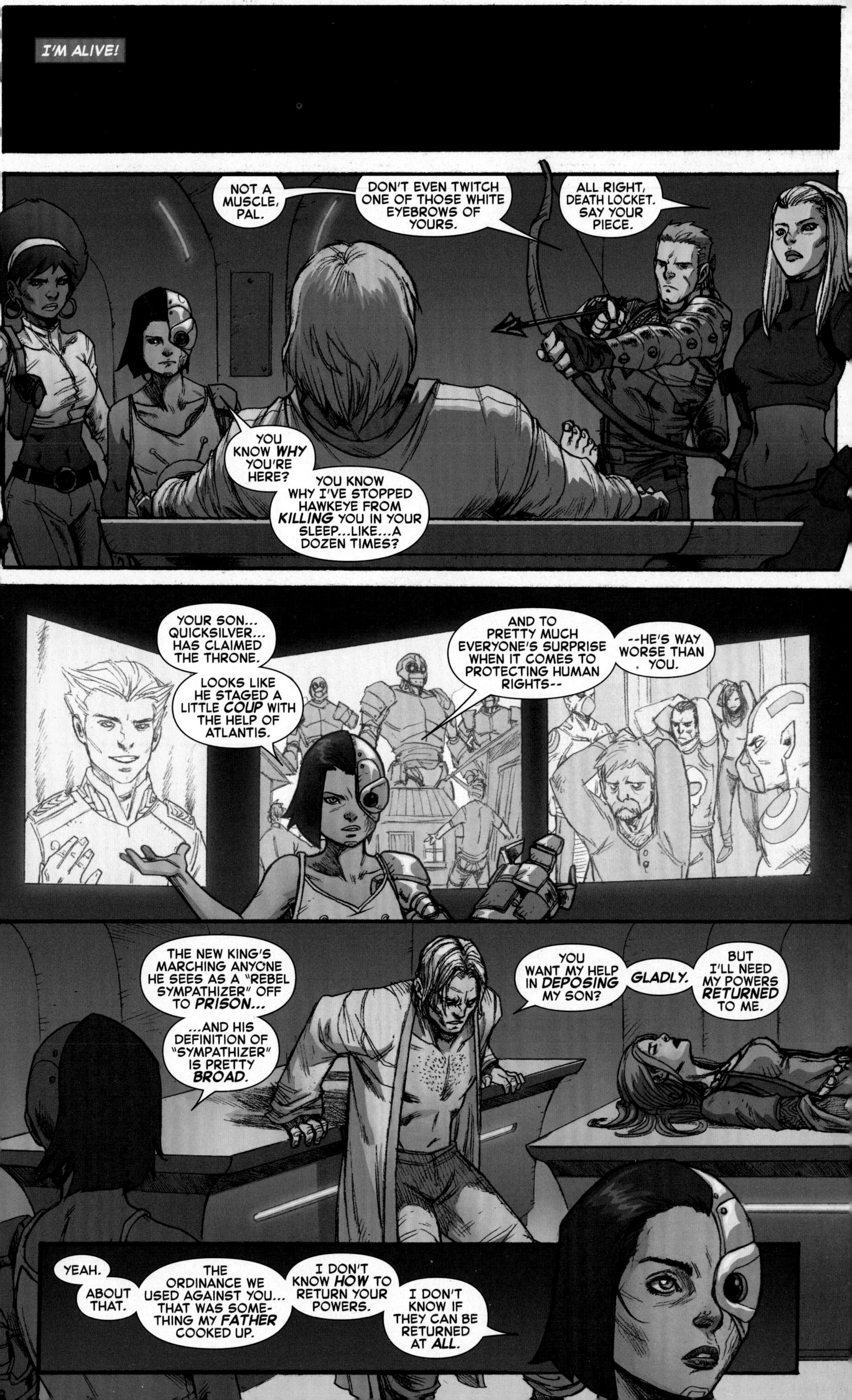

I'M ALIVE!
NOT A MUSCLE, PAL.
DON'T EVEN TWITCH ONE OF THOSE WHITE EYEBROWS OF YOURS.
ALL RIGHT, DEATH LOCKET. SAY YOUR PIECE.
YOU KNOW WHY YOU'RE HERE?
YOU KNOW WHY I'VE STOPPED HAWKEYE FROM KILLING YOU IN YOUR SLEEP...LIKE...A DOZEN TIMES?
YOUR SON... QUICKSILVER... HAS CLAIMED THE THRONE.
LOOKS LIKE HE STAGED A LITTLE COUP WITH THE HELP OF ATLANTIS.
AND TO PRETTY MUCH EVERYONE'S SURPRISE WHEN IT COMES TO PROTECTING HUMAN RIGHTS--
--HE'S WAY WORSE THAN YOU.
THE NEW KING'S MARCHING ANYONE HE SEES AS A "REBEL SYMPATHIZER" OFF TO PRISON...
...AND HIS DEFINITION OF "SYMPATHIZER" IS PRETTY BROAD.
YOU WANT MY HELP IN DEPOSING MY SON?
GLADLY.
BUT I'LL NEED MY POWERS RETURNED TO ME.
YEAH.
ABOUT THAT.
THE ORDINANCE WE USED AGAINST YOU... THAT WAS SOMETHING MY FATHER COOKED UP.
I DON'T KNOW HOW TO RETURN YOUR POWERS.
I DON'T KNOW IF THEY CAN BE RETURNED AT ALL.

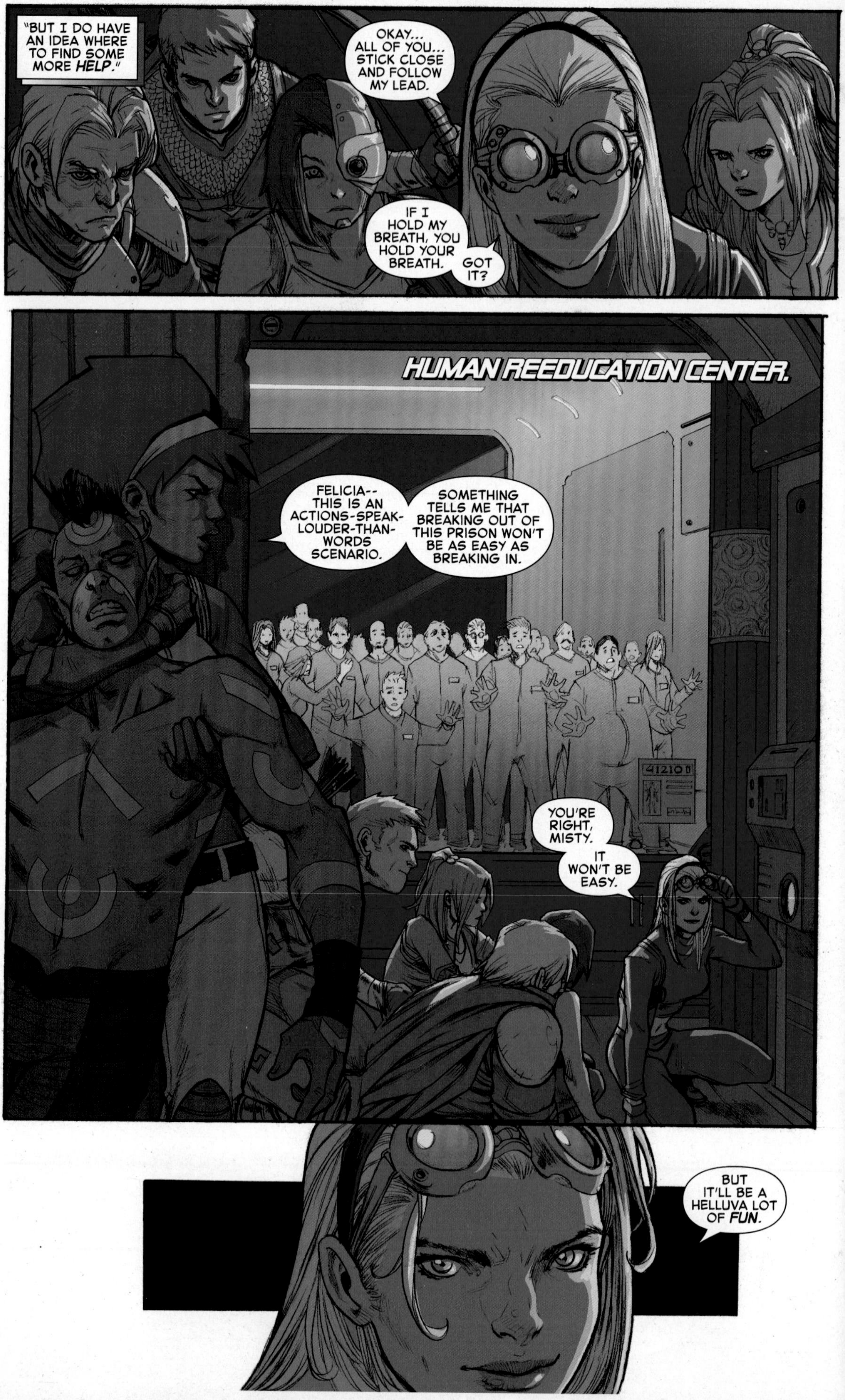
"BUT I DO HAVE AN IDEA WHERE TO FIND SOME MORE HELP."
OKAY... ALL OF YOU... STICK CLOSE AND FOLLOW MY LEAD.
IF I HOLD MY BREATH, YOU HOLD YOUR BREATH.
GOT IT?
HUMAN REEDUCATION CENTER.
FELICIA-- THIS IS AN ACTIONS-SPEAK-LOUDER-THAN-WORDS SCENARIO.
SOMETHING TELLS ME THAT BREAKING OUT OF THIS PRISON WON'T BE AS EASY AS BREAKING IN.
41210
YOU'RE RIGHT, MISTY.
IT WON'T BE EASY.
BUT IT'LL BE A HELLUVA LOT OF FUN.

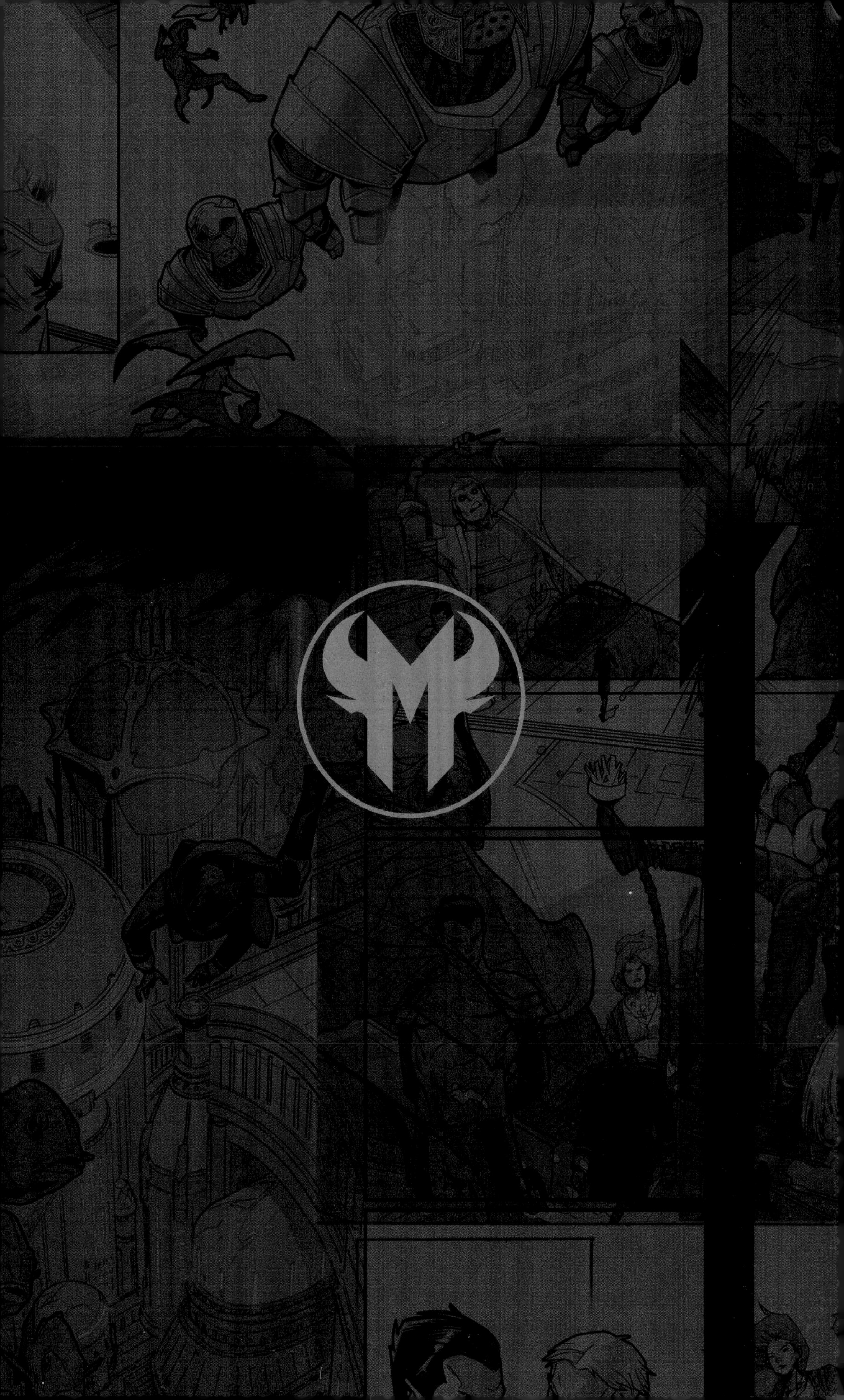

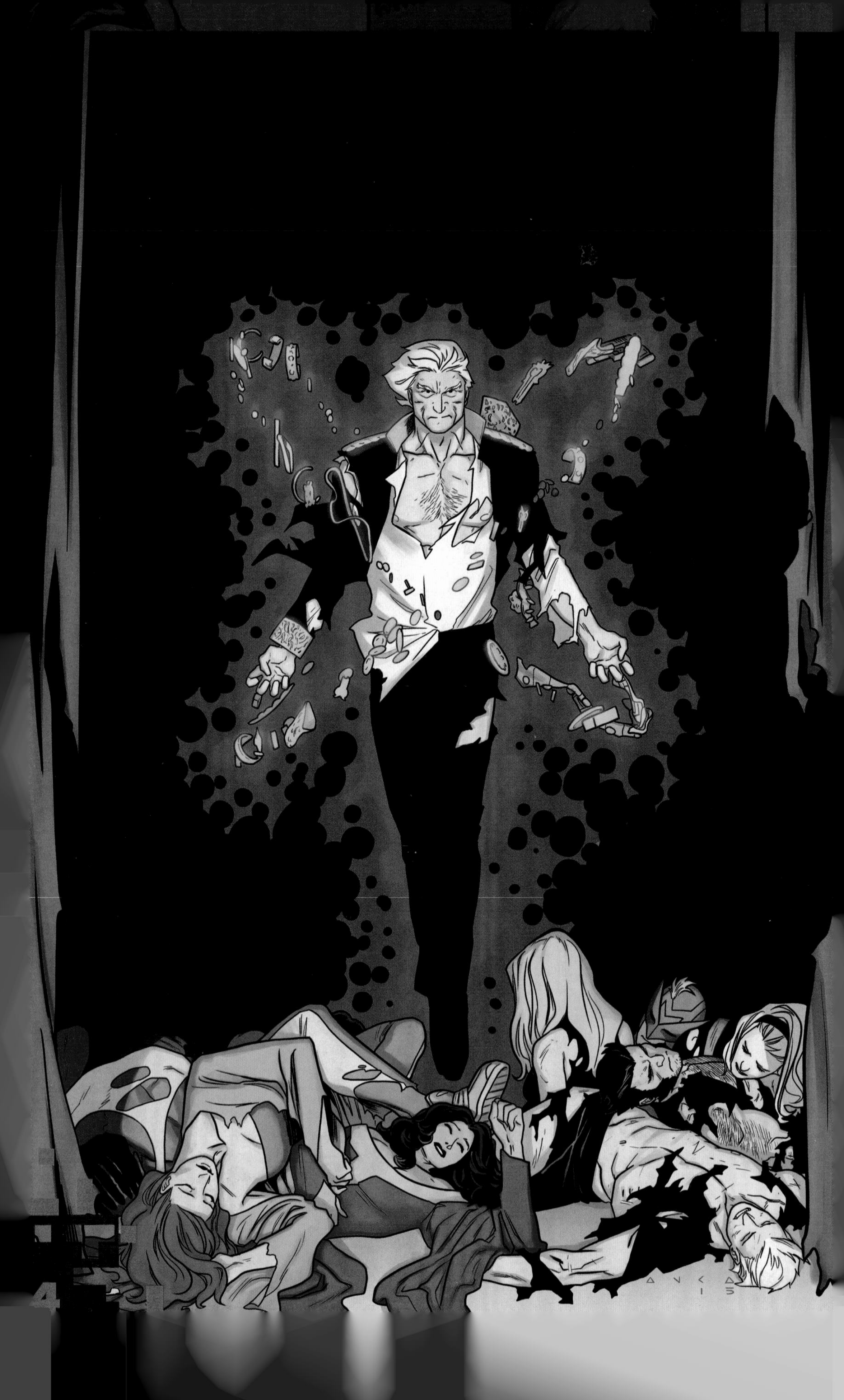

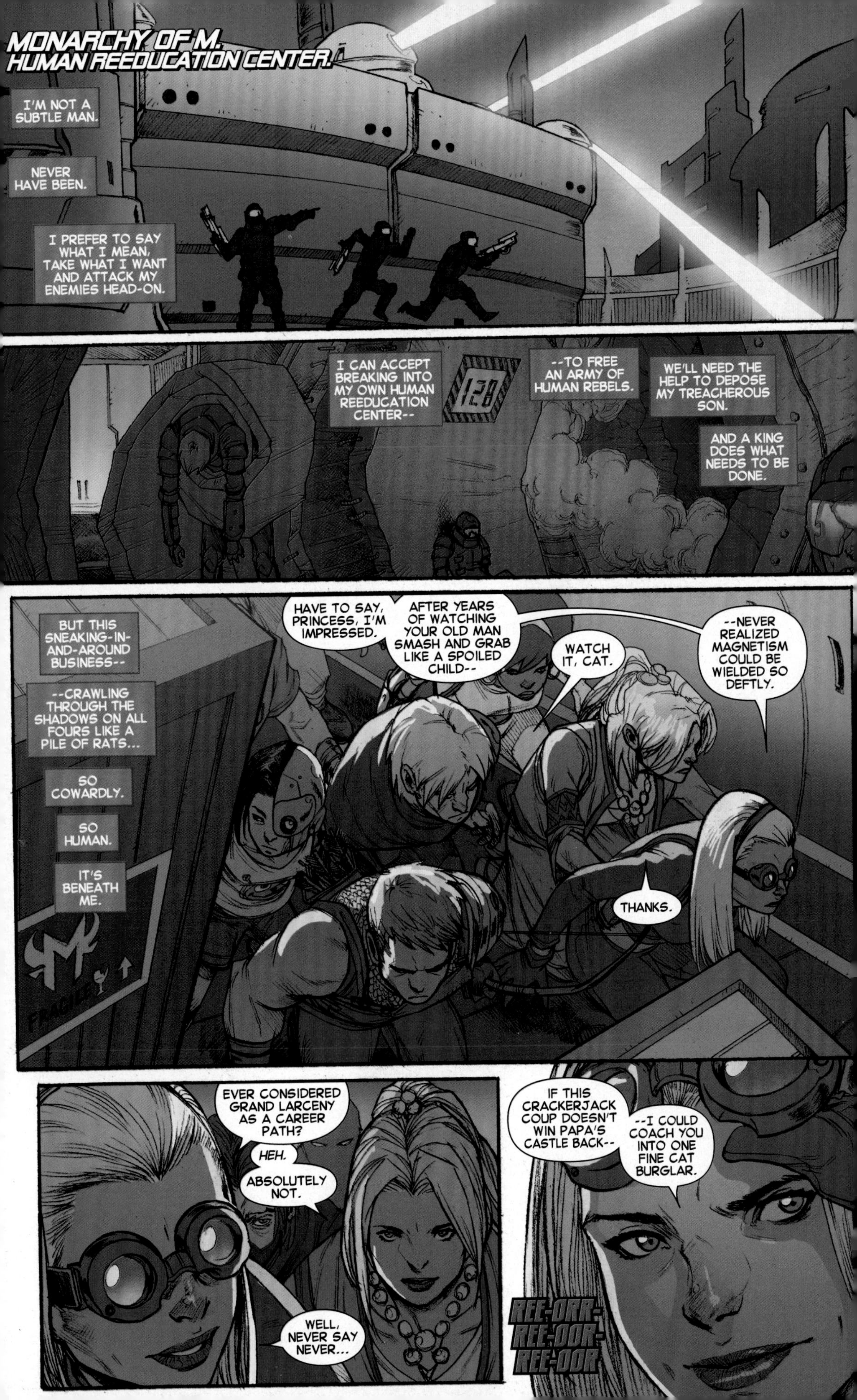
MONARCHY OF M.
HUMAN REEDUCATION CENTER.
I'M NOT A SUBTLE MAN.
NEVER HAVE BEEN.
I PREFER TO SAY WHAT I MEAN, TAKE WHAT I WANT AND ATTACK MY ENEMIES HEAD-ON.
I CAN ACCEPT BREAKING INTO MY OWN HUMAN REEDUCATION CENTER--
128
--TO FREE AN ARMY OF HUMAN REBELS.
WE'LL NEED THE HELP TO DEPOSE MY TREACHEROUS SON.
AND A KING DOES WHAT NEEDS TO BE DONE.
BUT THIS SNEAKING-IN-AND-AROUND BUSINESS--
--CRAWLING THROUGH THE SHADOWS ON ALL FOURS LIKE A PILE OF RATS...
SO COWARDLY.
SO HUMAN.
IT'S BENEATH ME.
HAVE TO SAY, PRINCESS, I'M IMPRESSED.
AFTER YEARS OF WATCHING YOUR OLD MAN SMASH AND GRAB LIKE A SPOILED CHILD--
--NEVER REALIZED MAGNETISM COULD BE WIELDED SO DEFTLY.
WATCH IT, CAT.
THANKS.
FRAGILE
EVER CONSIDERED GRAND LARCENY AS A CAREER PATH?
HEH.
ABSOLUTELY NOT.
WELL, NEVER SAY NEVER...
IF THIS CRACKERJACK COUP DOESN'T WIN PAPA'S CASTLE BACK--
--I COULD COACH YOU INTO ONE FINE CAT BURGLAR.
REE-ORR-REE-OOR-REE-OOR

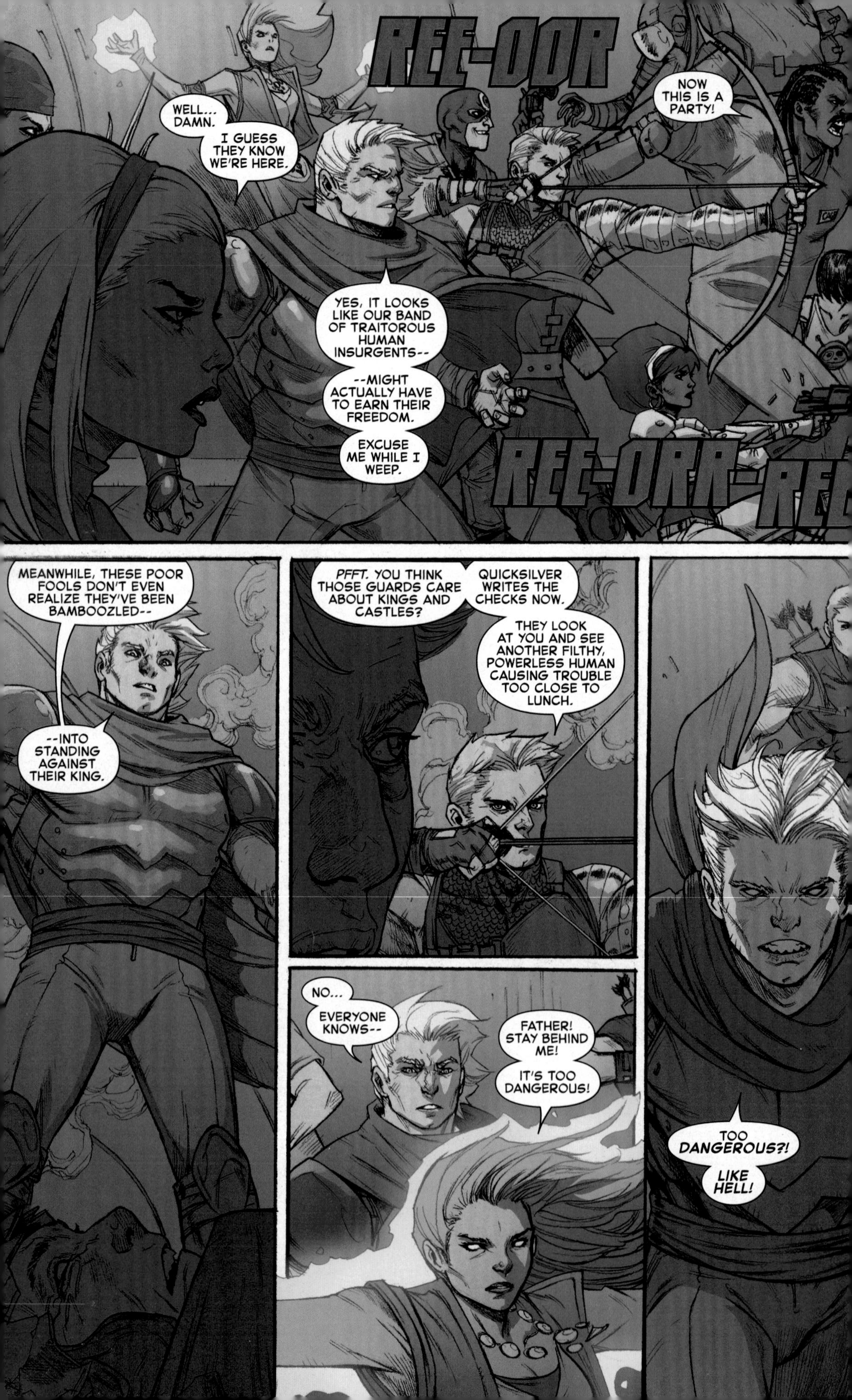
REE-OOR
WELL... DAMN.
I GUESS THEY KNOW WE'RE HERE.
NOW THIS IS A PARTY!
YES, IT LOOKS LIKE OUR BAND OF TRAITOROUS HUMAN INSURGENTS--
--MIGHT ACTUALLY HAVE TO EARN THEIR FREEDOM.
EXCUSE ME WHILE I WEEP.
REE-ORR-REE
MEANWHILE, THESE POOR FOOLS DON'T EVEN REALIZE THEY'VE BEEN BAMBOOZLED--
--INTO STANDING AGAINST THEIR KING.
PFFT. YOU THINK THOSE GUARDS CARE ABOUT KINGS AND CASTLES?
QUICKSILVER WRITES THE CHECKS NOW.
THEY LOOK AT YOU AND SEE ANOTHER FILTHY, POWERLESS HUMAN CAUSING TROUBLE TOO CLOSE TO LUNCH.
NO...
EVERYONE KNOWS--
FATHER! STAY BEHIND ME!
IT'S TOO DANGEROUS!
TOO DANGEROUS?!
LIKE HELL!

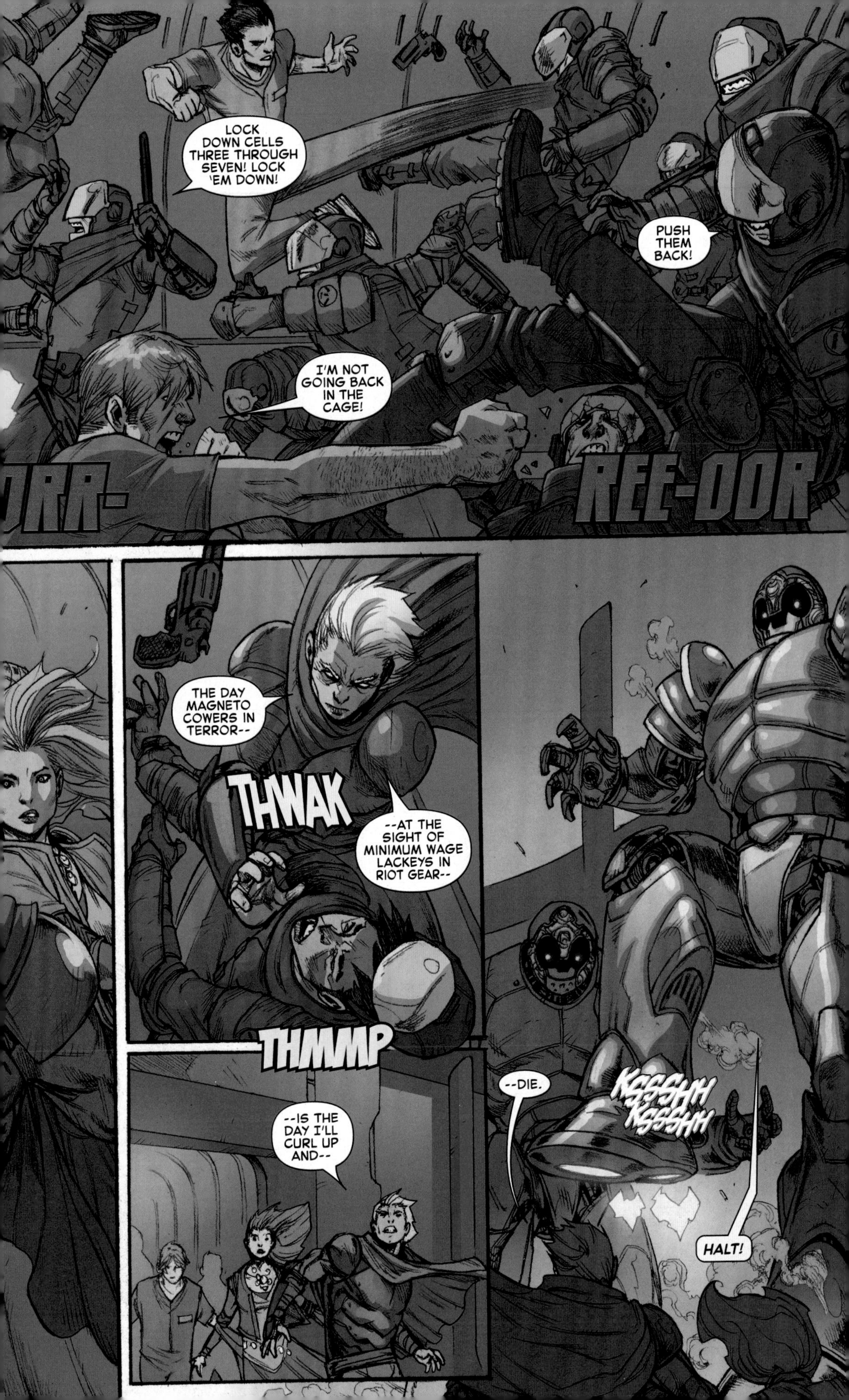

LOCK DOWN CELLS THREE THROUGH SEVEN! LOCK 'EM DOWN!
PUSH THEM BACK!
I'M NOT GOING BACK IN THE CAGE!
DRR-
REE-DOR
THE DAY MAGNETO COWERS IN TERROR--
THWAK
--AT THE SIGHT OF MINIMUM WAGE LACKEYS IN RIOT GEAR--
THMMP
--IS THE DAY I'LL CURL UP AND--
--DIE.
KSSSHH KSSSHH
HALT!

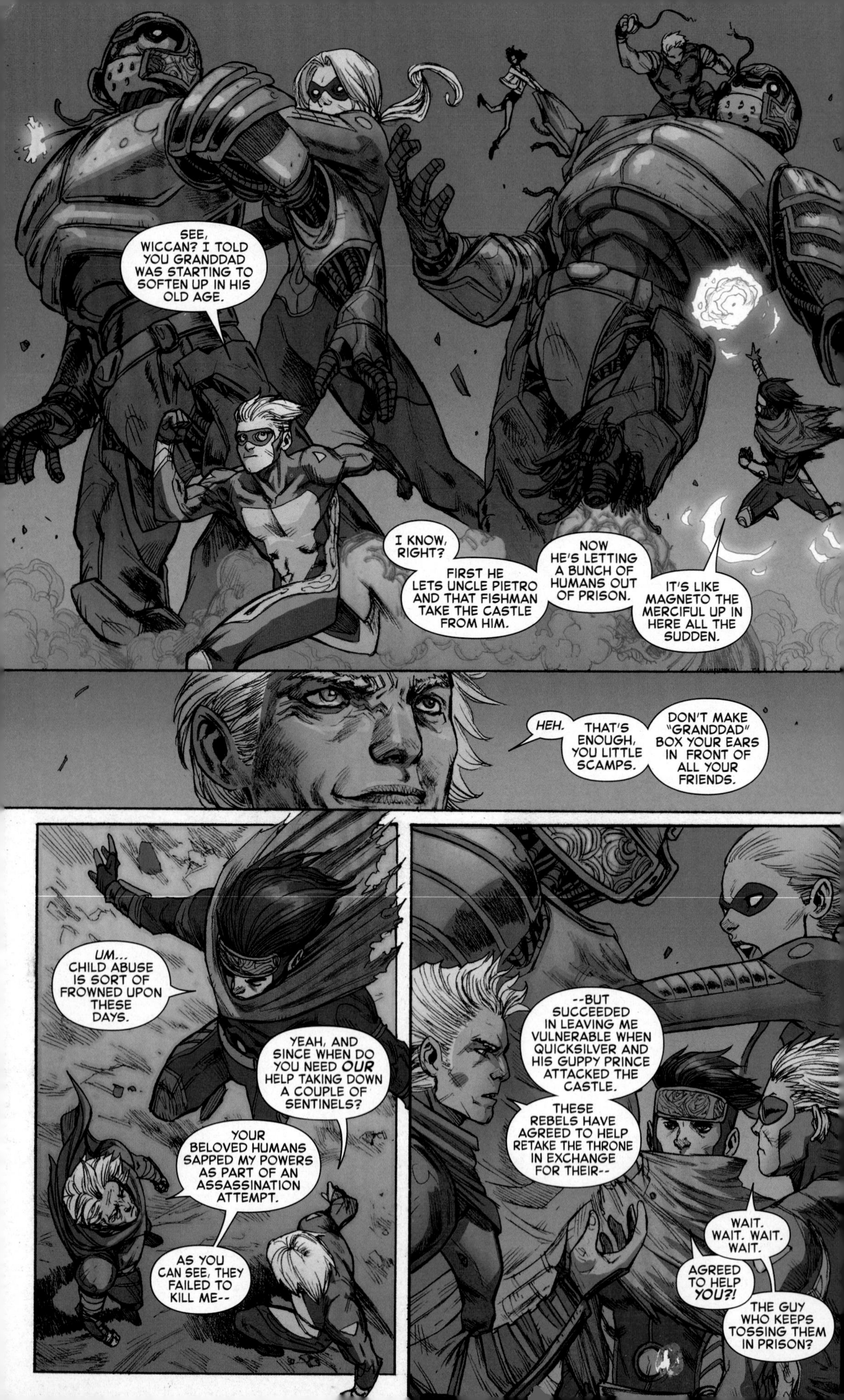
SEE, WICCAN? I TOLD YOU GRANDDAD WAS STARTING TO SOFTEN UP IN HIS OLD AGE.
I KNOW, RIGHT?
FIRST HE LETS UNCLE PIETRO AND THAT FISHMAN TAKE THE CASTLE FROM HIM.
NOW HE'S LETTING A BUNCH OF HUMANS OUT OF PRISON.
IT'S LIKE MAGNETO THE MERCIFUL UP IN HERE ALL THE SUDDEN.
HEH.
THAT'S ENOUGH, YOU LITTLE SCAMPS.
DON'T MAKE "GRANDDAD" BOX YOUR EARS IN FRONT OF ALL YOUR FRIENDS.
UM... CHILD ABUSE IS SORT OF FROWNED UPON THESE DAYS.
YEAH, AND SINCE WHEN DO YOU NEED *OUR* HELP TAKING DOWN A COUPLE OF SENTINELS?
YOUR BELOVED HUMANS SAPPED MY POWERS AS PART OF AN ASSASSINATION ATTEMPT.
AS YOU CAN SEE, THEY FAILED TO KILL ME--
--BUT SUCCEEDED IN LEAVING ME VULNERABLE WHEN QUICKSILVER AND HIS GUPPY PRINCE ATTACKED THE CASTLE.
THESE REBELS HAVE AGREED TO HELP RETAKE THE THRONE IN EXCHANGE FOR THEIR--
WAIT. WAIT. WAIT. WAIT.
AGREED TO HELP *YOU?!*
THE GUY WHO KEEPS TOSSING THEM IN PRISON?

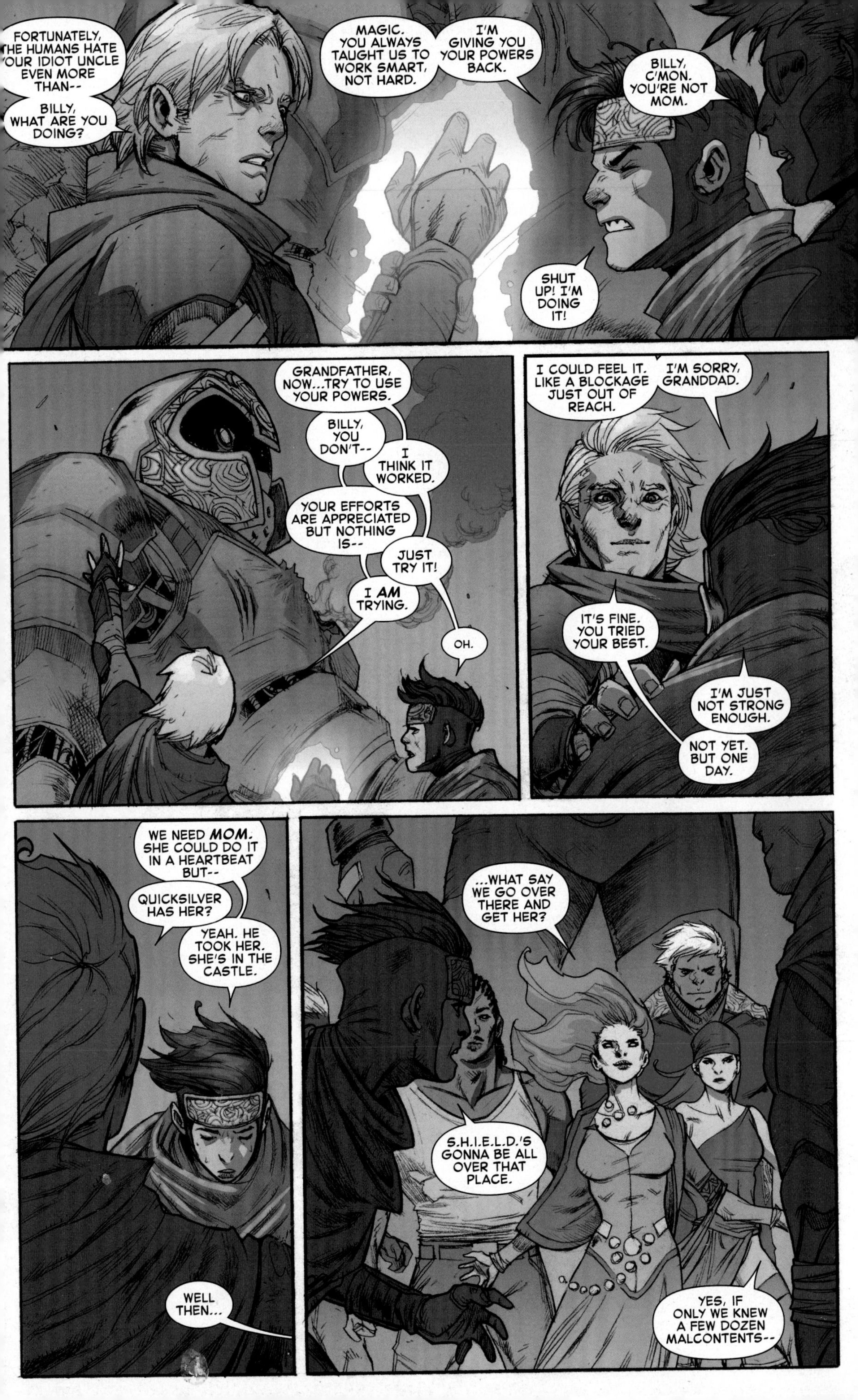
FORTUNATELY, THE HUMANS HATE YOUR IDIOT UNCLE EVEN MORE THAN--
BILLY, WHAT ARE YOU DOING?
MAGIC. YOU ALWAYS TAUGHT US TO WORK SMART, NOT HARD.
I'M GIVING YOU YOUR POWERS BACK.
BILLY, C'MON. YOU'RE NOT MOM.
SHUT UP! I'M DOING IT!
GRANDFATHER, NOW...TRY TO USE YOUR POWERS.
BILLY, YOU DON'T--
I THINK IT WORKED.
YOUR EFFORTS ARE APPRECIATED BUT NOTHING IS--
JUST TRY IT!
I AM TRYING.
OH.
I COULD FEEL IT. LIKE A BLOCKAGE JUST OUT OF REACH.
I'M SORRY, GRANDDAD.
IT'S FINE. YOU TRIED YOUR BEST.
I'M JUST NOT STRONG ENOUGH.
NOT YET. BUT ONE DAY.
WE NEED MOM. SHE COULD DO IT IN A HEARTBEAT BUT--
QUICKSILVER HAS HER?
YEAH. HE TOOK HER. SHE'S IN THE CASTLE.
WELL THEN...
...WHAT SAY WE GO OVER THERE AND GET HER?
S.H.I.E.L.D.'S GONNA BE ALL OVER THAT PLACE.
YES, IF ONLY WE KNEW A FEW DOZEN MALCONTENTS--

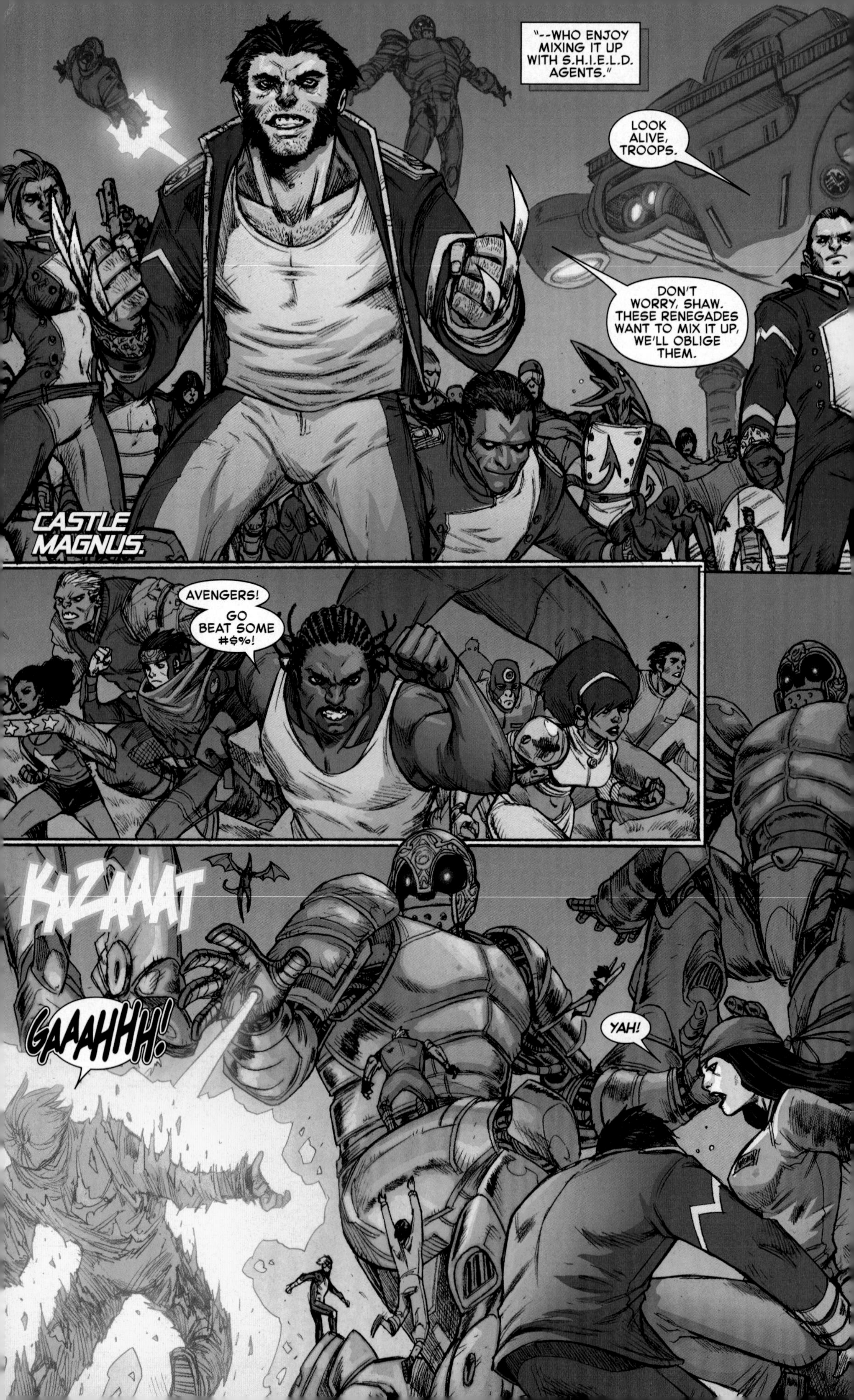
"--WHO ENJOY MIXING IT UP WITH S.H.I.E.L.D. AGENTS."
LOOK ALIVE, TROOPS.
DON'T WORRY, SHAW. THESE RENEGADES WANT TO MIX IT UP, WE'LL OBLIGE THEM.
CASTLE MAGNUS.
AVENGERS! GO BEAT SOME #$%!
KAZAAAT
GAAAHHH!
YAH!

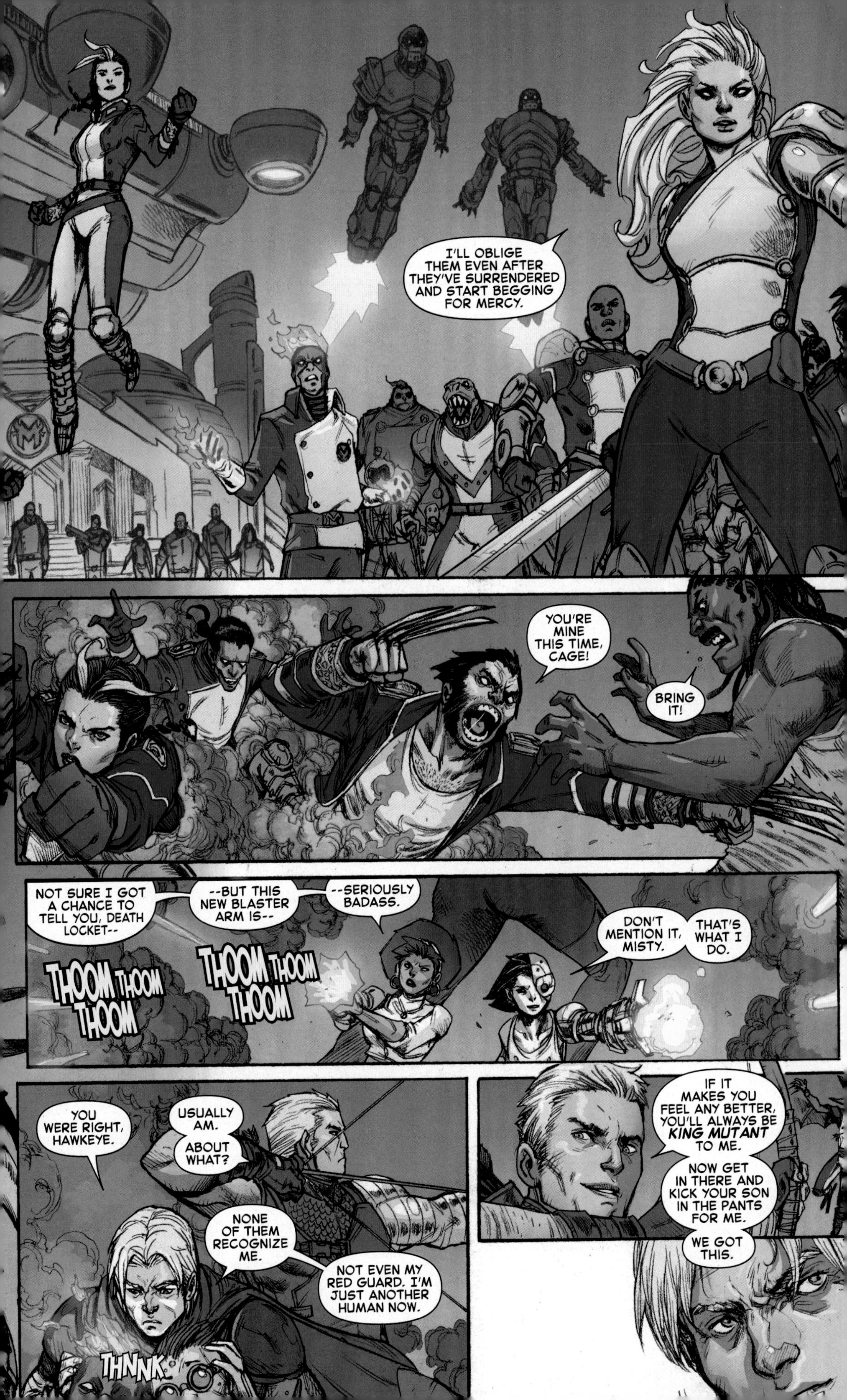
I'LL OBLIGE THEM EVEN AFTER THEY'VE SURRENDERED AND START BEGGING FOR MERCY.
YOU'RE MINE THIS TIME, CAGE!
BRING IT!
NOT SURE I GOT A CHANCE TO TELL YOU, DEATH LOCKET--
--BUT THIS NEW BLASTER ARM IS--
--SERIOUSLY BADASS.
THOOM THOOM THOOM
THOOM THOOM THOOM
DON'T MENTION IT, MISTY.
THAT'S WHAT I DO.
YOU WERE RIGHT, HAWKEYE.
USUALLY AM.
ABOUT WHAT?
NONE OF THEM RECOGNIZE ME.
NOT EVEN MY RED GUARD. I'M JUST ANOTHER HUMAN NOW.
THNNK
IF IT MAKES YOU FEEL ANY BETTER, YOU'LL ALWAYS BE *KING MUTANT* TO ME.
NOW GET IN THERE AND KICK YOUR SON IN THE PANTS FOR ME.
WE GOT THIS.

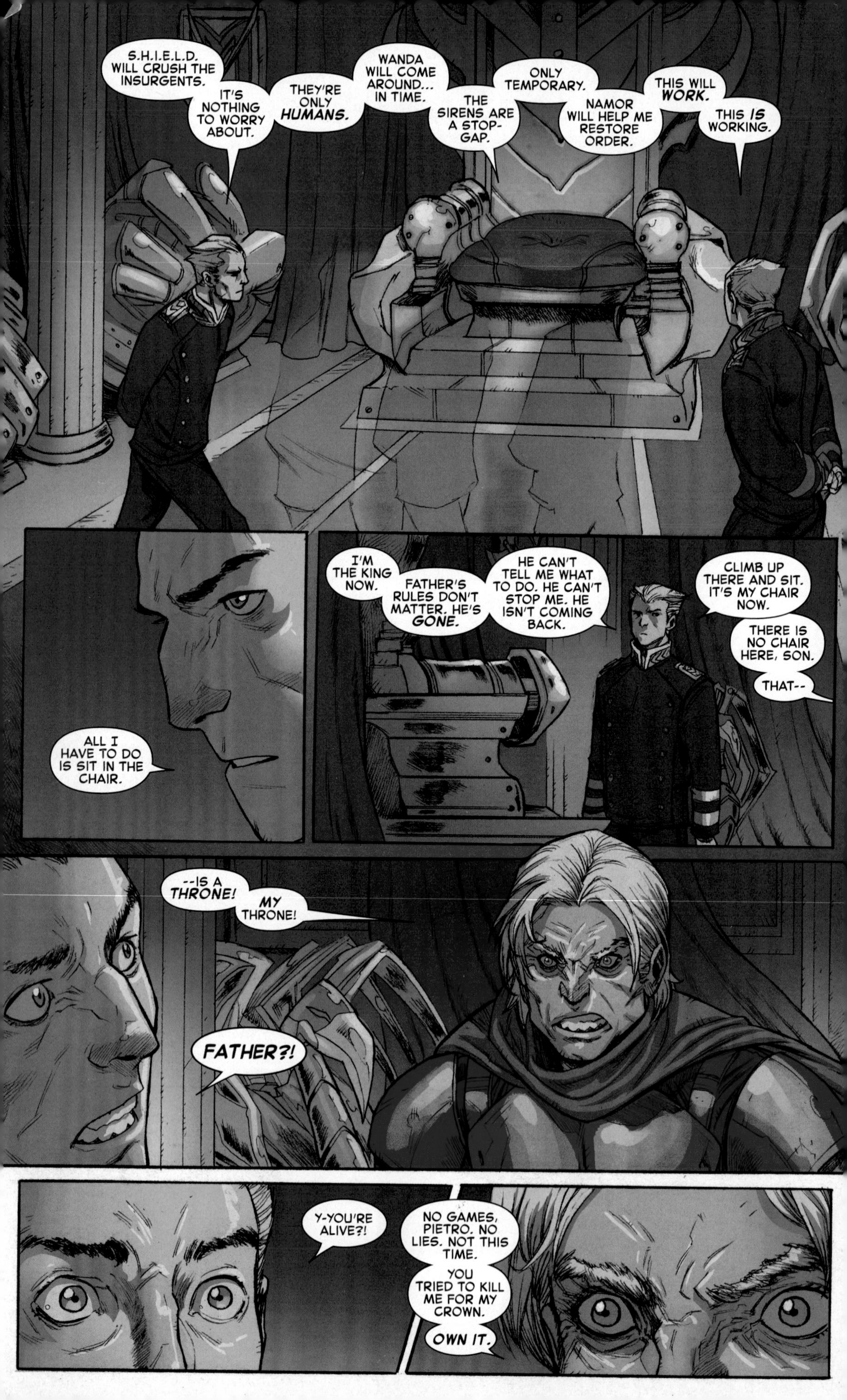
S.H.I.E.L.D. WILL CRUSH THE INSURGENTS.
IT'S NOTHING TO WORRY ABOUT.
THEY'RE ONLY HUMANS.
WANDA WILL COME AROUND... IN TIME.
THE SIRENS ARE A STOP-GAP.
ONLY TEMPORARY.
NAMOR WILL HELP ME RESTORE ORDER.
THIS WILL WORK.
THIS IS WORKING.
ALL I HAVE TO DO IS SIT IN THE CHAIR.
I'M THE KING NOW.
FATHER'S RULES DON'T MATTER. HE'S GONE.
HE CAN'T TELL ME WHAT TO DO. HE CAN'T STOP ME. HE ISN'T COMING BACK.
CLIMB UP THERE AND SIT. IT'S MY CHAIR NOW.
THERE IS NO CHAIR HERE, SON.
THAT--
--IS A THRONE!
MY THRONE!
FATHER?!
Y-YOU'RE ALIVE?!
NO GAMES, PIETRO. NO LIES. NOT THIS TIME.
YOU TRIED TO KILL ME FOR MY CROWN.
OWN IT.

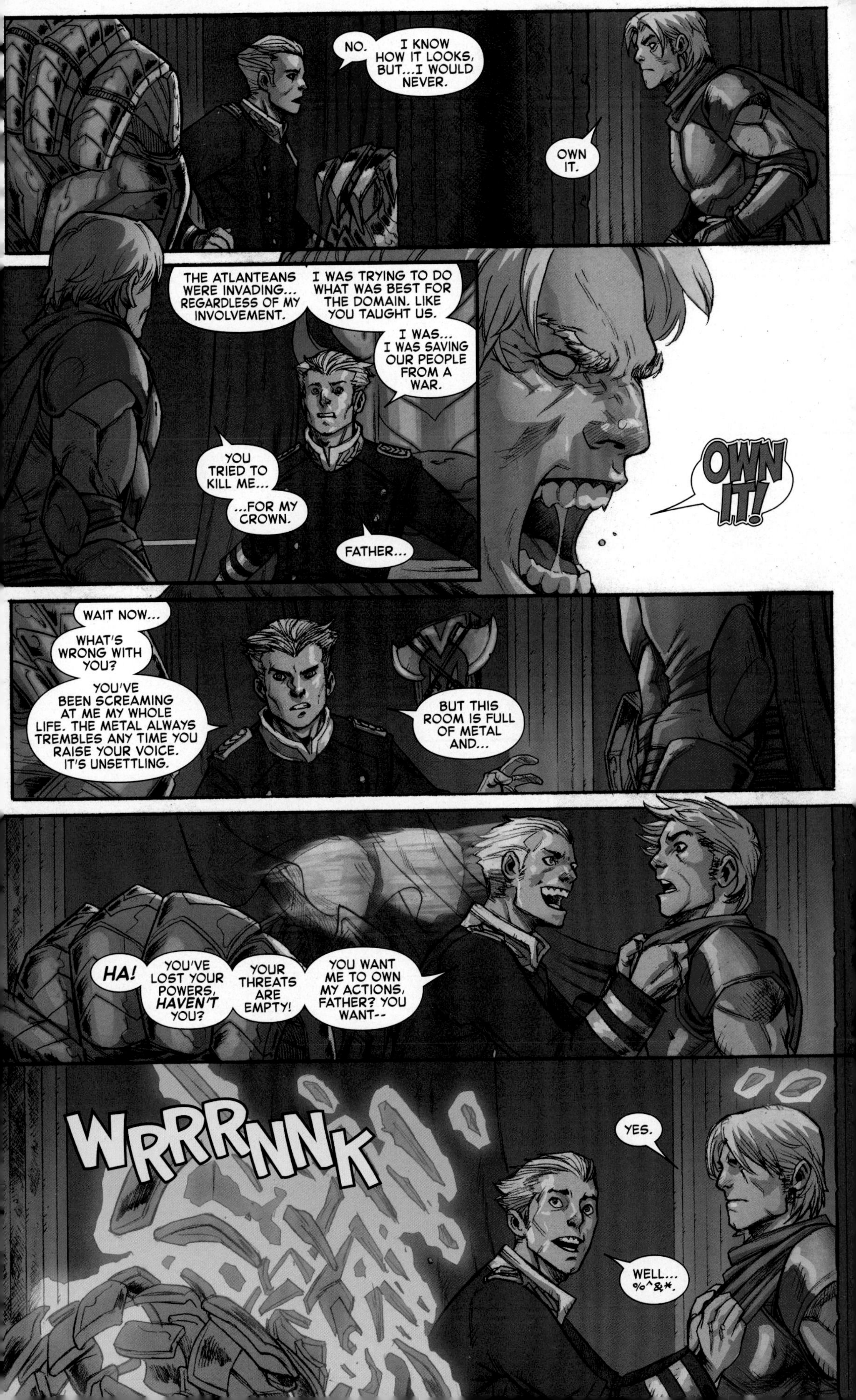
NO.
I KNOW HOW IT LOOKS, BUT...I WOULD NEVER.
OWN IT.
THE ATLANTEANS WERE INVADING... REGARDLESS OF MY INVOLVEMENT.
I WAS TRYING TO DO WHAT WAS BEST FOR THE DOMAIN. LIKE YOU TAUGHT US.
I WAS... I WAS SAVING OUR PEOPLE FROM A WAR.
YOU TRIED TO KILL ME...
...FOR MY CROWN.
FATHER...
OWN IT!
WAIT NOW...
WHAT'S WRONG WITH YOU?
YOU'VE BEEN SCREAMING AT ME MY WHOLE LIFE. THE METAL ALWAYS TREMBLES ANY TIME YOU RAISE YOUR VOICE. IT'S UNSETTLING.
BUT THIS ROOM IS FULL OF METAL AND...
HA!
YOU'VE LOST YOUR POWERS, HAVEN'T YOU?
YOUR THREATS ARE EMPTY!
YOU WANT ME TO OWN MY ACTIONS, FATHER? YOU WANT--
WRRRNNK
YES.
WELL... %^&*.

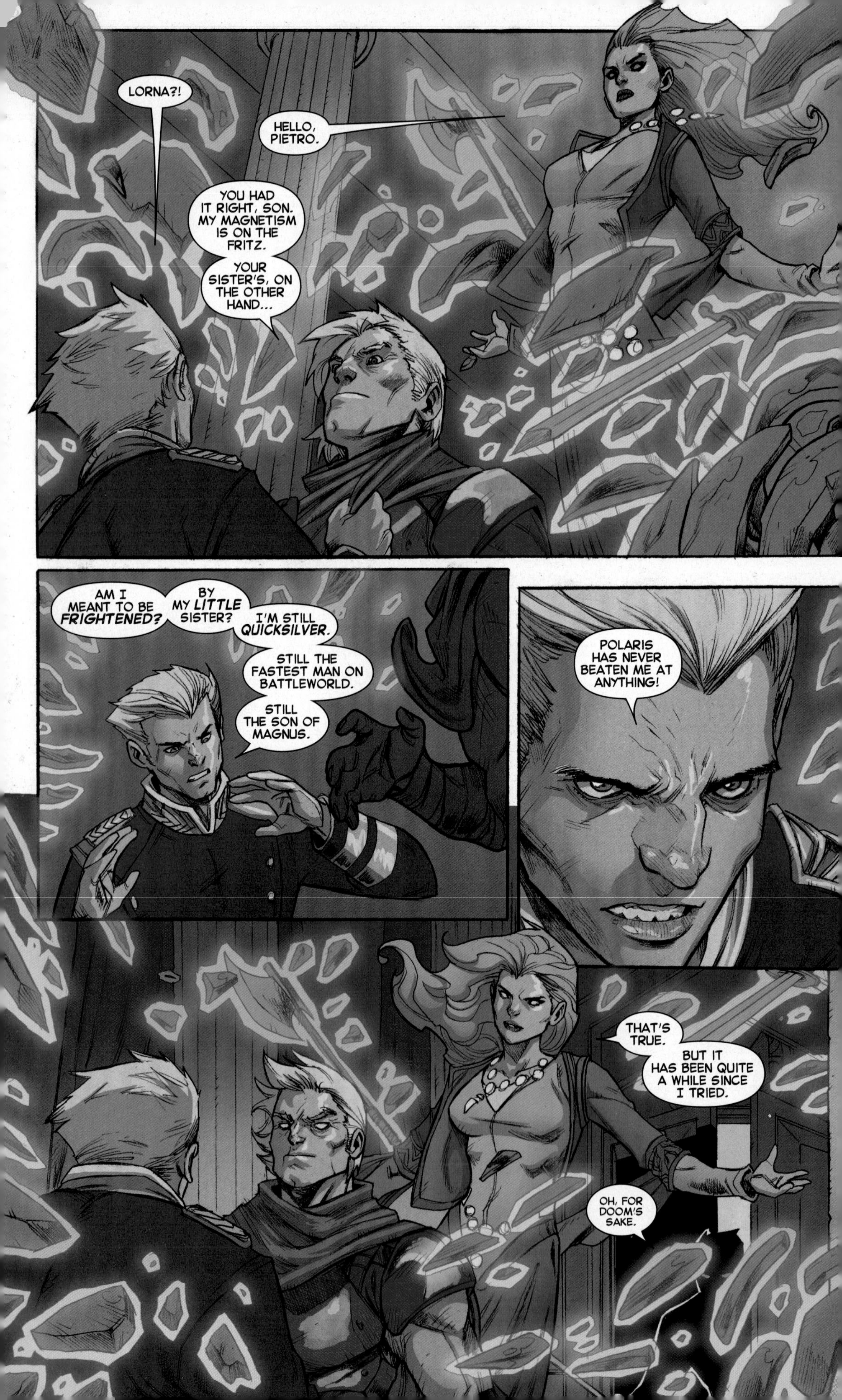
LORNA?!
HELLO, PIETRO.
YOU HAD IT RIGHT, SON. MY MAGNETISM IS ON THE FRITZ.
YOUR SISTER'S, ON THE OTHER HAND...
AM I MEANT TO BE *FRIGHTENED?*
BY MY *LITTLE* SISTER?
I'M STILL *QUICKSILVER*.
STILL THE FASTEST MAN ON BATTLEWORLD.
STILL THE SON OF MAGNUS.
POLARIS HAS NEVER BEATEN ME AT ANYTHING!
THAT'S TRUE.
BUT IT HAS BEEN QUITE A WHILE SINCE I TRIED.
OH, FOR DOOM'S SAKE.

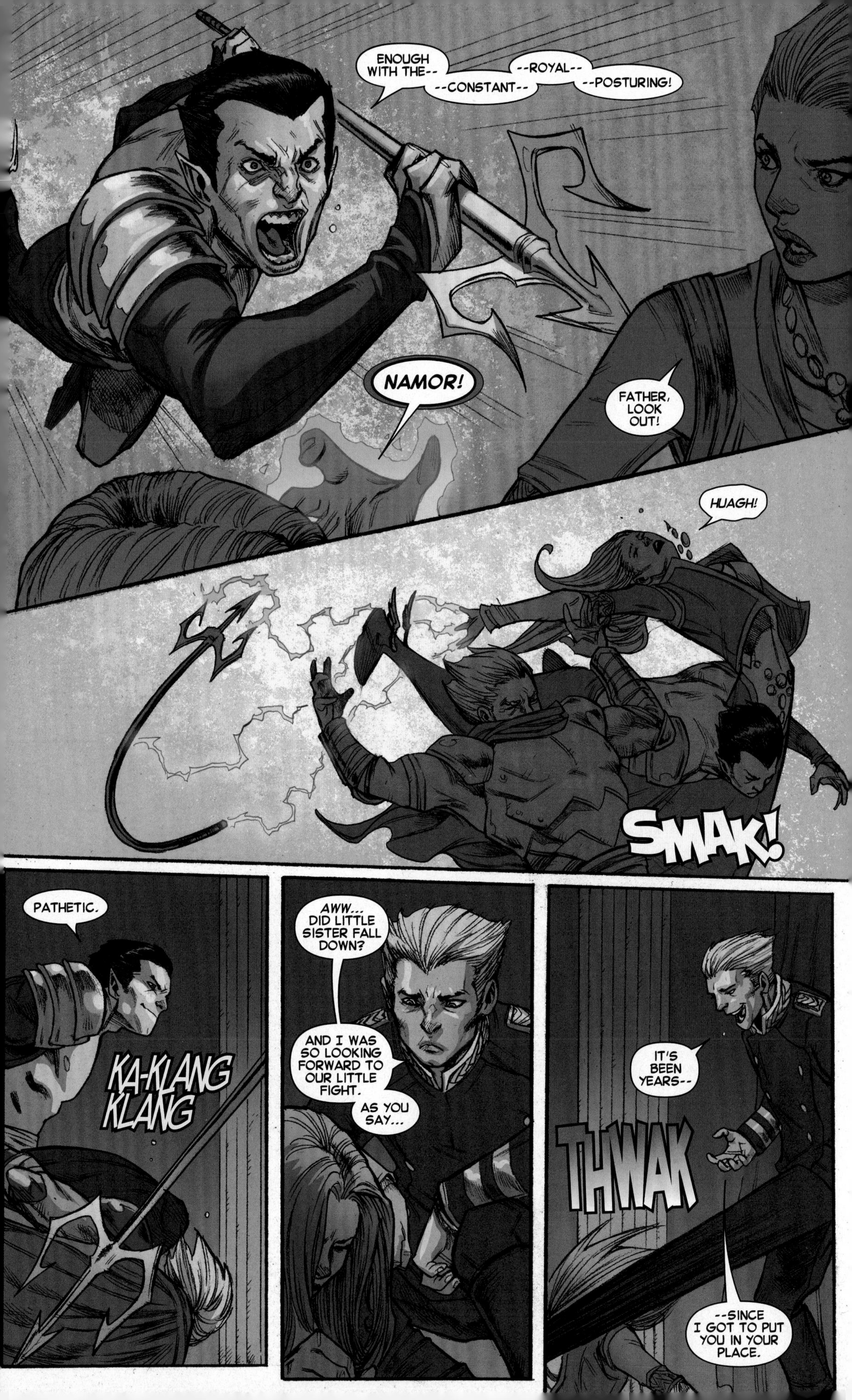
ENOUGH WITH THE--
--CONSTANT--
--ROYAL--
--POSTURING!
NAMOR!
FATHER, LOOK OUT!
HUAGH!
SMAK!
PATHETIC.
KA-KLANG KLANG
AWW... DID LITTLE SISTER FALL DOWN?
AND I WAS SO LOOKING FORWARD TO OUR LITTLE FIGHT.
AS YOU SAY...
IT'S BEEN YEARS--
THWAK
--SINCE I GOT TO PUT YOU IN YOUR PLACE.

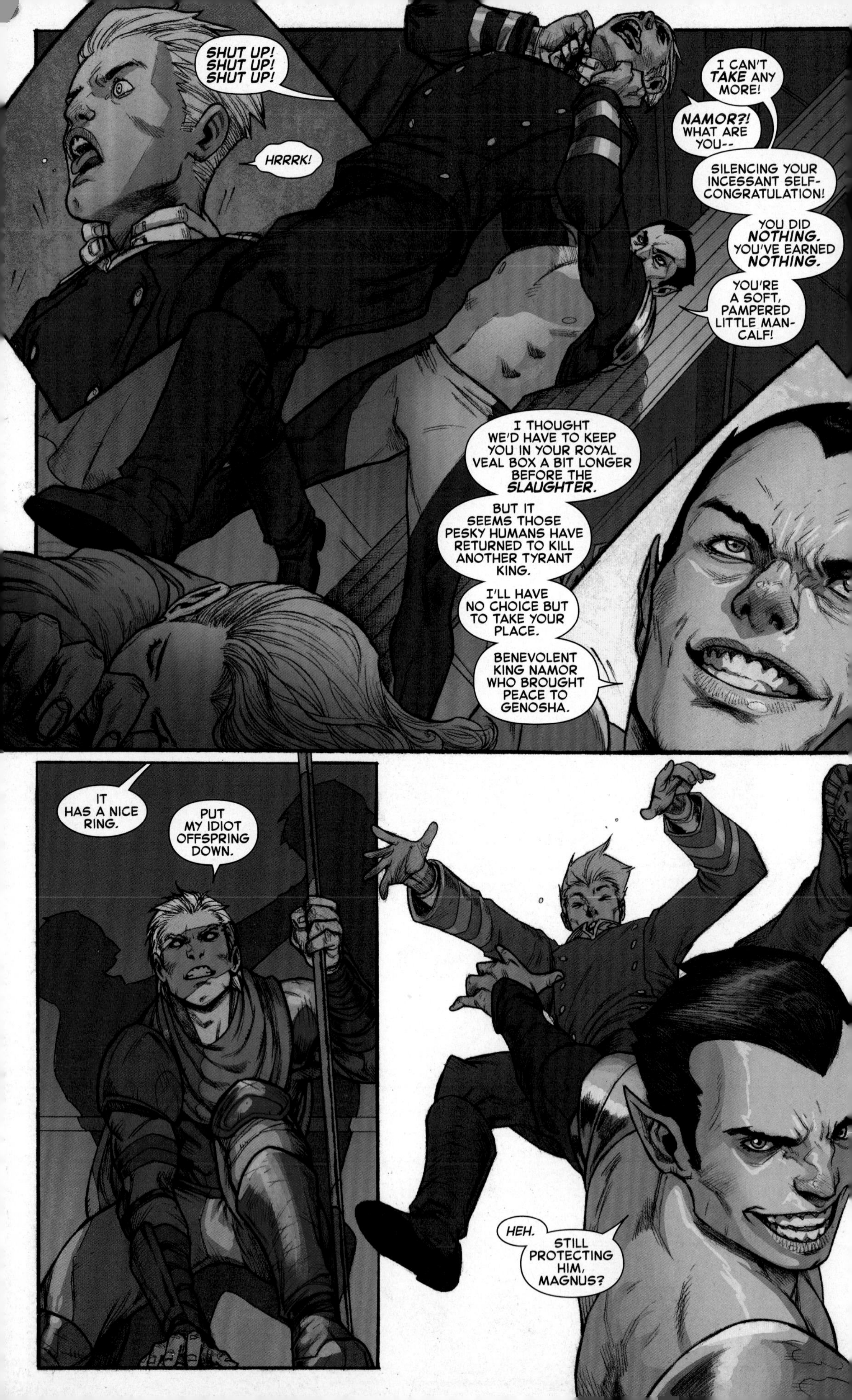
SHUT UP! SHUT UP! SHUT UP!
HRRRK!
I CAN'T TAKE ANY MORE!
NAMOR?! WHAT ARE YOU--
SILENCING YOUR INCESSANT SELF-CONGRATULATION!
YOU DID NOTHING. YOU'VE EARNED NOTHING.
YOU'RE A SOFT, PAMPERED LITTLE MAN-CALF!
I THOUGHT WE'D HAVE TO KEEP YOU IN YOUR ROYAL VEAL BOX A BIT LONGER BEFORE THE SLAUGHTER.
BUT IT SEEMS THOSE PESKY HUMANS HAVE RETURNED TO KILL ANOTHER TYRANT KING.
I'LL HAVE NO CHOICE BUT TO TAKE YOUR PLACE.
BENEVOLENT KING NAMOR WHO BROUGHT PEACE TO GENOSHA.
IT HAS A NICE RING.
PUT MY IDIOT OFFSPRING DOWN.
HEH.
STILL PROTECTING HIM, MAGNUS?

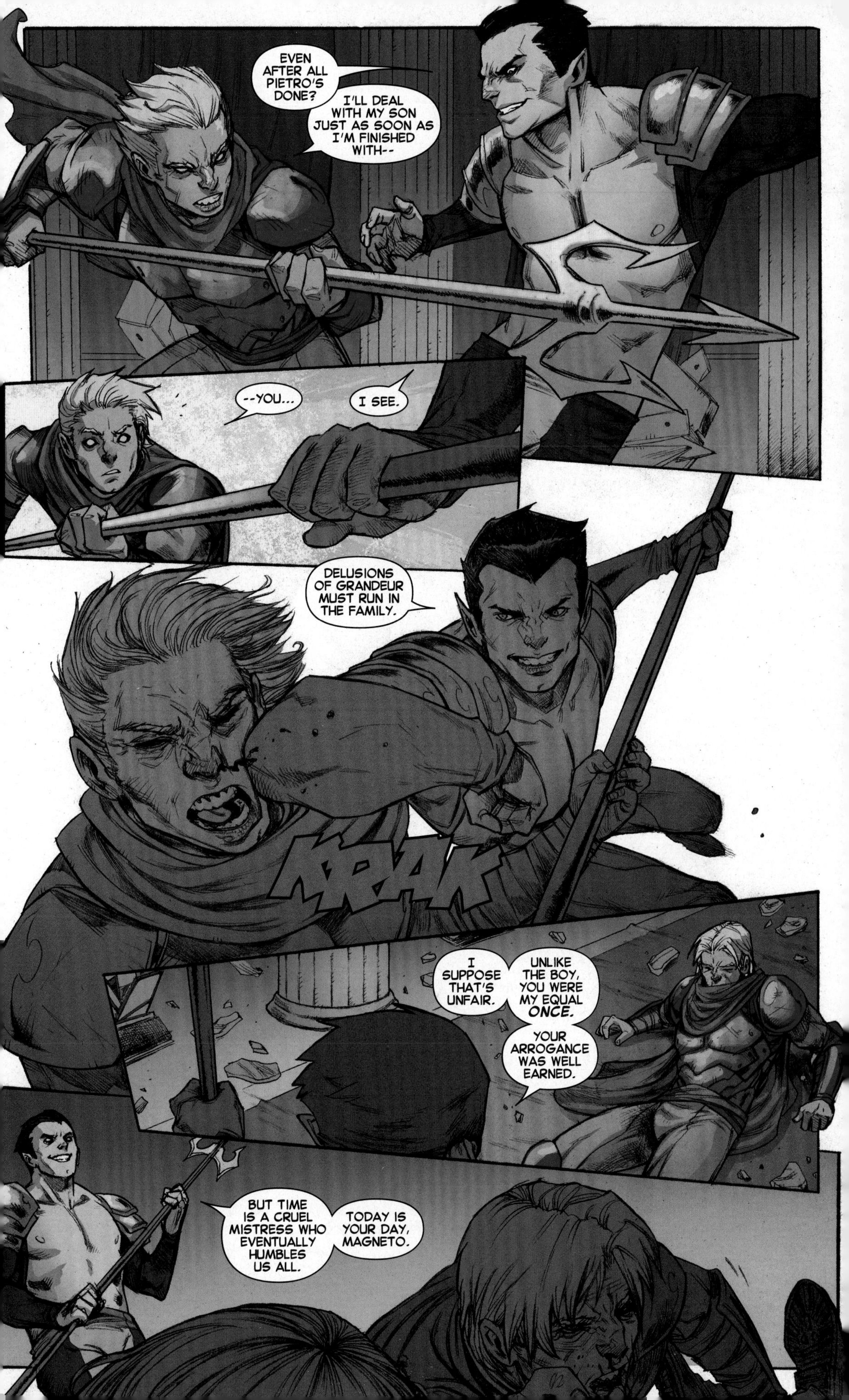
EVEN AFTER ALL PIETRO'S DONE?
I'LL DEAL WITH MY SON JUST AS SOON AS I'M FINISHED WITH--
--YOU...
I SEE.
DELUSIONS OF GRANDEUR MUST RUN IN THE FAMILY.
KRAK
I SUPPOSE THAT'S UNFAIR.
UNLIKE THE BOY, YOU WERE MY EQUAL ONCE.
YOUR ARROGANCE WAS WELL EARNED.
BUT TIME IS A CRUEL MISTRESS WHO EVENTUALLY HUMBLES US ALL.
TODAY IS YOUR DAY, MAGNETO.

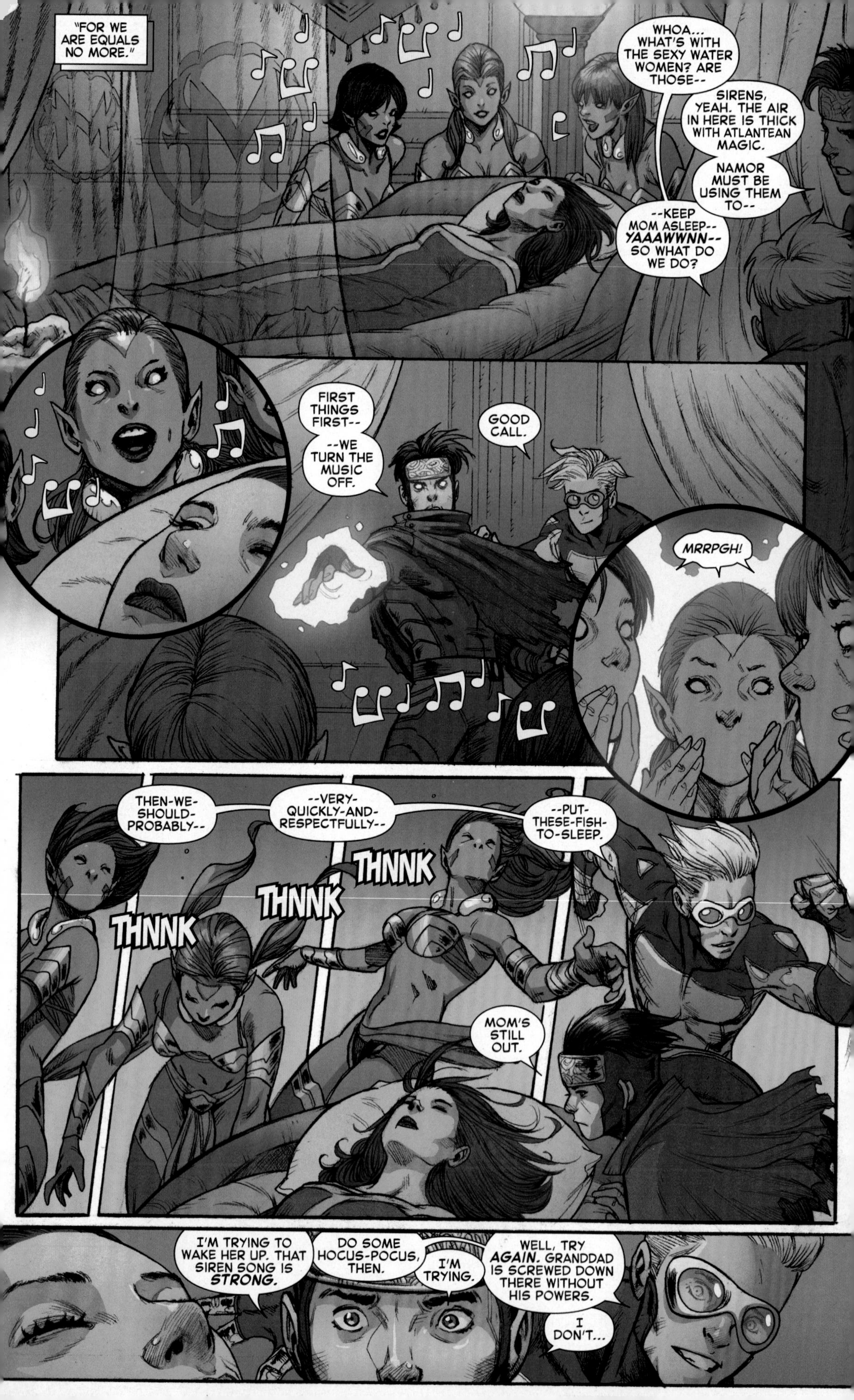
"FOR WE ARE EQUALS NO MORE."
WHOA... WHAT'S WITH THE SEXY WATER WOMEN? ARE THOSE--
SIRENS, YEAH. THE AIR IN HERE IS THICK WITH ATLANTEAN MAGIC.
NAMOR MUST BE USING THEM TO--
--KEEP MOM ASLEEP-- YAAAWWNN-- SO WHAT DO WE DO?
FIRST THINGS FIRST--
--WE TURN THE MUSIC OFF.
GOOD CALL.
MRRPGH!
THEN-WE-SHOULD-PROBABLY--
--VERY-QUICKLY-AND-RESPECTFULLY--
--PUT-THESE-FISH-TO-SLEEP.
THNNK
THNNK
THNNK
MOM'S STILL OUT.
I'M TRYING TO WAKE HER UP. THAT SIREN SONG IS STRONG.
DO SOME HOCUS-POCUS, THEN.
I'M TRYING.
WELL, TRY AGAIN. GRANDDAD IS SCREWED DOWN THERE WITHOUT HIS POWERS.
I DON'T...

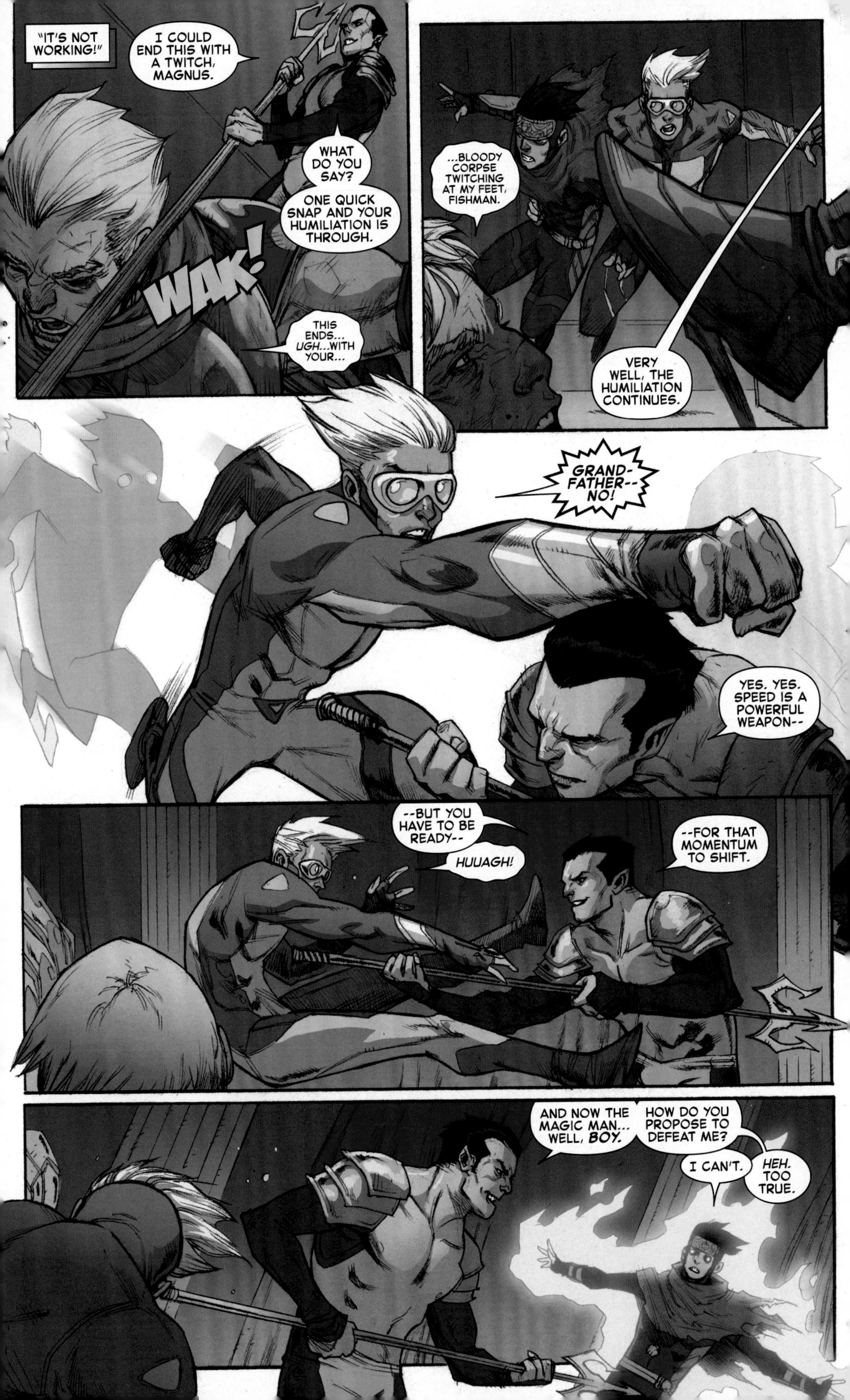
"IT'S NOT WORKING!"
I COULD END THIS WITH A TWITCH, MAGNUS.
WHAT DO YOU SAY?
ONE QUICK SNAP AND YOUR HUMILIATION IS THROUGH.
WAK!
THIS ENDS... UGH...WITH YOUR...
...BLOODY CORPSE TWITCHING AT MY FEET, FISHMAN.
VERY WELL, THE HUMILIATION CONTINUES.
GRAND-FATHER--NO!
YES. YES. SPEED IS A POWERFUL WEAPON--
--BUT YOU HAVE TO BE READY--
HUUAGH!
--FOR THAT MOMENTUM TO SHIFT.
AND NOW THE MAGIC MAN... WELL, BOY.
HOW DO YOU PROPOSE TO DEFEAT ME?
I CAN'T.
HEH. TOO TRUE.

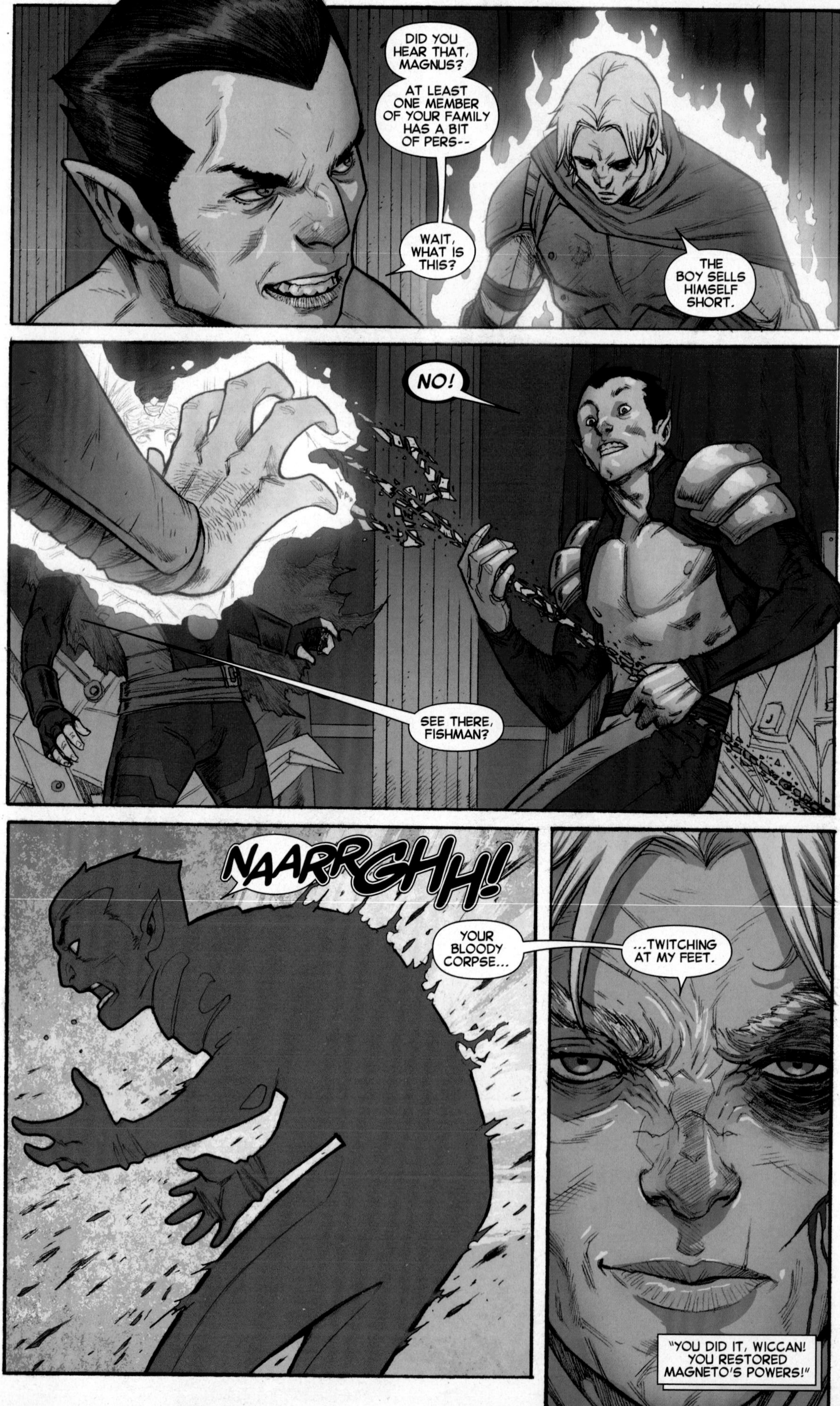
DID YOU HEAR THAT, MAGNUS?
AT LEAST ONE MEMBER OF YOUR FAMILY HAS A BIT OF PERS--
WAIT, WHAT IS THIS?
THE BOY SELLS HIMSELF SHORT.
NO!
SEE THERE, FISHMAN?
NAARRGHH!
YOUR BLOODY CORPSE...
...TWITCHING AT MY FEET.
"YOU DID IT, WICCAN! YOU RESTORED MAGNETO'S POWERS!"

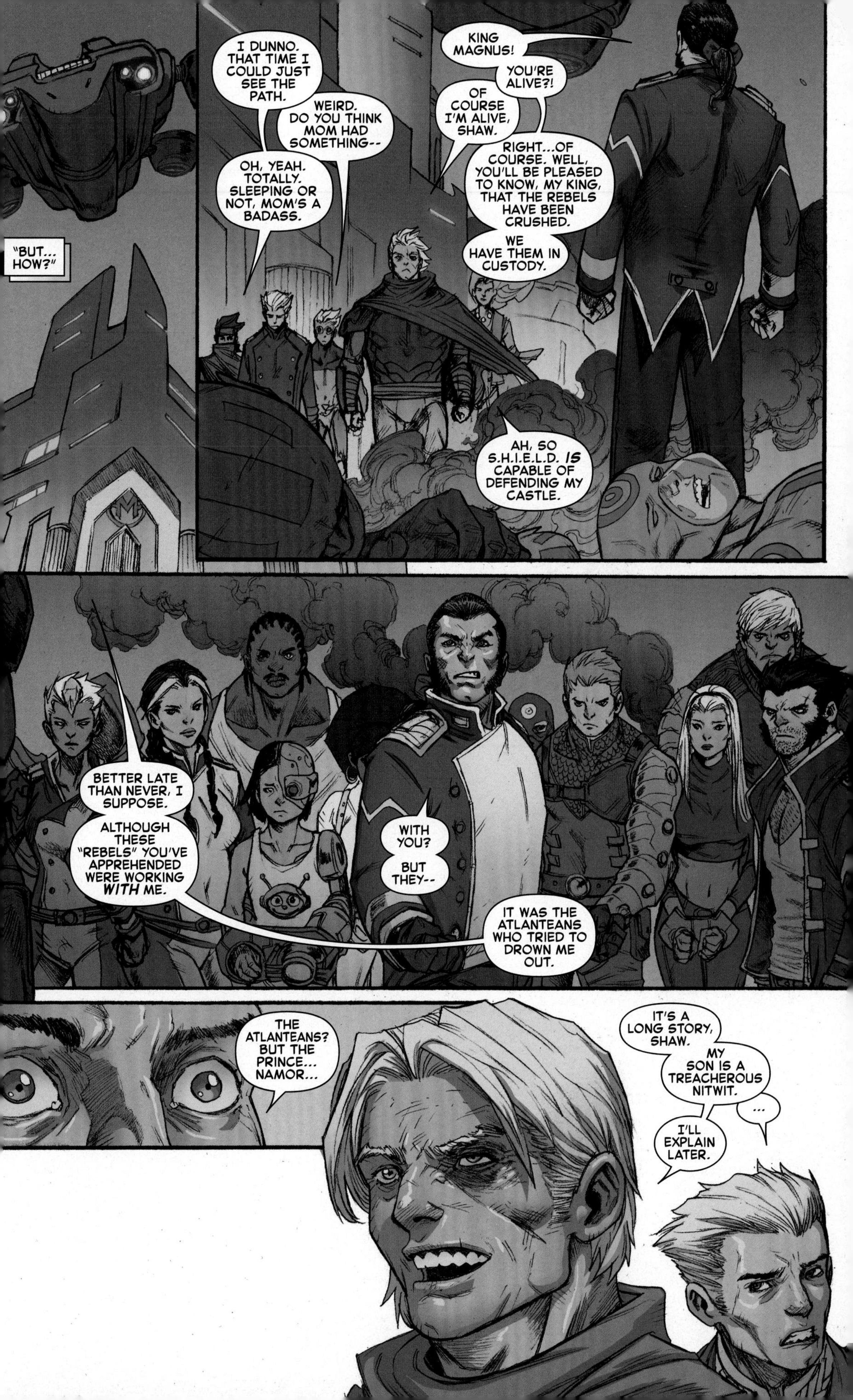
"BUT... HOW?"
I DUNNO. THAT TIME I COULD JUST SEE THE PATH.
WEIRD. DO YOU THINK MOM HAD SOMETHING--
OH, YEAH. TOTALLY. SLEEPING OR NOT, MOM'S A BADASS.
KING MAGNUS!
YOU'RE ALIVE?!
OF COURSE I'M ALIVE, SHAW.
RIGHT...OF COURSE. WELL, YOU'LL BE PLEASED TO KNOW, MY KING, THAT THE REBELS HAVE BEEN CRUSHED.
WE HAVE THEM IN CUSTODY.
AH, SO S.H.I.E.L.D. IS CAPABLE OF DEFENDING MY CASTLE.
BETTER LATE THAN NEVER, I SUPPOSE.
ALTHOUGH THESE "REBELS" YOU'VE APPREHENDED WERE WORKING WITH ME.
WITH YOU?
BUT THEY--
IT WAS THE ATLANTEANS WHO TRIED TO DROWN ME OUT.
THE ATLANTEANS? BUT THE PRINCE... NAMOR...
IT'S A LONG STORY, SHAW.
MY SON IS A TREACHEROUS NITWIT.
...
I'LL EXPLAIN LATER.

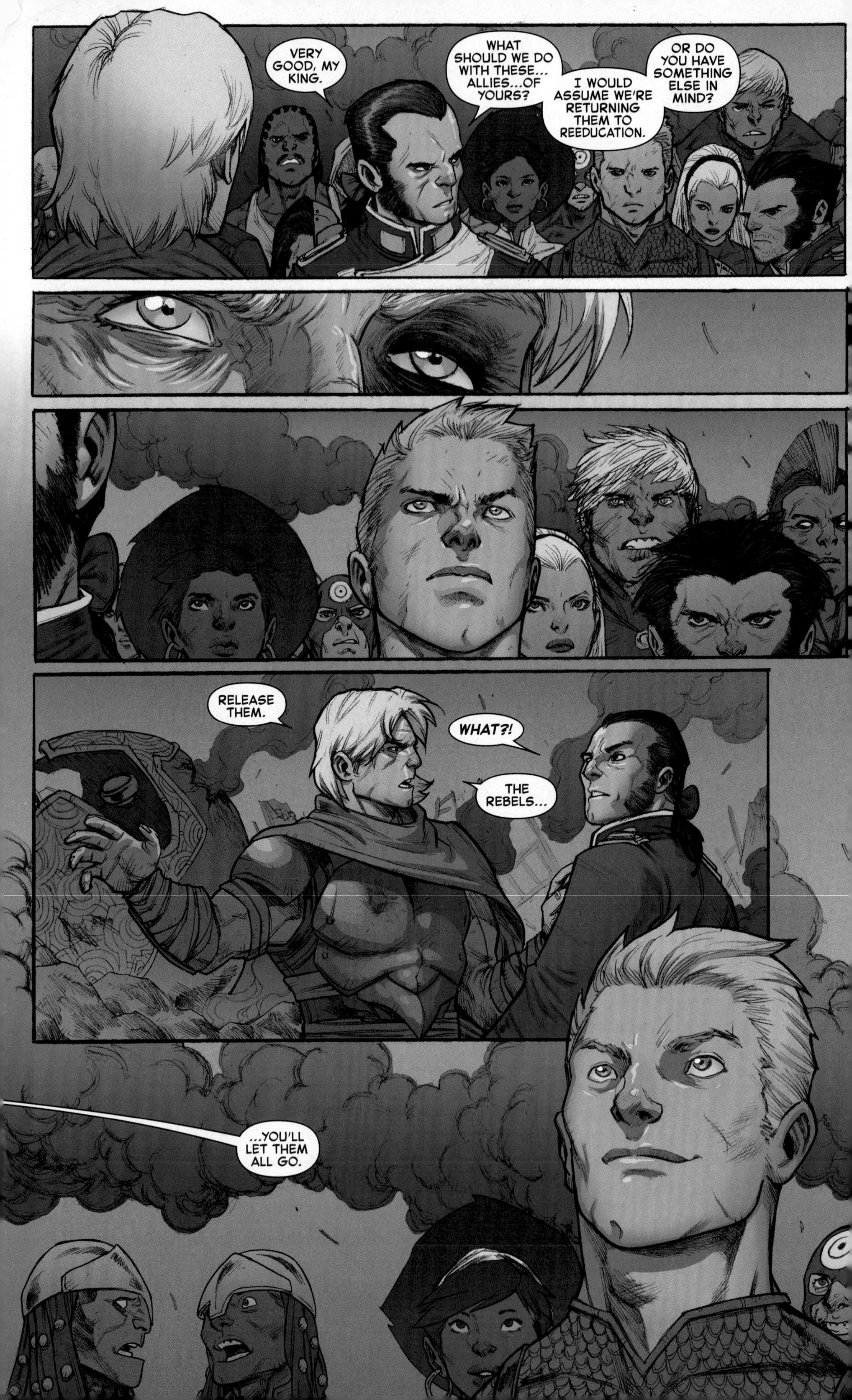
VERY GOOD, MY KING.
WHAT SHOULD WE DO WITH THESE... ALLIES...OF YOURS?
I WOULD ASSUME WE'RE RETURNING THEM TO REEDUCATION.
OR DO YOU HAVE SOMETHING ELSE IN MIND?
RELEASE THEM.
WHAT?!
THE REBELS...
...YOU'LL LET THEM ALL GO.

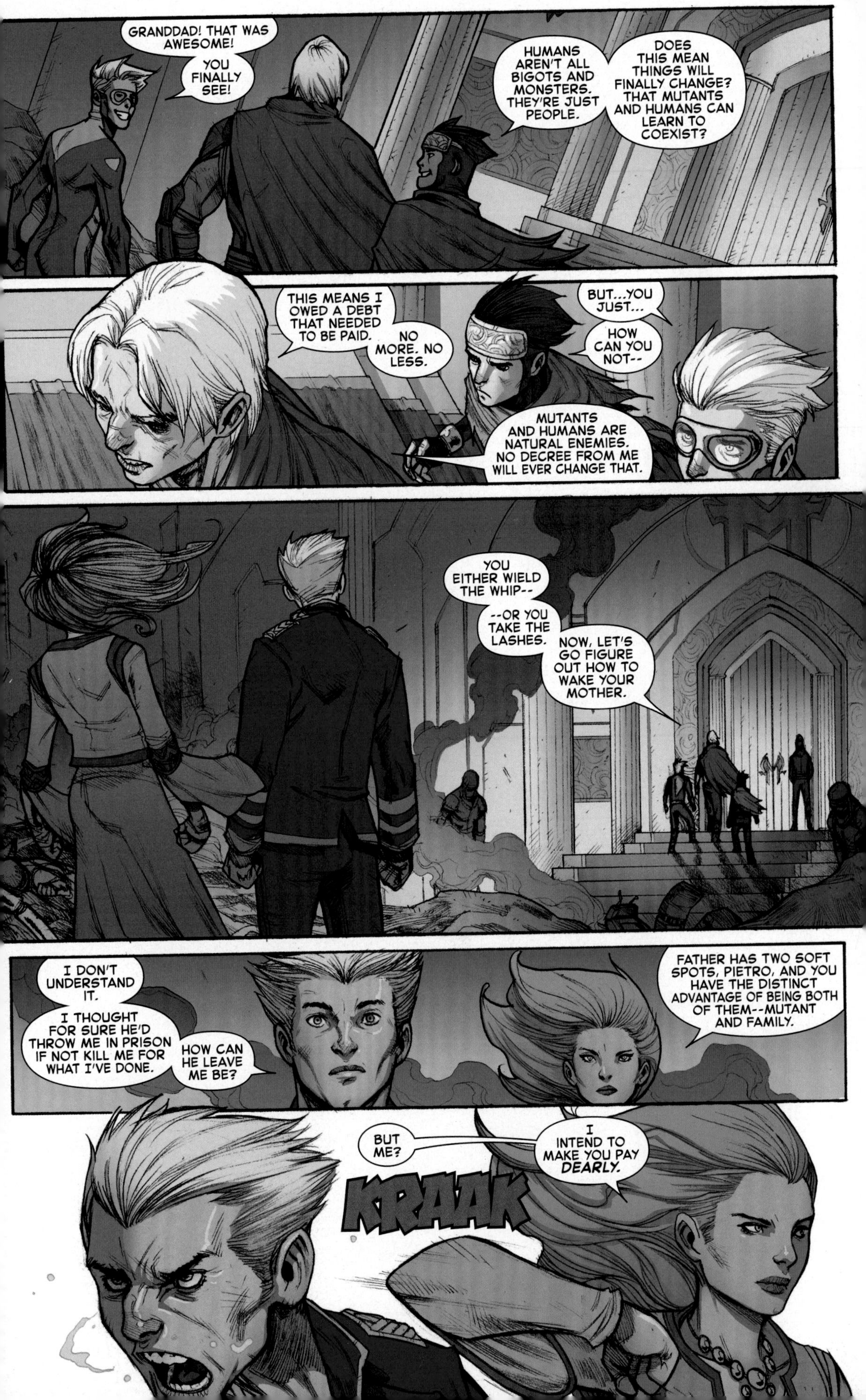
GRANDDAD! THAT WAS AWESOME!
YOU FINALLY SEE!
HUMANS AREN'T ALL BIGOTS AND MONSTERS. THEY'RE JUST PEOPLE.
DOES THIS MEAN THINGS WILL FINALLY CHANGE? THAT MUTANTS AND HUMANS CAN LEARN TO COEXIST?
THIS MEANS I OWED A DEBT THAT NEEDED TO BE PAID.
NO MORE. NO LESS.
BUT...YOU JUST...
HOW CAN YOU NOT--
MUTANTS AND HUMANS ARE NATURAL ENEMIES. NO DECREE FROM ME WILL EVER CHANGE THAT.
YOU EITHER WIELD THE WHIP--
--OR YOU TAKE THE LASHES.
NOW, LET'S GO FIGURE OUT HOW TO WAKE YOUR MOTHER.
I DON'T UNDERSTAND IT.
I THOUGHT FOR SURE HE'D THROW ME IN PRISON IF NOT KILL ME FOR WHAT I'VE DONE.
HOW CAN HE LEAVE ME BE?
FATHER HAS TWO SOFT SPOTS, PIETRO, AND YOU HAVE THE DISTINCT ADVANTAGE OF BEING BOTH OF THEM--MUTANT AND FAMILY.
BUT ME?
I INTEND TO MAKE YOU PAY *DEARLY.*
KRAAK

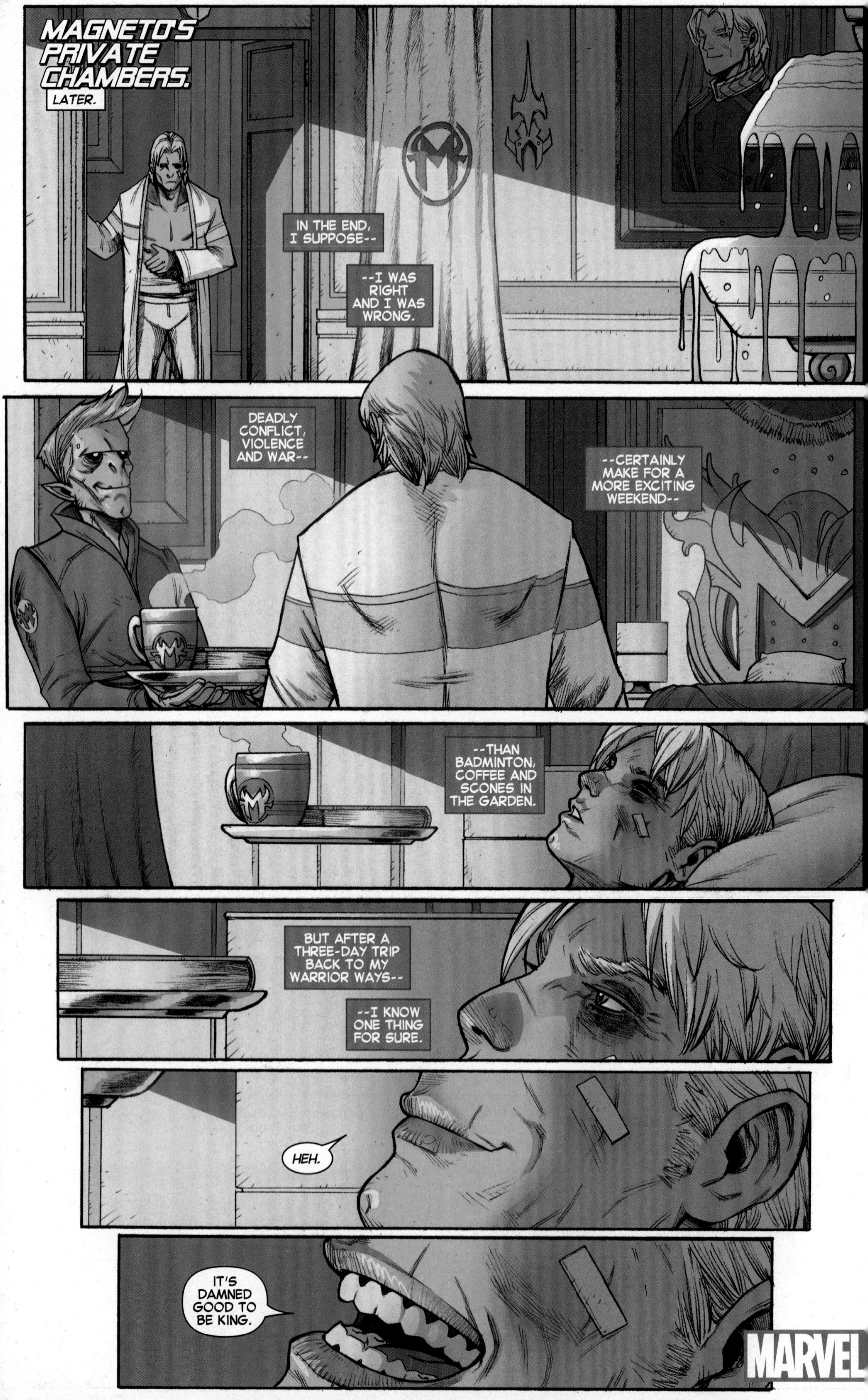
MAGNETO'S PRIVATE CHAMBERS.
LATER.
IN THE END, I SUPPOSE--
--I WAS RIGHT AND I WAS WRONG.
DEADLY CONFLICT, VIOLENCE AND WAR--
--CERTAINLY MAKE FOR A MORE EXCITING WEEKEND--
--THAN BADMINTON, COFFEE AND SCONES IN THE GARDEN.
BUT AFTER A THREE-DAY TRIP BACK TO MY WARRIOR WAYS--
--I KNOW ONE THING FOR SURE.
HEH.
IT'S DAMNED GOOD TO BE KING.
MARVEL

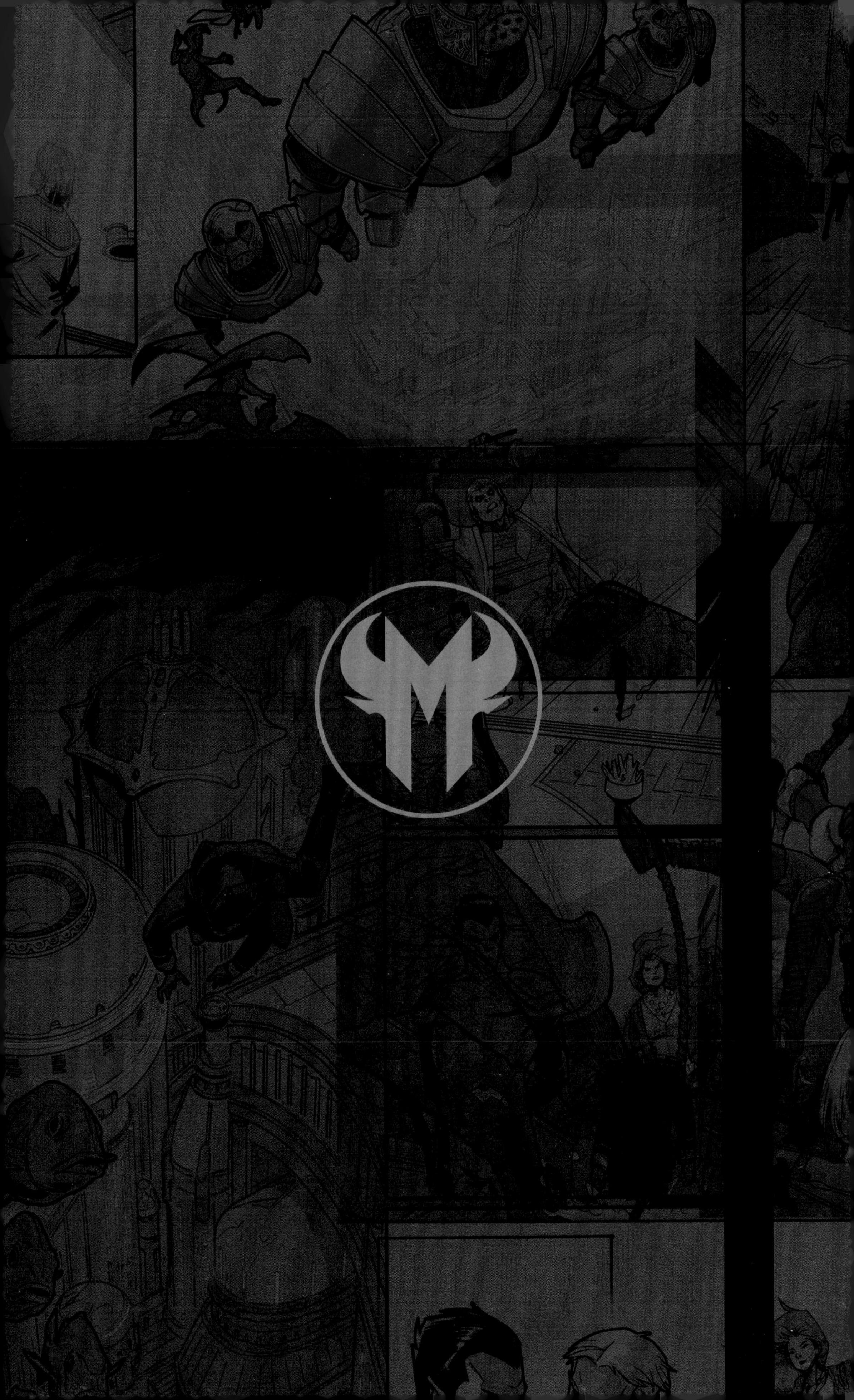

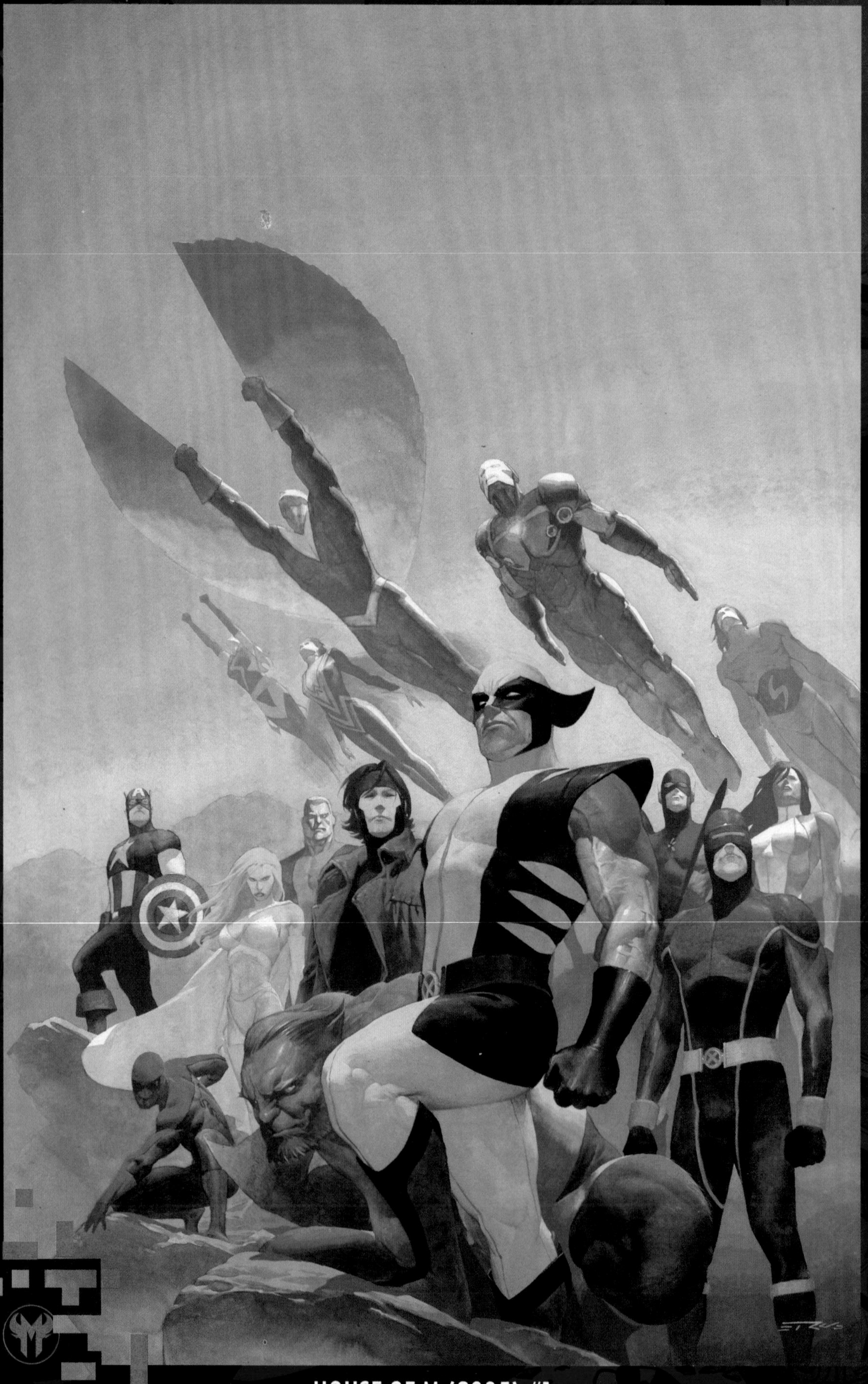

HOUSE OF M (2005) #1

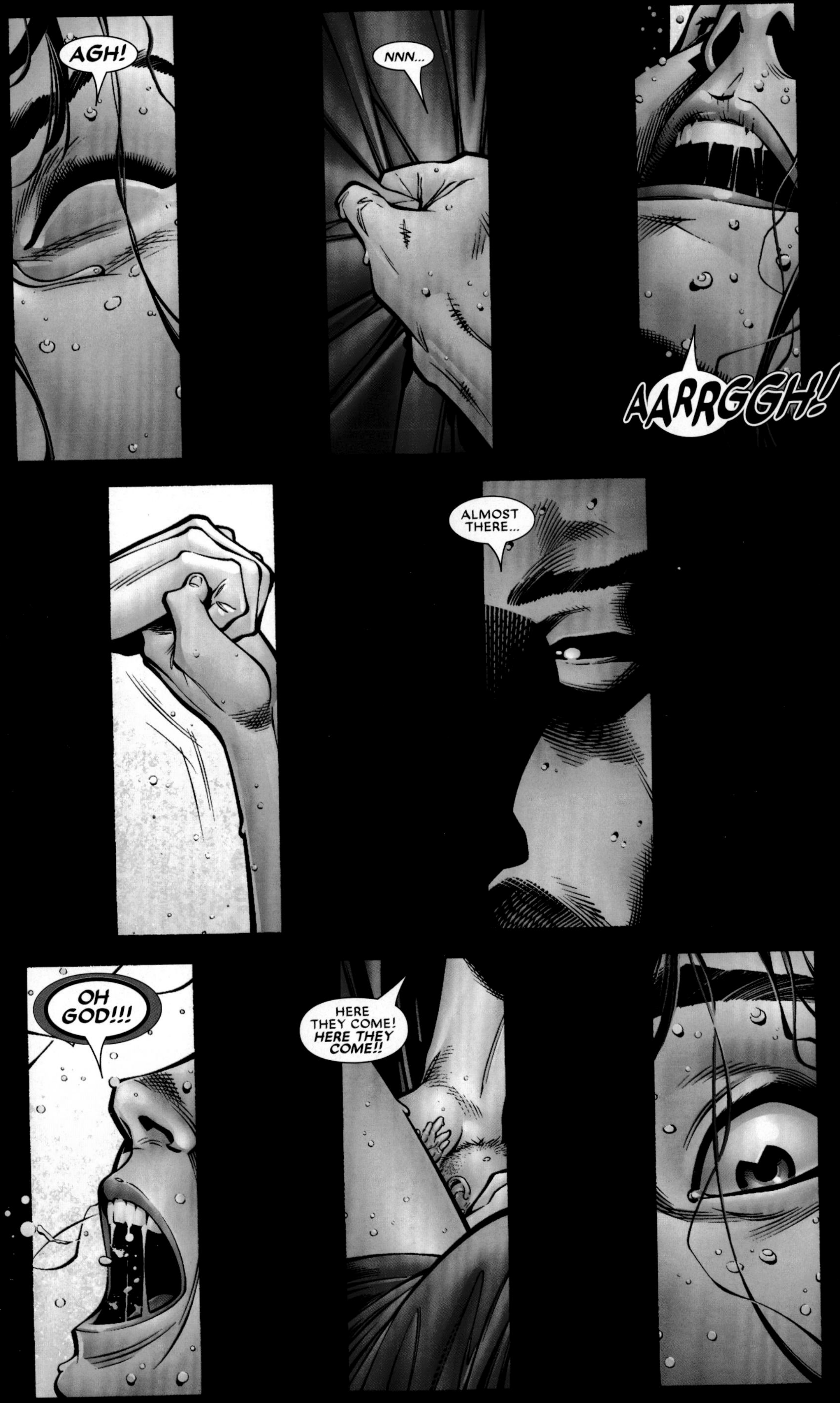
AGH!
NNN...
AARRGGH!
ALMOST THERE...
OH GOD!!!
HERE THEY COME! HERE THEY COME!!

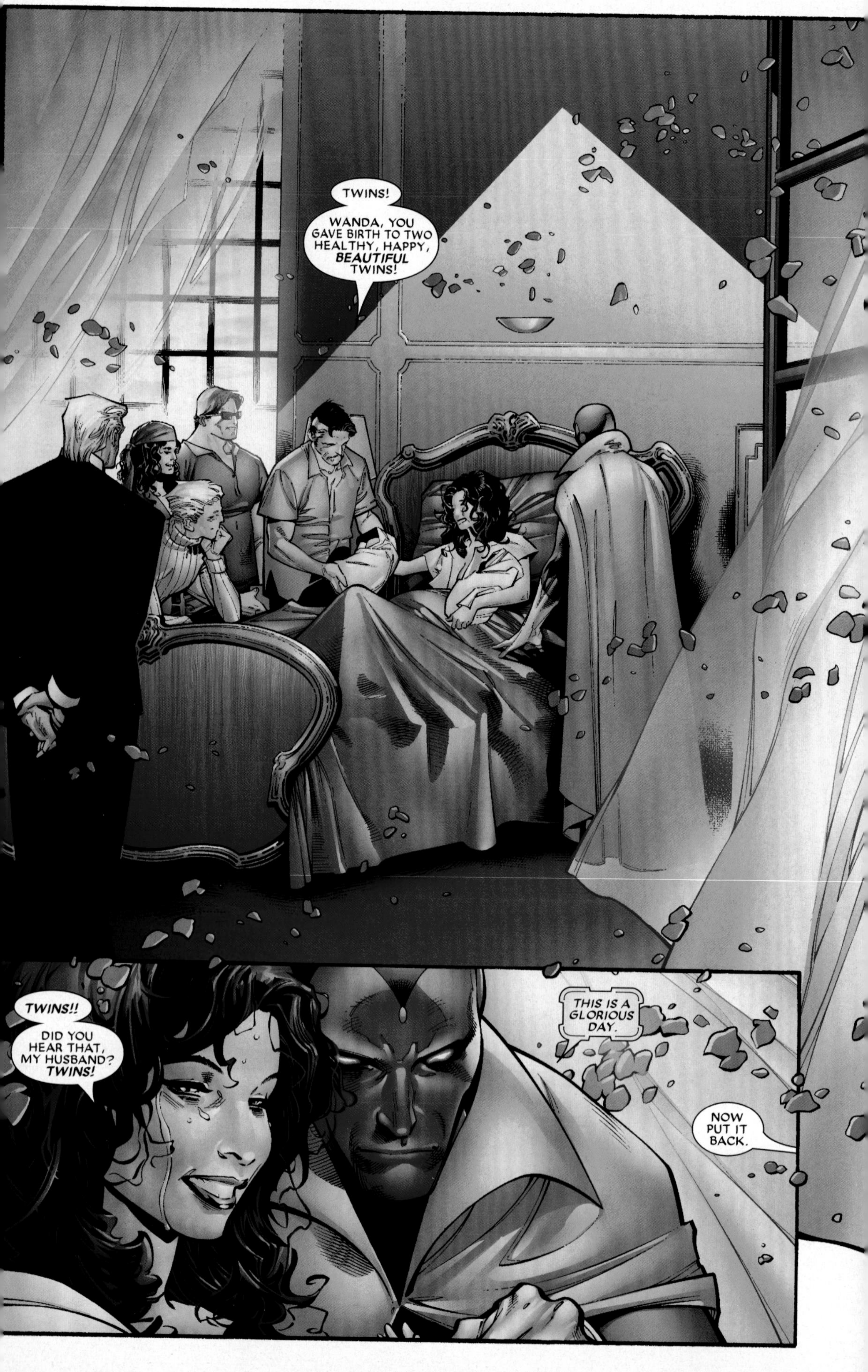
TWINS!
WANDA, YOU GAVE BIRTH TO TWO HEALTHY, HAPPY, *BEAUTIFUL* TWINS!
TWINS!!
DID YOU HEAR THAT, MY HUSBAND? *TWINS!*
THIS IS A GLORIOUS DAY.
NOW PUT IT BACK.

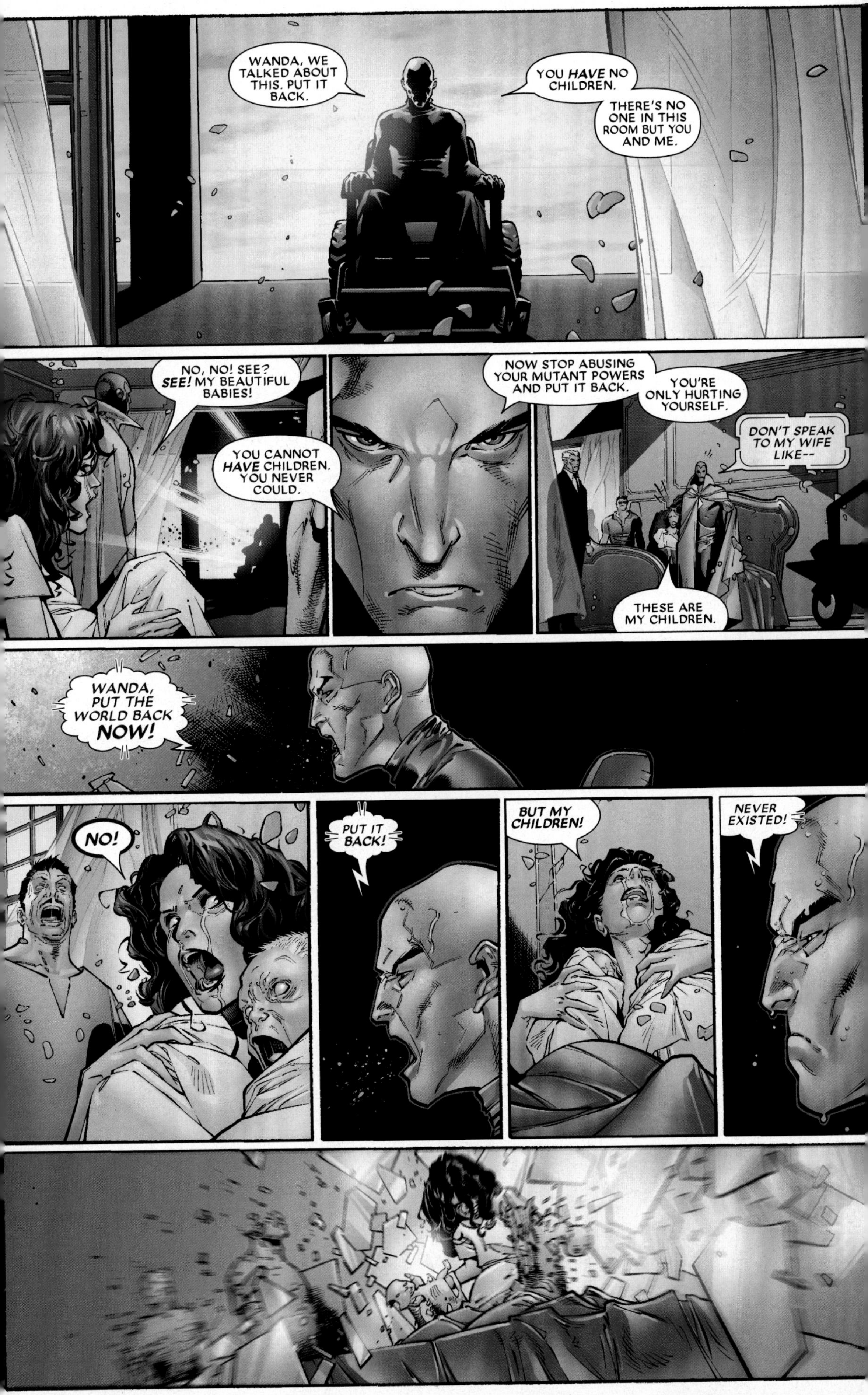

WANDA, WE TALKED ABOUT THIS. PUT IT BACK.
YOU HAVE NO CHILDREN.
THERE'S NO ONE IN THIS ROOM BUT YOU AND ME.
NO, NO! SEE? SEE! MY BEAUTIFUL BABIES!
YOU CANNOT HAVE CHILDREN. YOU NEVER COULD.
NOW STOP ABUSING YOUR MUTANT POWERS AND PUT IT BACK.
YOU'RE ONLY HURTING YOURSELF.
DON'T SPEAK TO MY WIFE LIKE--
THESE ARE MY CHILDREN.
WANDA, PUT THE WORLD BACK NOW!
NO!
PUT IT BACK!
BUT MY CHILDREN!
NEVER EXISTED!

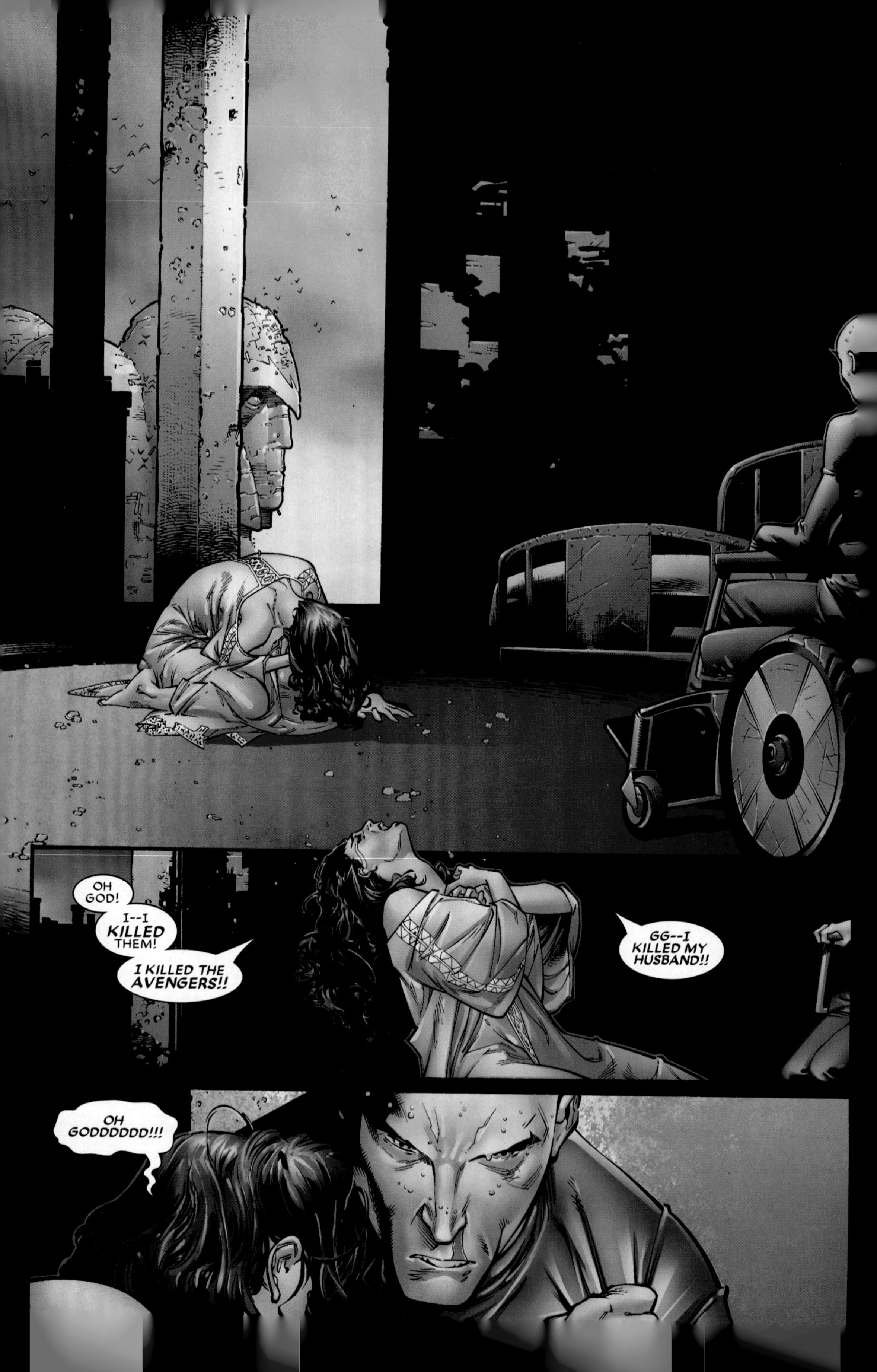
OH GOD!
I--I KILLED THEM!
I KILLED THE AVENGERS!!
GG--I KILLED MY HUSBAND!!
OH GODDDDDD!!!

And there came a day, a day unlike any other, when Earth's mightiest heroes found themselves united against a common threat! On that day, the Avengers were born — to fight the foes no single super hero could withstand!

Born with strange powers, the mutants known as the X-MEN use their awesome abilities to protect a world that hates and fears them!

Professor Charles Xavier — legendary founder of the X-Men who dreams of a peaceful coexistence between humans and mutants — has come to Genosha with one intention: to rebuild a mutant nation from its devastated ashes.

It was the worst day in Avengers history. The Scarlet Witch suffered a total nervous breakdown after losing control of her reality-altering powers. In the chaos created around the breakdown, beloved Avengers Hawkeye, Ant-Man and the Vision lost their lives. Many of the other Avengers were hurt, both emotionally and physically.

That was six months ago.

HOUSE OF M

Writer	Penciler	Inker	Colorist	Letterer	Production
Brian Michael Bendis	Olivier Coipel	Tim Townsend	Frank D'Armata	Chris Eliopoulos	James Taveras

Assistant Editors	Associate Editor	Editor	Editor in Chief	Publisher
Stephanie Moore &	Andy Schmidt	Tom Brevoort	Joe Quesada	Dan Buckley

HOW DID IT GO?

I HEARD THE SCREAMING.

I'M SORRY, CHARLES.

ERIK, EVERY TIME YOUR DAUGHTER USES HER POWERS TO *ALTER* REALITY, SHE LOSES MORE OF HER *GRASP* ON REALITY.

AND IT'S NOT GETTING BETTER.

IS SHE ASLEEP?

YES, I "SUGGESTED" SHE SLEEP.

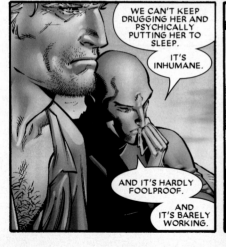

WE CAN'T KEEP DRUGGING HER AND PSYCHICALLY PUTTING HER TO SLEEP.

IT'S INHUMANE.

AND IT'S HARDLY FOOLPROOF.

AND IT'S BARELY WORKING.

STOP BLAMING YOURSELF, ERIK. SHE'S A GROWN WOMAN.

STOP READING MY MIND WITHOUT PERMISSION.

I WASN'T.

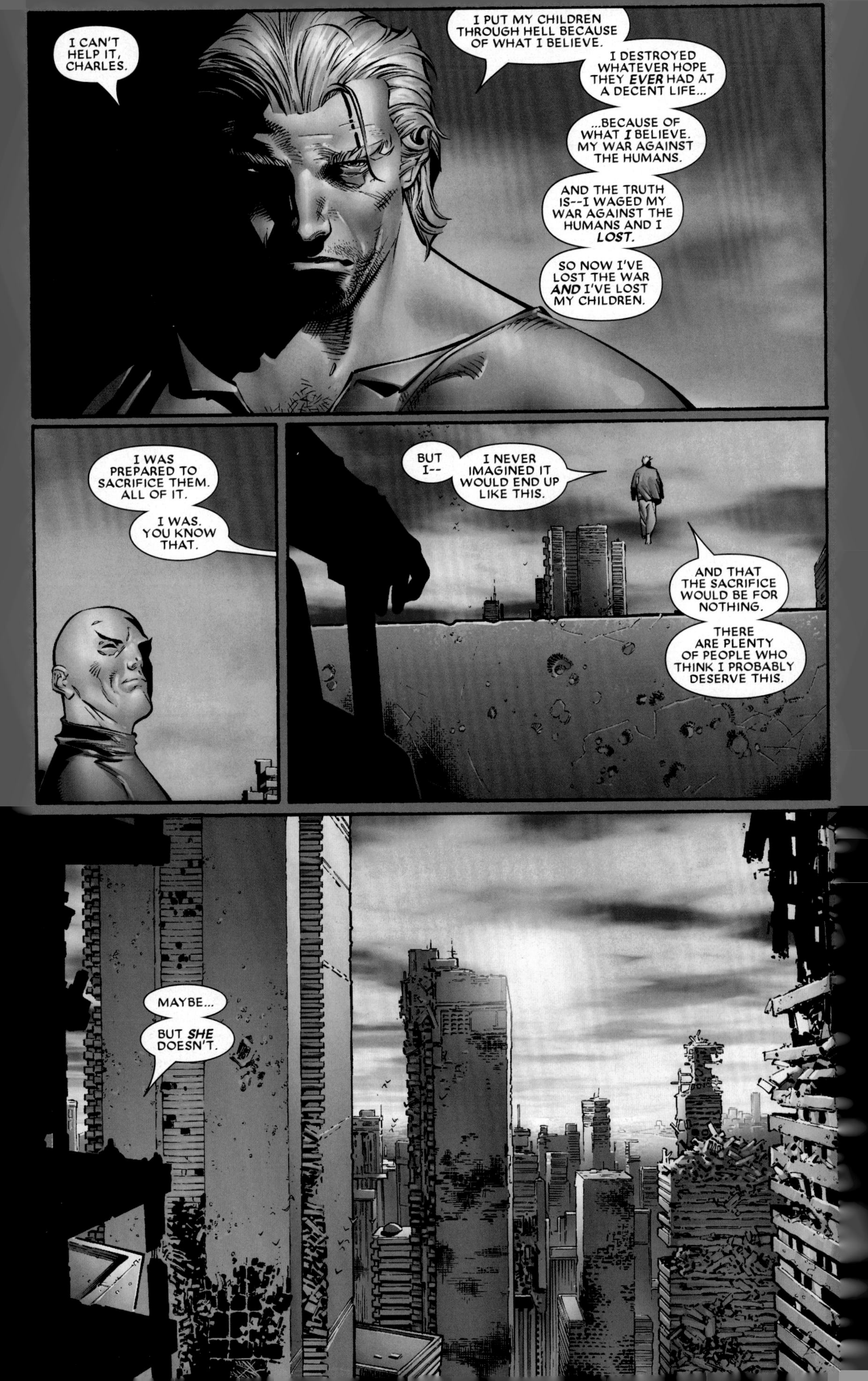
I CAN'T HELP IT, CHARLES.
I PUT MY CHILDREN THROUGH HELL BECAUSE OF WHAT I BELIEVE.
I DESTROYED WHATEVER HOPE THEY EVER HAD AT A DECENT LIFE...
...BECAUSE OF WHAT I BELIEVE. MY WAR AGAINST THE HUMANS.
AND THE TRUTH IS--I WAGED MY WAR AGAINST THE HUMANS AND I LOST.
SO NOW I'VE LOST THE WAR AND I'VE LOST MY CHILDREN.
I WAS PREPARED TO SACRIFICE THEM. ALL OF IT.
I WAS. YOU KNOW THAT.
BUT I--
I NEVER IMAGINED IT WOULD END UP LIKE THIS.
AND THAT THE SACRIFICE WOULD BE FOR NOTHING.
THERE ARE PLENTY OF PEOPLE WHO THINK I PROBABLY DESERVE THIS.
MAYBE...
BUT SHE DOESN'T.

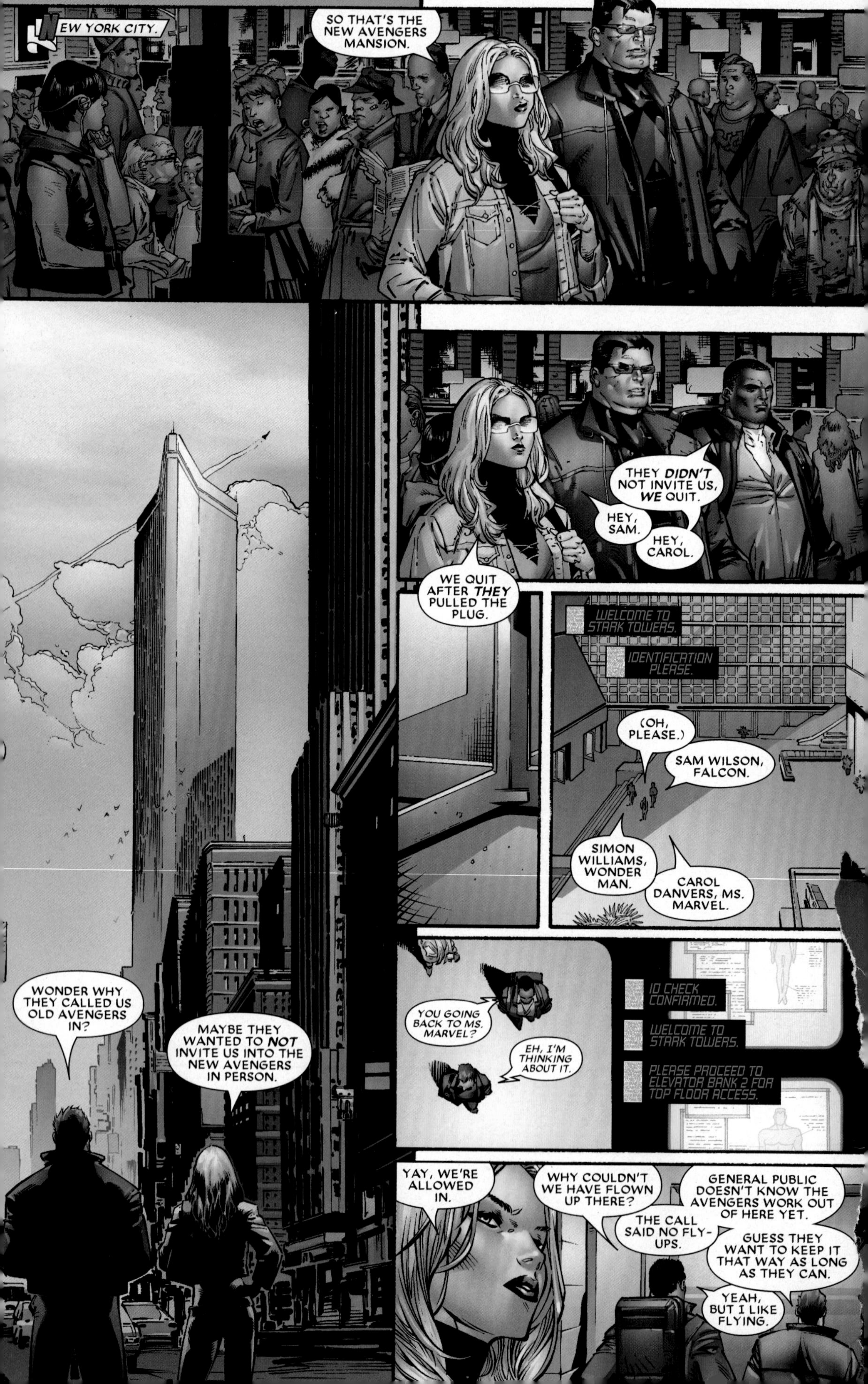
NEW YORK CITY.
SO THAT'S THE NEW AVENGERS MANSION.
WONDER WHY THEY CALLED US OLD AVENGERS IN?
MAYBE THEY WANTED TO NOT INVITE US INTO THE NEW AVENGERS IN PERSON.
THEY DIDN'T NOT INVITE US, WE QUIT.
HEY, SAM.
HEY, CAROL.
WE QUIT AFTER THEY PULLED THE PLUG.
WELCOME TO STARK TOWERS.
IDENTIFICATION PLEASE.
(OH, PLEASE.)
SAM WILSON, FALCON.
SIMON WILLIAMS, WONDER MAN.
CAROL DANVERS, MS. MARVEL.
YOU GOING BACK TO MS. MARVEL?
EH, I'M THINKING ABOUT IT.
ID CHECK CONFIRMED.
WELCOME TO STARK TOWERS.
PLEASE PROCEED TO ELEVATOR BANK 2 FOR TOP FLOOR ACCESS.
YAY, WE'RE ALLOWED IN.
WHY COULDN'T WE HAVE FLOWN UP THERE?
THE CALL SAID NO FLY-UPS.
GENERAL PUBLIC DOESN'T KNOW THE AVENGERS WORK OUT OF HERE YET.
GUESS THEY WANT TO KEEP IT THAT WAY AS LONG AS THEY CAN.
YEAH, BUT I LIKE FLYING.

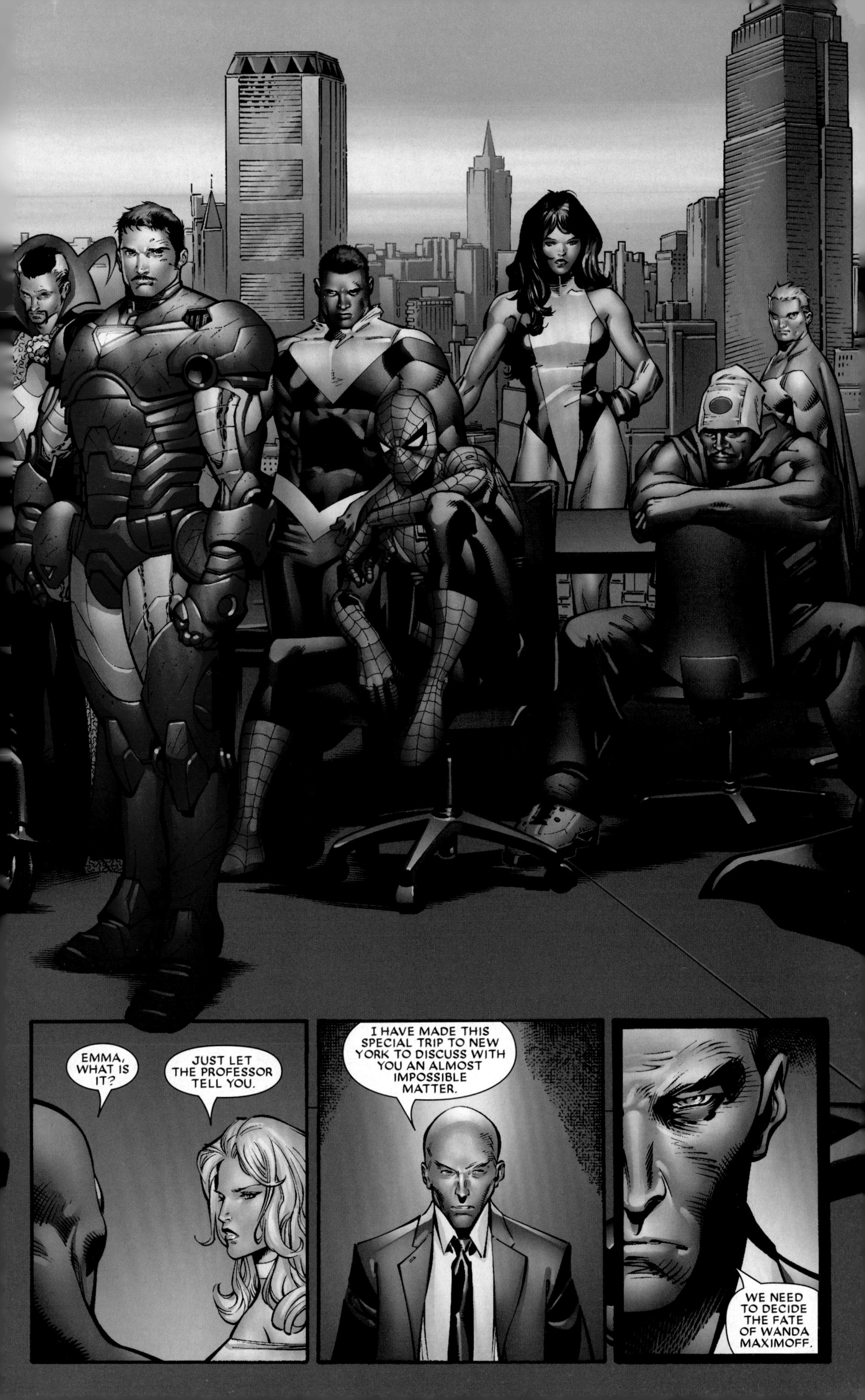
EMMA, WHAT IS IT?
JUST LET THE PROFESSOR TELL YOU.
I HAVE MADE THIS SPECIAL TRIP TO NEW YORK TO DISCUSS WITH YOU AN ALMOST IMPOSSIBLE MATTER.
WE NEED TO DECIDE THE FATE OF WANDA MAXIMOFF.

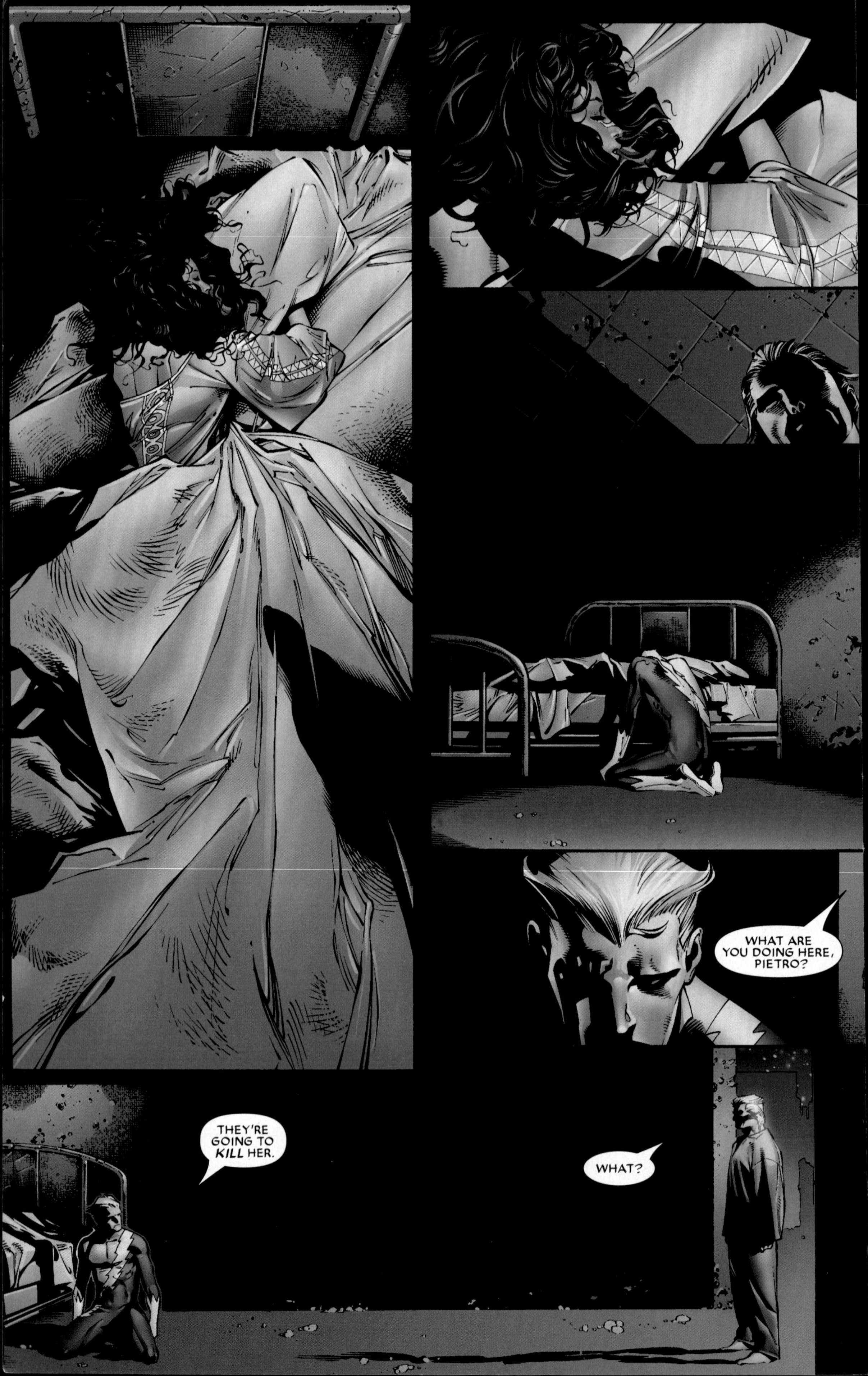
WHAT ARE YOU DOING HERE, PIETRO?
THEY'RE GOING TO *KILL* HER.
WHAT?

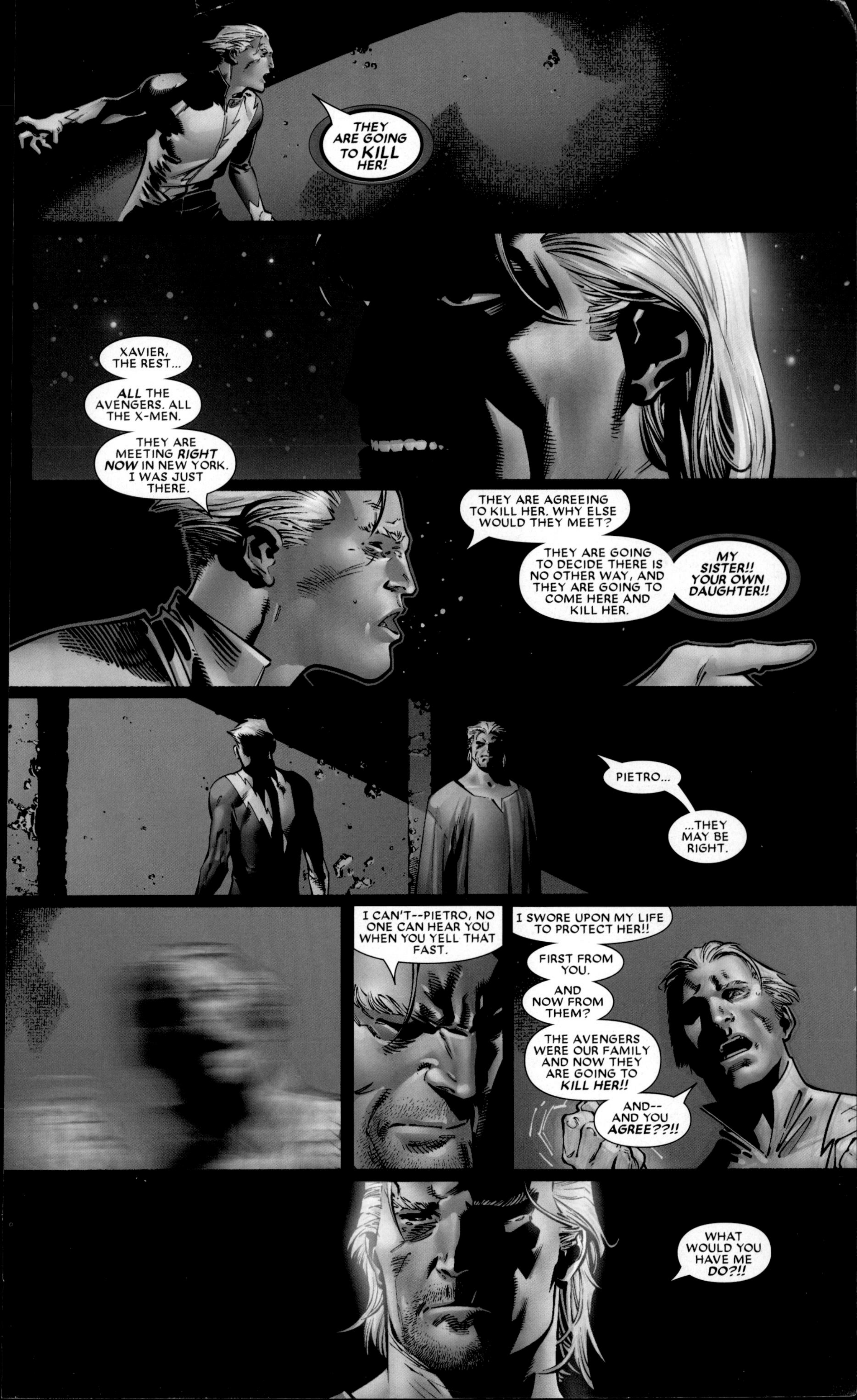
THEY ARE GOING TO KILL HER!
XAVIER, THE REST...
ALL THE AVENGERS. ALL THE X-MEN.
THEY ARE MEETING RIGHT NOW IN NEW YORK. I WAS JUST THERE.
THEY ARE AGREEING TO KILL HER. WHY ELSE WOULD THEY MEET?
THEY ARE GOING TO DECIDE THERE IS NO OTHER WAY, AND THEY ARE GOING TO COME HERE AND KILL HER.
MY SISTER!! YOUR OWN DAUGHTER!!
PIETRO...
...THEY MAY BE RIGHT.
I CAN'T--PIETRO, NO ONE CAN HEAR YOU WHEN YOU YELL THAT FAST.
I SWORE UPON MY LIFE TO PROTECT HER!!
FIRST FROM YOU.
AND NOW FROM THEM?
THE AVENGERS WERE OUR FAMILY AND NOW THEY ARE GOING TO KILL HER!!
AND--AND YOU AGREE??!!
WHAT WOULD YOU HAVE ME DO?!!

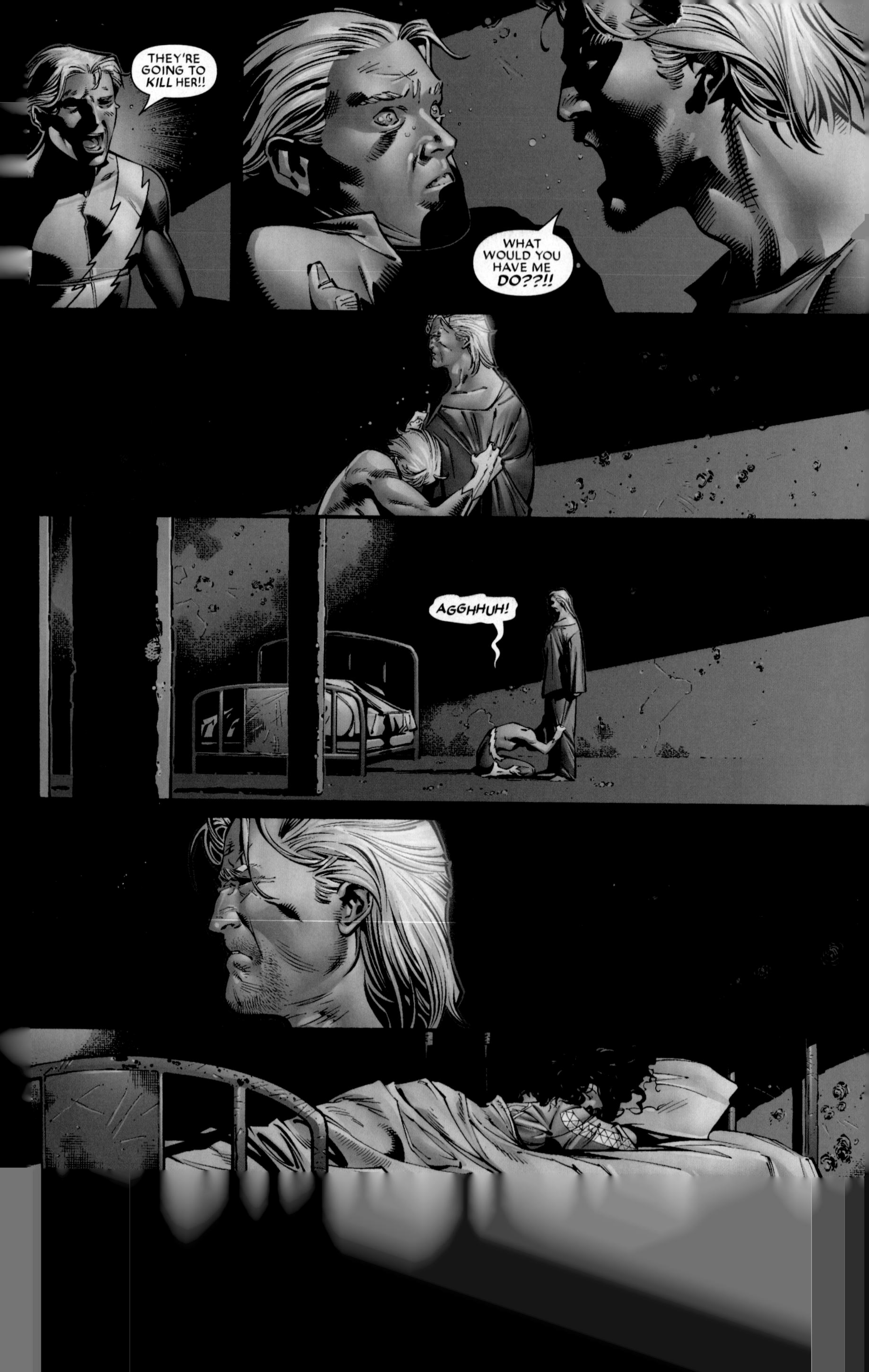
THEY'RE GOING TO KILL HER!!
WHAT WOULD YOU HAVE ME DO??!!
AGGHHUH!

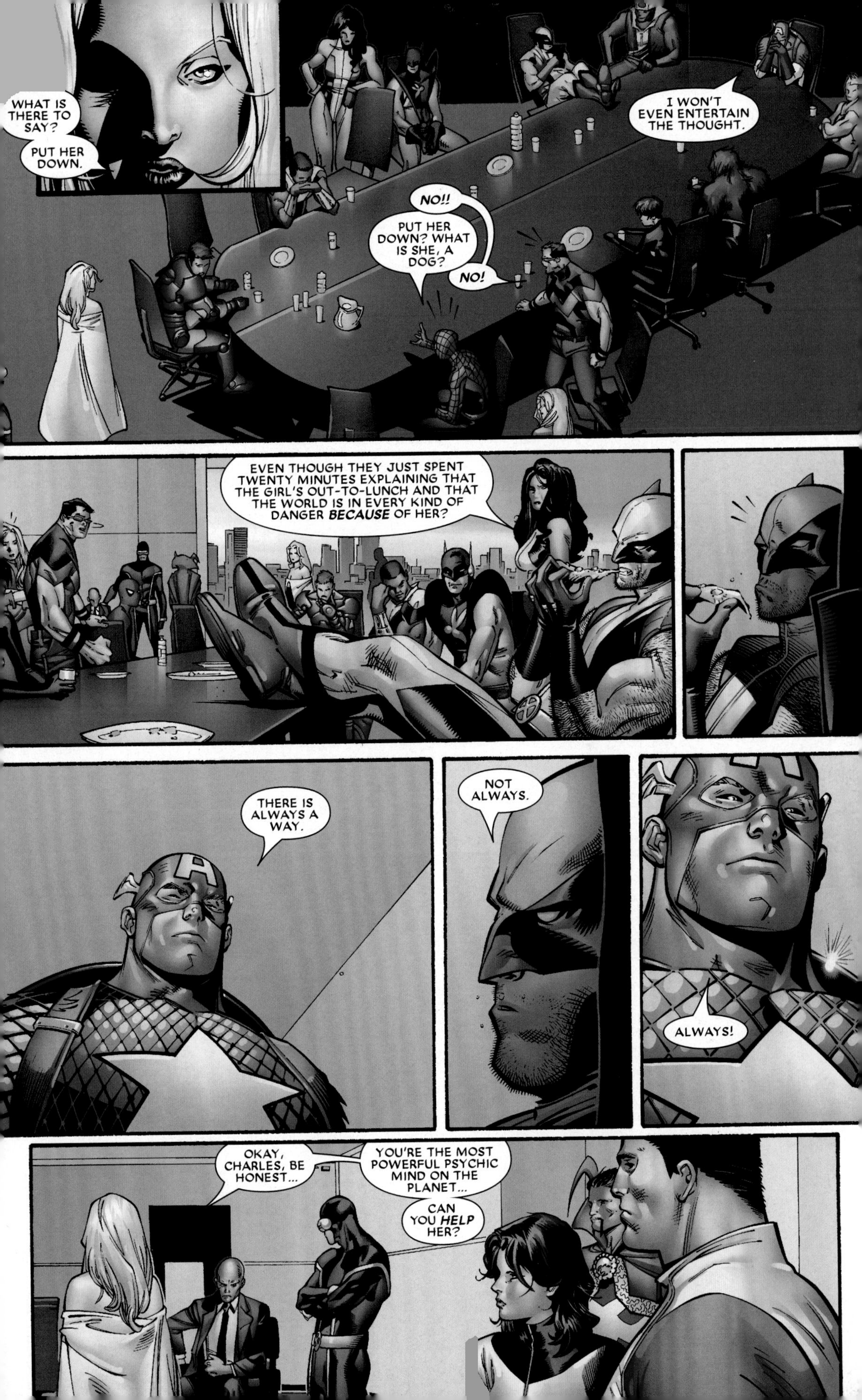
WHAT IS THERE TO SAY?
PUT HER DOWN.
I WON'T EVEN ENTERTAIN THE THOUGHT.
NO!!
PUT HER DOWN? WHAT IS SHE, A DOG?
NO!
EVEN THOUGH THEY JUST SPENT TWENTY MINUTES EXPLAINING THAT THE GIRL'S OUT-TO-LUNCH AND THAT THE WORLD IS IN EVERY KIND OF DANGER BECAUSE OF HER?
THERE IS ALWAYS A WAY.
NOT ALWAYS.
ALWAYS!
OKAY, CHARLES, BE HONEST...
YOU'RE THE MOST POWERFUL PSYCHIC MIND ON THE PLANET...
CAN YOU HELP HER?

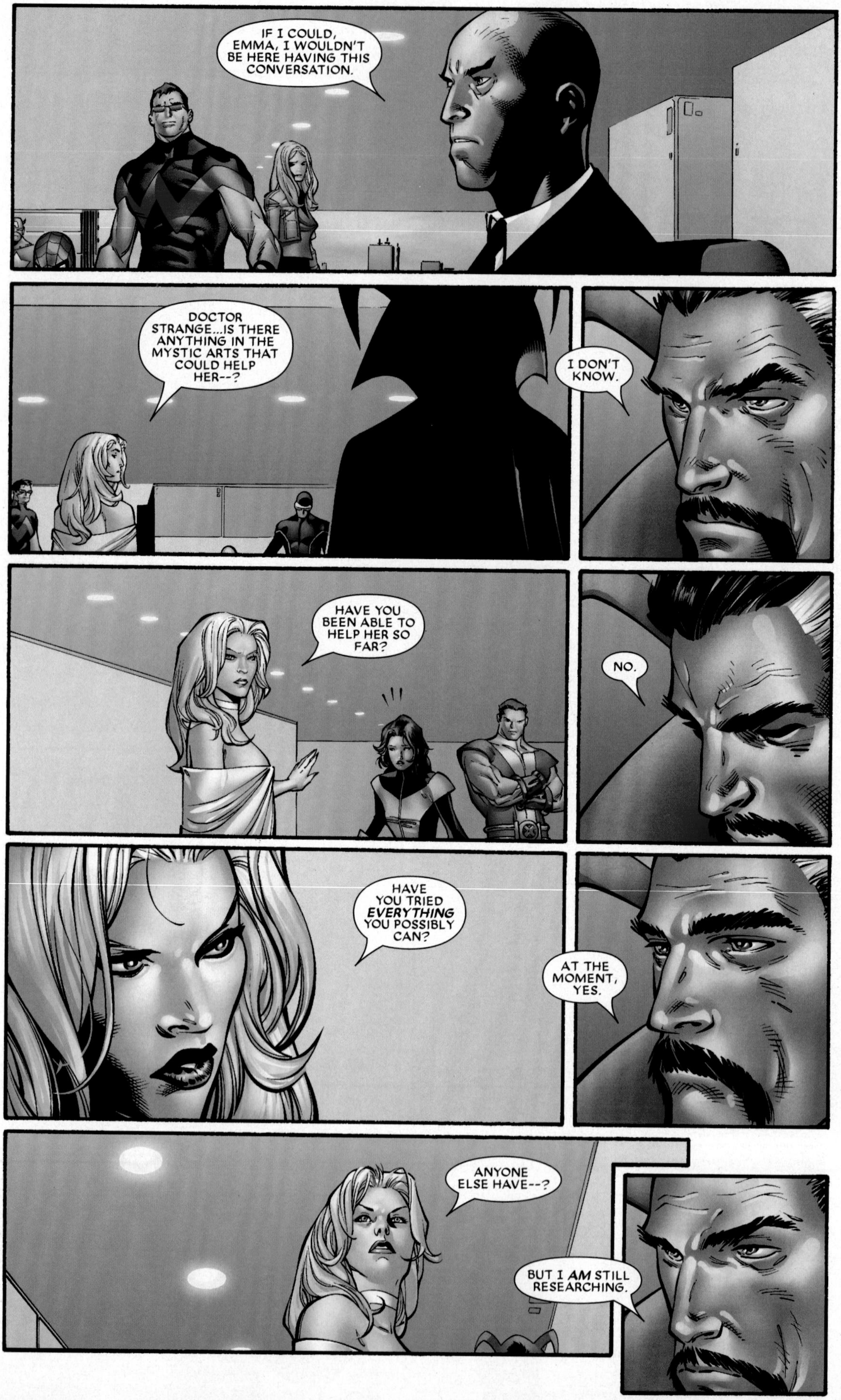
IF I COULD, EMMA, I WOULDN'T BE HERE HAVING THIS CONVERSATION.
DOCTOR STRANGE...IS THERE ANYTHING IN THE MYSTIC ARTS THAT COULD HELP HER--?
I DON'T KNOW.
HAVE YOU BEEN ABLE TO HELP HER SO FAR?
NO.
HAVE YOU TRIED *EVERYTHING* YOU POSSIBLY CAN?
AT THE MOMENT, YES.
ANYONE ELSE HAVE--?
BUT I *AM* STILL RESEARCHING.

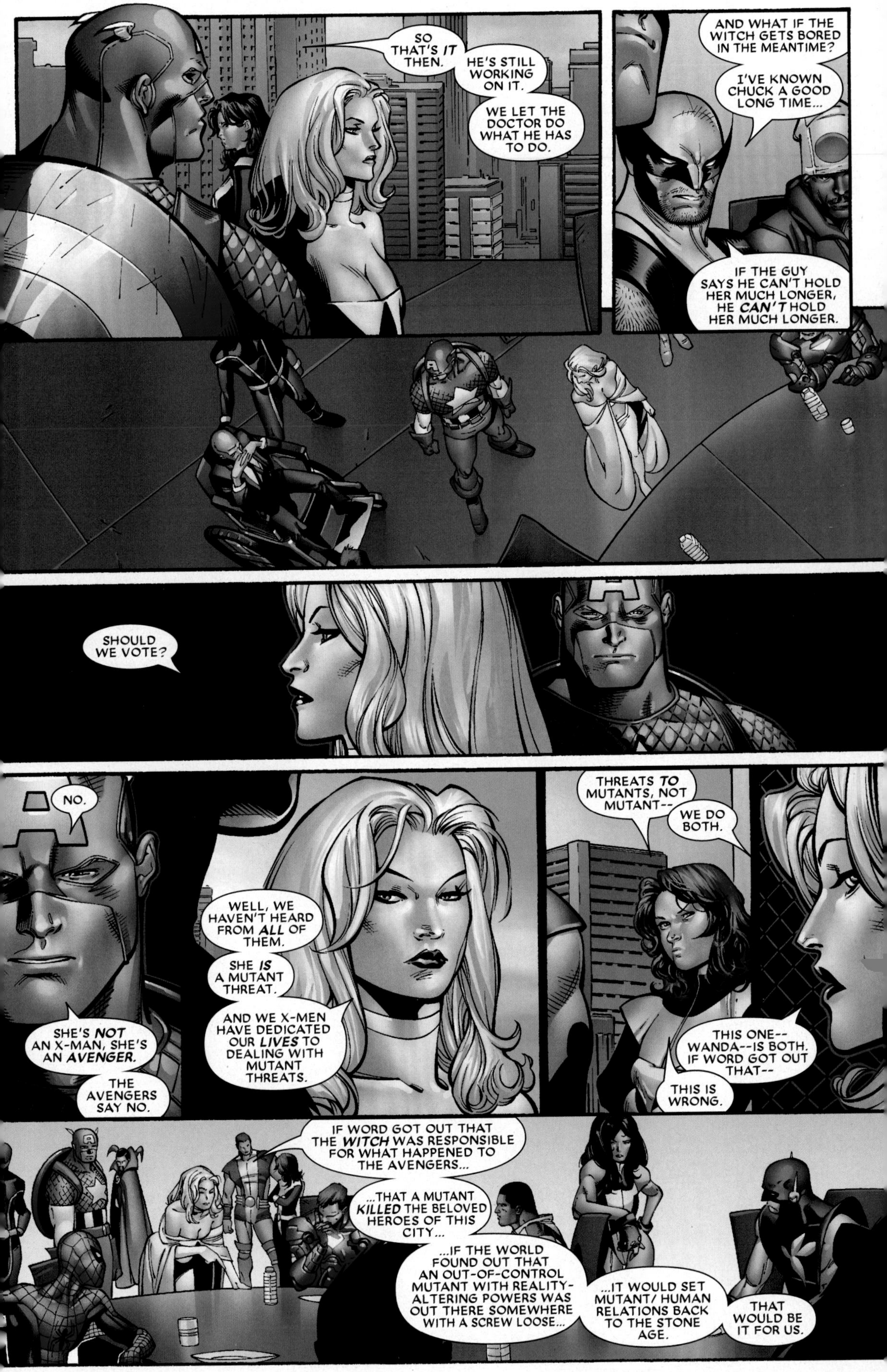
SO THAT'S *IT* THEN.
HE'S STILL WORKING ON IT.
WE LET THE DOCTOR DO WHAT HE HAS TO DO.
AND WHAT IF THE WITCH GETS BORED IN THE MEANTIME?
I'VE KNOWN CHUCK A GOOD LONG TIME...
IF THE GUY SAYS HE CAN'T HOLD HER MUCH LONGER, HE *CAN'T* HOLD HER MUCH LONGER.
SHOULD WE VOTE?
NO.
SHE'S *NOT* AN X-MAN, SHE'S AN *AVENGER.*
THE AVENGERS SAY NO.
WELL, WE HAVEN'T HEARD FROM *ALL* OF THEM.
SHE *IS* A MUTANT THREAT.
AND WE X-MEN HAVE DEDICATED OUR *LIVES* TO DEALING WITH MUTANT THREATS.
THREATS *TO* MUTANTS, NOT MUTANT--
WE DO BOTH.
THIS ONE-- WANDA--IS BOTH. IF WORD GOT OUT THAT--
THIS IS WRONG.
IF WORD GOT OUT THAT THE *WITCH* WAS RESPONSIBLE FOR WHAT HAPPENED TO THE AVENGERS...
...THAT A MUTANT *KILLED* THE BELOVED HEROES OF THIS CITY...
...IF THE WORLD FOUND OUT THAT AN OUT-OF-CONTROL MUTANT WITH REALITY-ALTERING POWERS WAS OUT THERE SOMEWHERE WITH A SCREW LOOSE...
...IT WOULD SET MUTANT/ HUMAN RELATIONS BACK TO THE STONE AGE.
THAT WOULD BE IT FOR US.

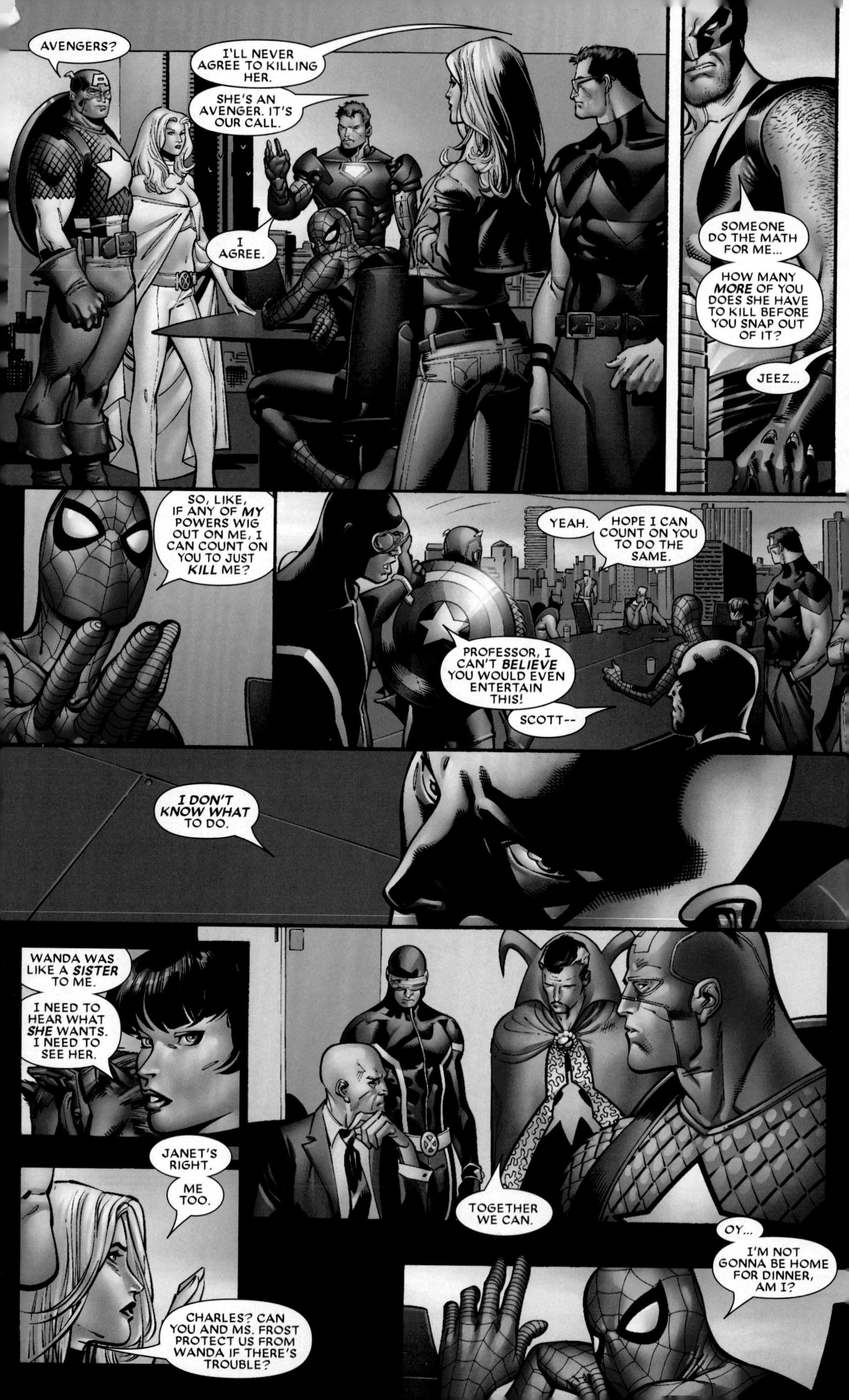

AVENGERS?
I'LL NEVER AGREE TO KILLING HER.
SHE'S AN AVENGER. IT'S OUR CALL.
I AGREE.
SOMEONE DO THE MATH FOR ME...
HOW MANY MORE OF YOU DOES SHE HAVE TO KILL BEFORE YOU SNAP OUT OF IT?
JEEZ...
SO, LIKE, IF ANY OF MY POWERS WIG OUT ON ME, I CAN COUNT ON YOU TO JUST KILL ME?
YEAH.
HOPE I CAN COUNT ON YOU TO DO THE SAME.
PROFESSOR, I CAN'T BELIEVE YOU WOULD EVEN ENTERTAIN THIS!
SCOTT--
I DON'T KNOW WHAT TO DO.
WANDA WAS LIKE A SISTER TO ME.
I NEED TO HEAR WHAT SHE WANTS. I NEED TO SEE HER.
TOGETHER WE CAN.
JANET'S RIGHT.
ME TOO.
CHARLES? CAN YOU AND MS. FROST PROTECT US FROM WANDA IF THERE'S TROUBLE?
OY...
I'M NOT GONNA BE HOME FOR DINNER, AM I?

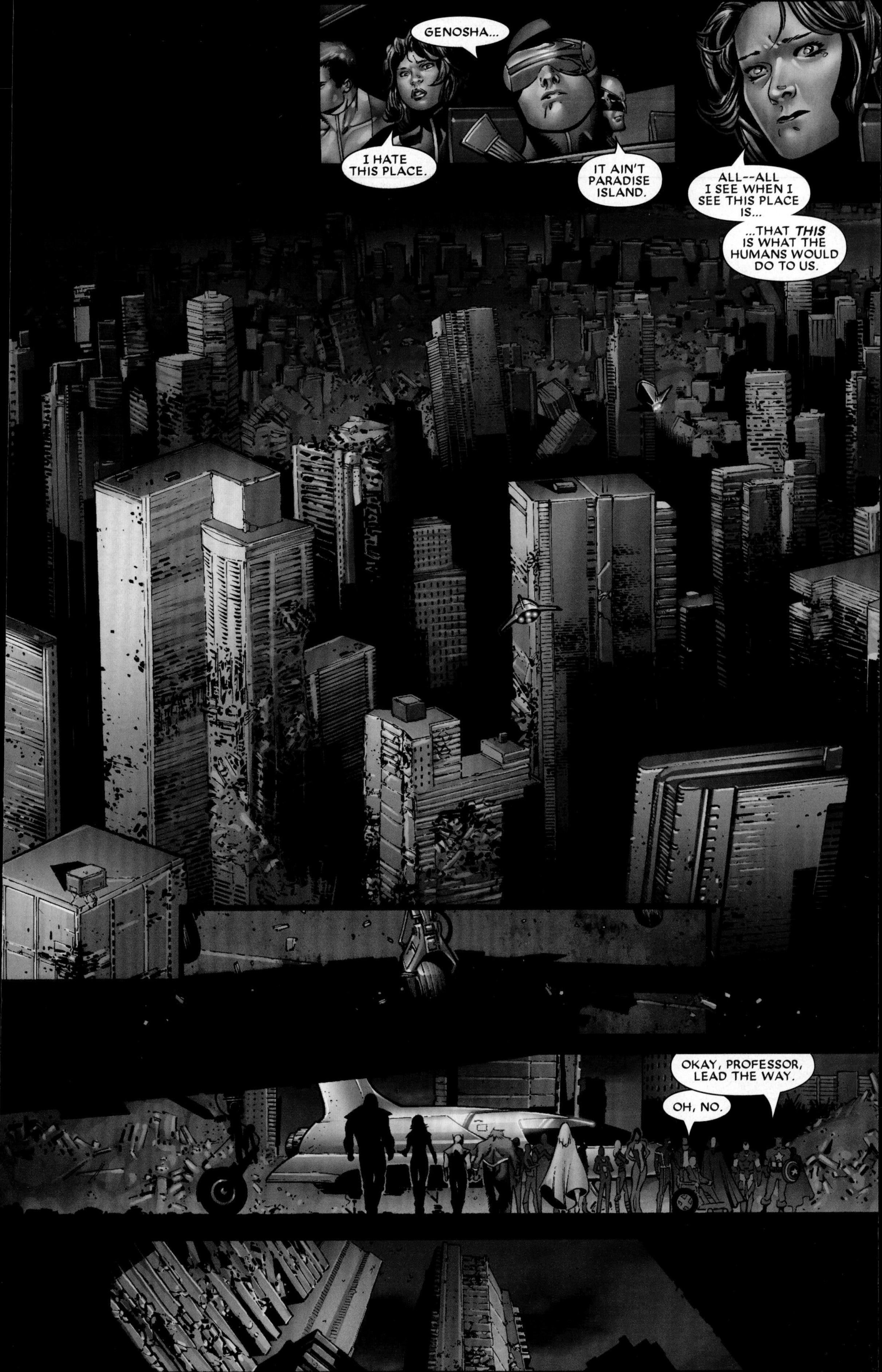
GENOSHA...
I HATE THIS PLACE.
IT AIN'T PARADISE ISLAND.
ALL--ALL I SEE WHEN I SEE THIS PLACE IS...
...THAT THIS IS WHAT THE HUMANS WOULD DO TO US.
OKAY, PROFESSOR, LEAD THE WAY.
OH, NO.

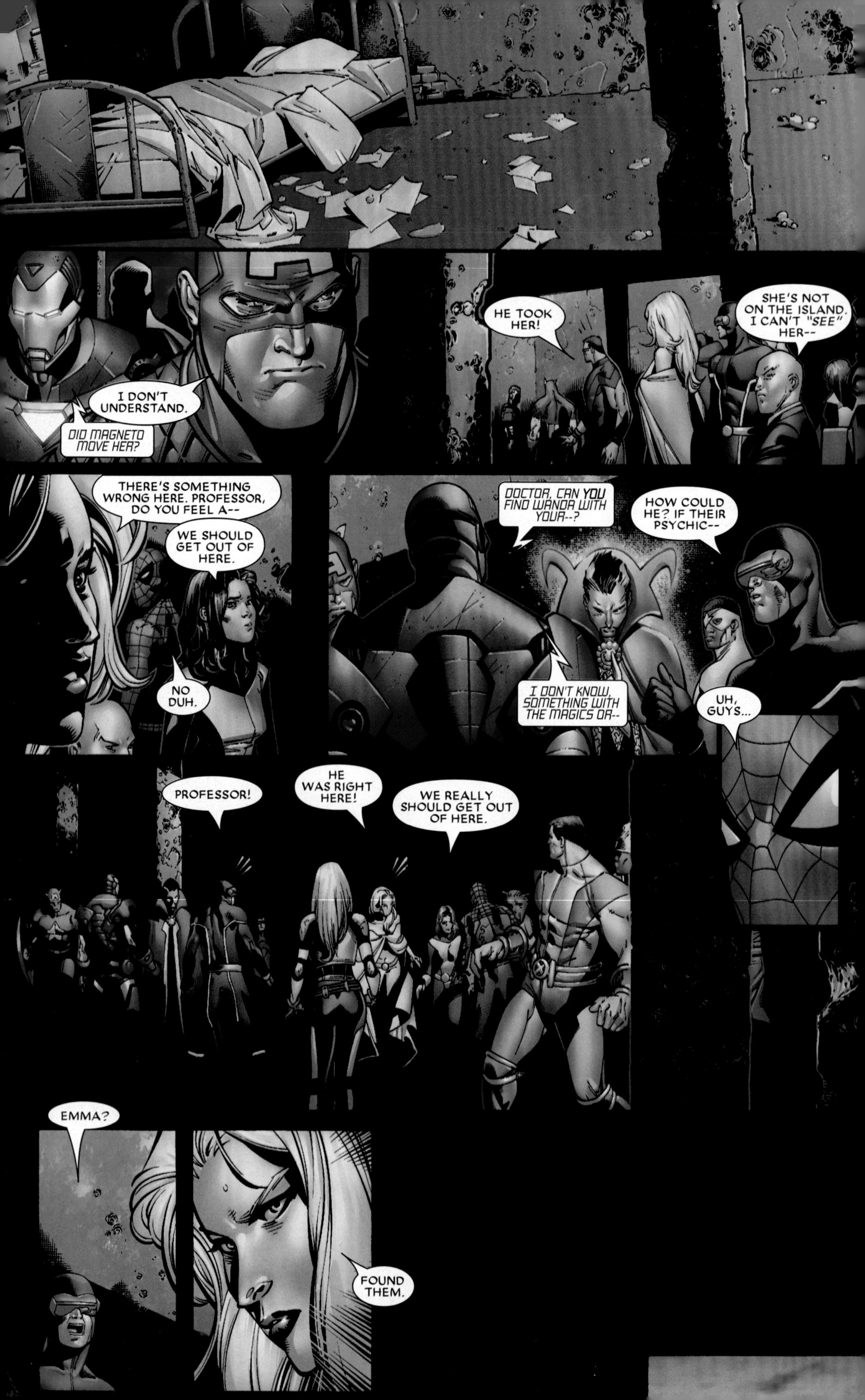
I DON'T UNDERSTAND.
DID MAGNETO MOVE HER?
HE TOOK HER!
SHE'S NOT ON THE ISLAND. I CAN'T "SEE" HER--
THERE'S SOMETHING WRONG HERE. PROFESSOR, DO YOU FEEL A--
WE SHOULD GET OUT OF HERE.
NO DUH.
DOCTOR, CAN YOU FIND WANDA WITH YOUR--?
HOW COULD HE? IF THEIR PSYCHIC--
I DON'T KNOW, SOMETHING WITH THE MAGICS OR--
UH, GUYS...
PROFESSOR!
HE WAS RIGHT HERE!
WE REALLY SHOULD GET OUT OF HERE.
EMMA?
FOUND THEM.

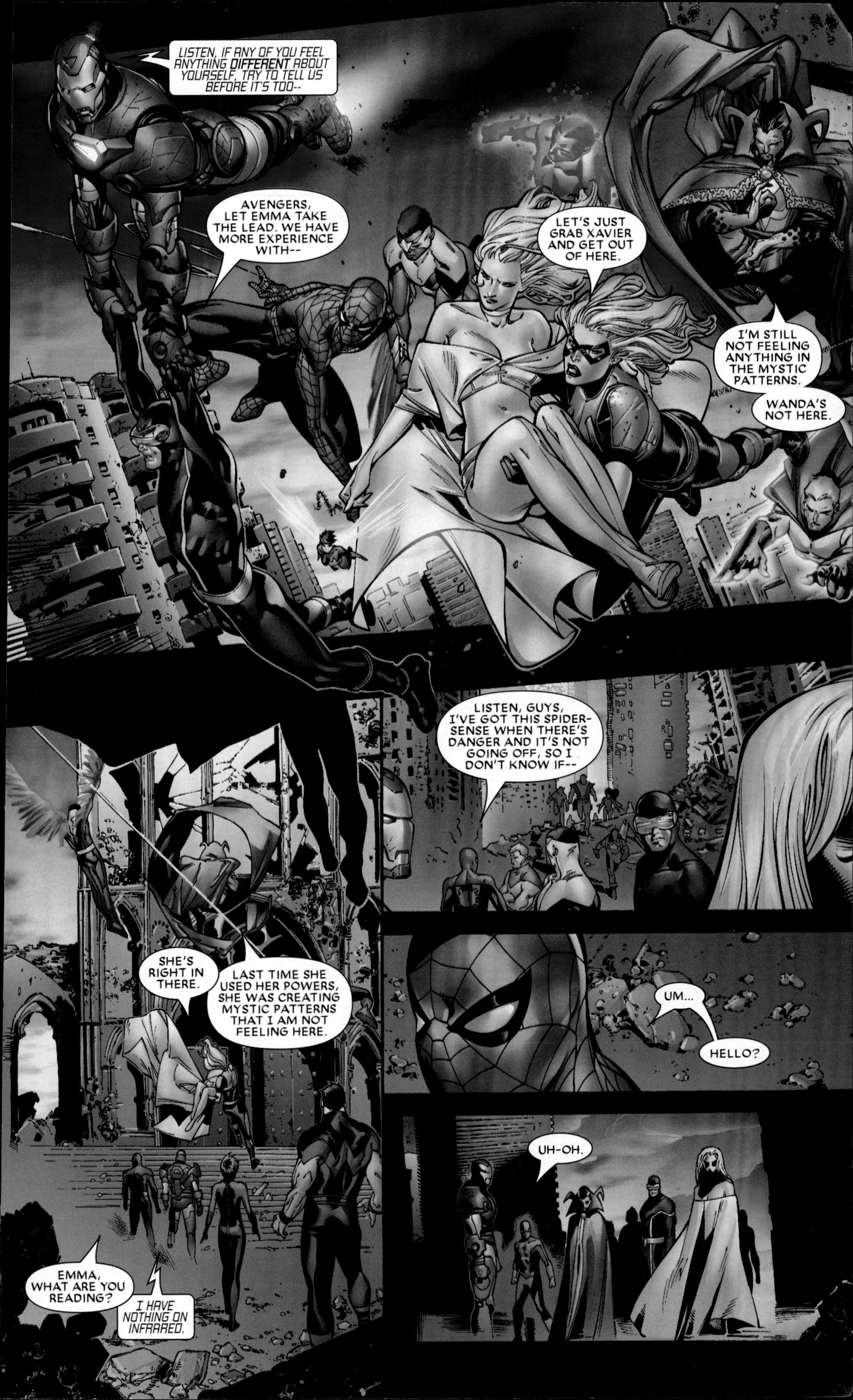

LISTEN, IF ANY OF YOU FEEL ANYTHING **DIFFERENT** ABOUT YOURSELF, TRY TO TELL US BEFORE IT'S TOO--
AVENGERS, LET EMMA TAKE THE LEAD. WE HAVE MORE EXPERIENCE WITH--
LET'S JUST GRAB XAVIER AND GET OUT OF HERE.
I'M STILL NOT FEELING ANYTHING IN THE MYSTIC PATTERNS.
WANDA'S NOT HERE.
LISTEN, GUYS, I'VE GOT THIS SPIDER-SENSE WHEN THERE'S DANGER AND IT'S NOT GOING OFF, SO I DON'T KNOW IF--
SHE'S RIGHT IN THERE.
LAST TIME SHE USED HER POWERS, SHE WAS CREATING MYSTIC PATTERNS THAT I AM NOT FEELING HERE.
EMMA, WHAT ARE YOU READING?
I HAVE NOTHING ON INFRARED.
UM...
HELLO?
UH-OH.

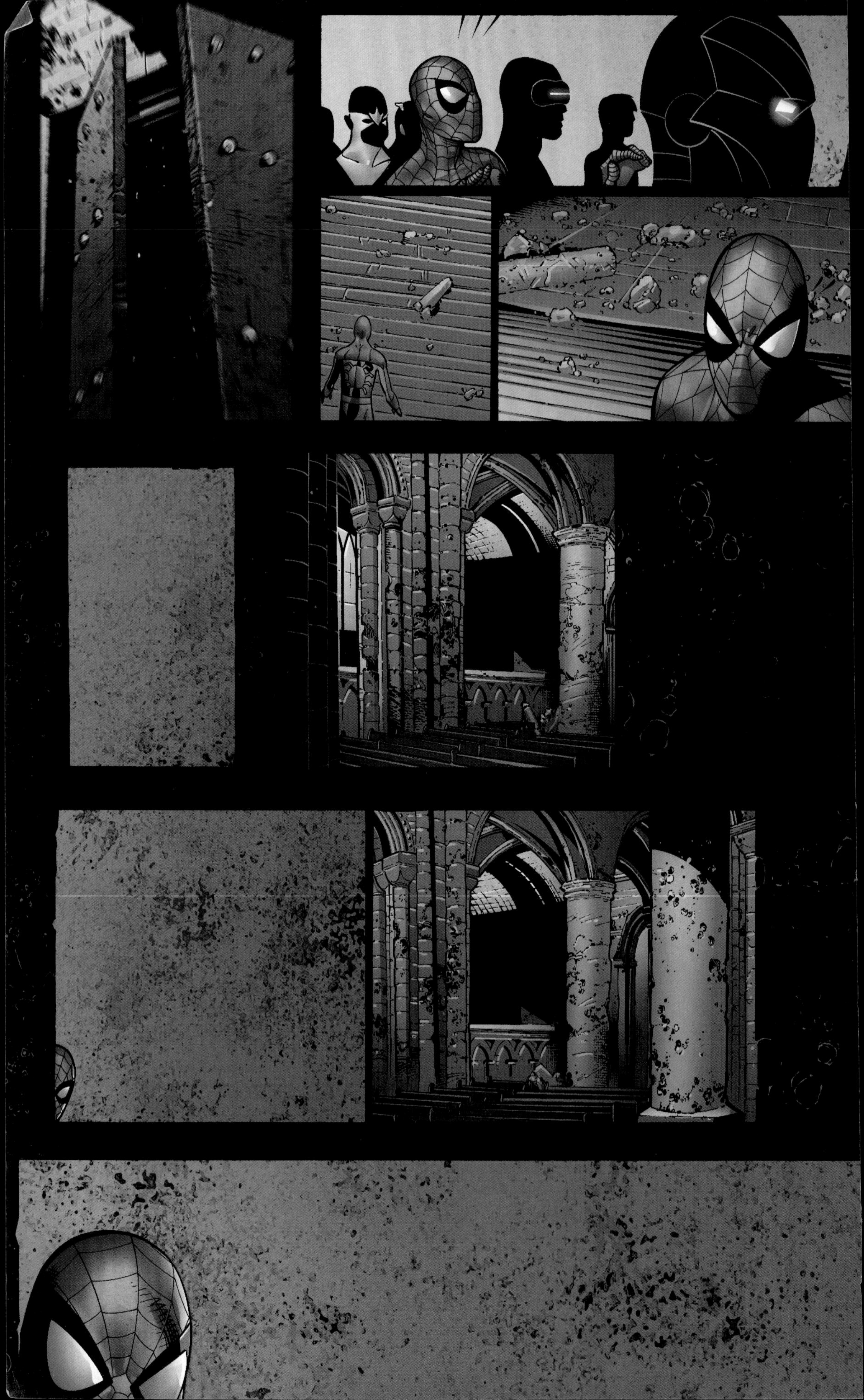

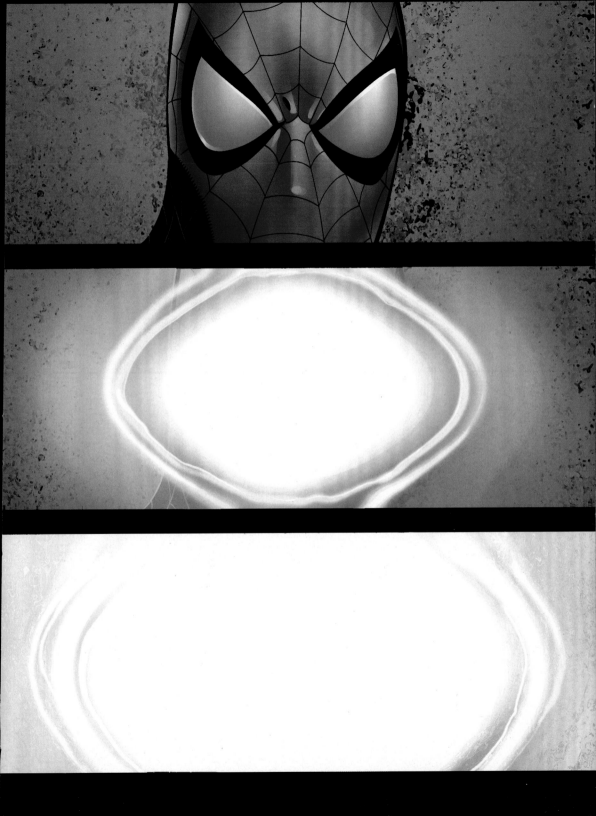

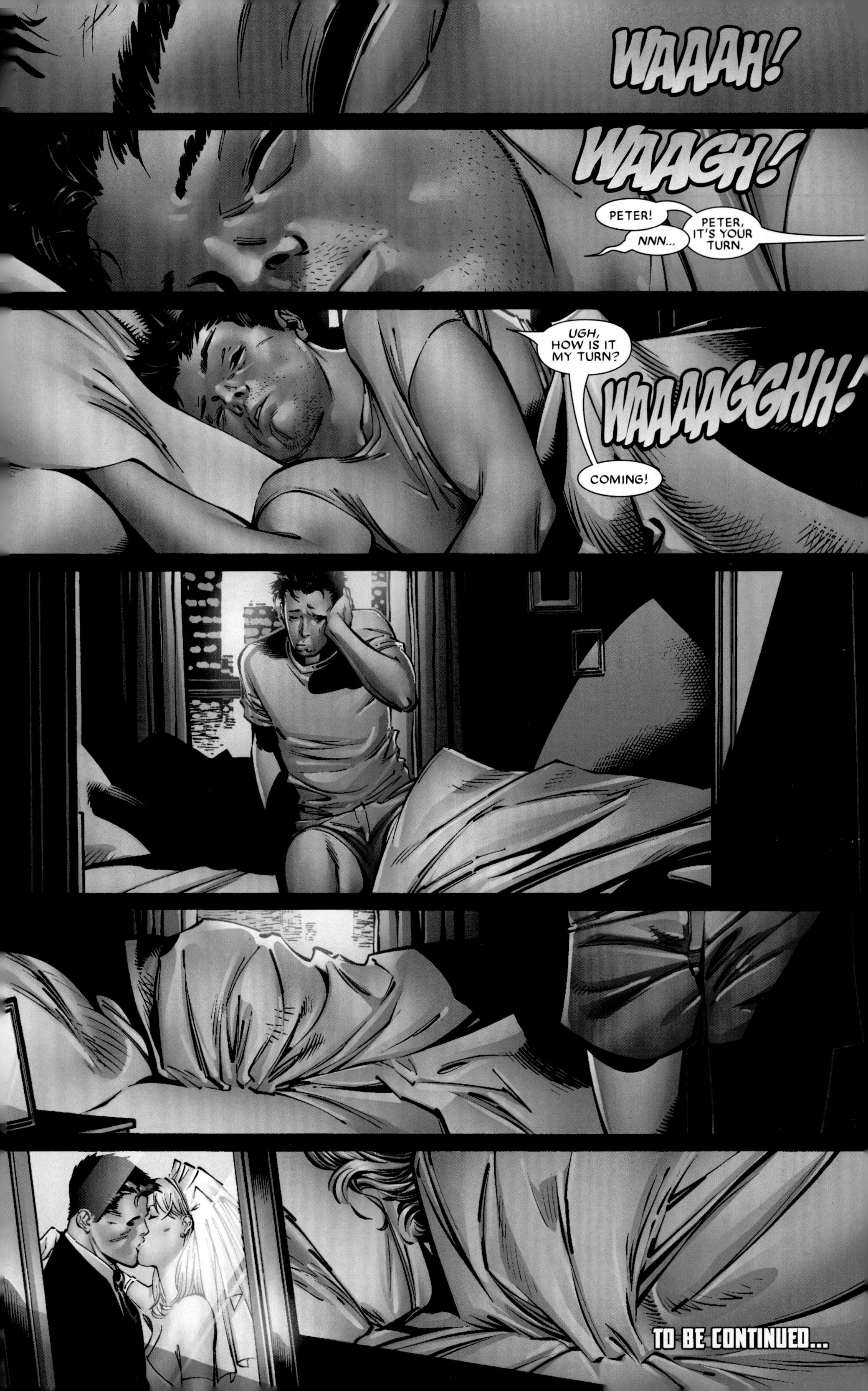
WAAAH!
WAAGH!
PETER!
NNN...
PETER, IT'S YOUR TURN.
UGH, HOW IS IT MY TURN?
WAAAAGGHH!
COMING!
TO BE CONTINUED...

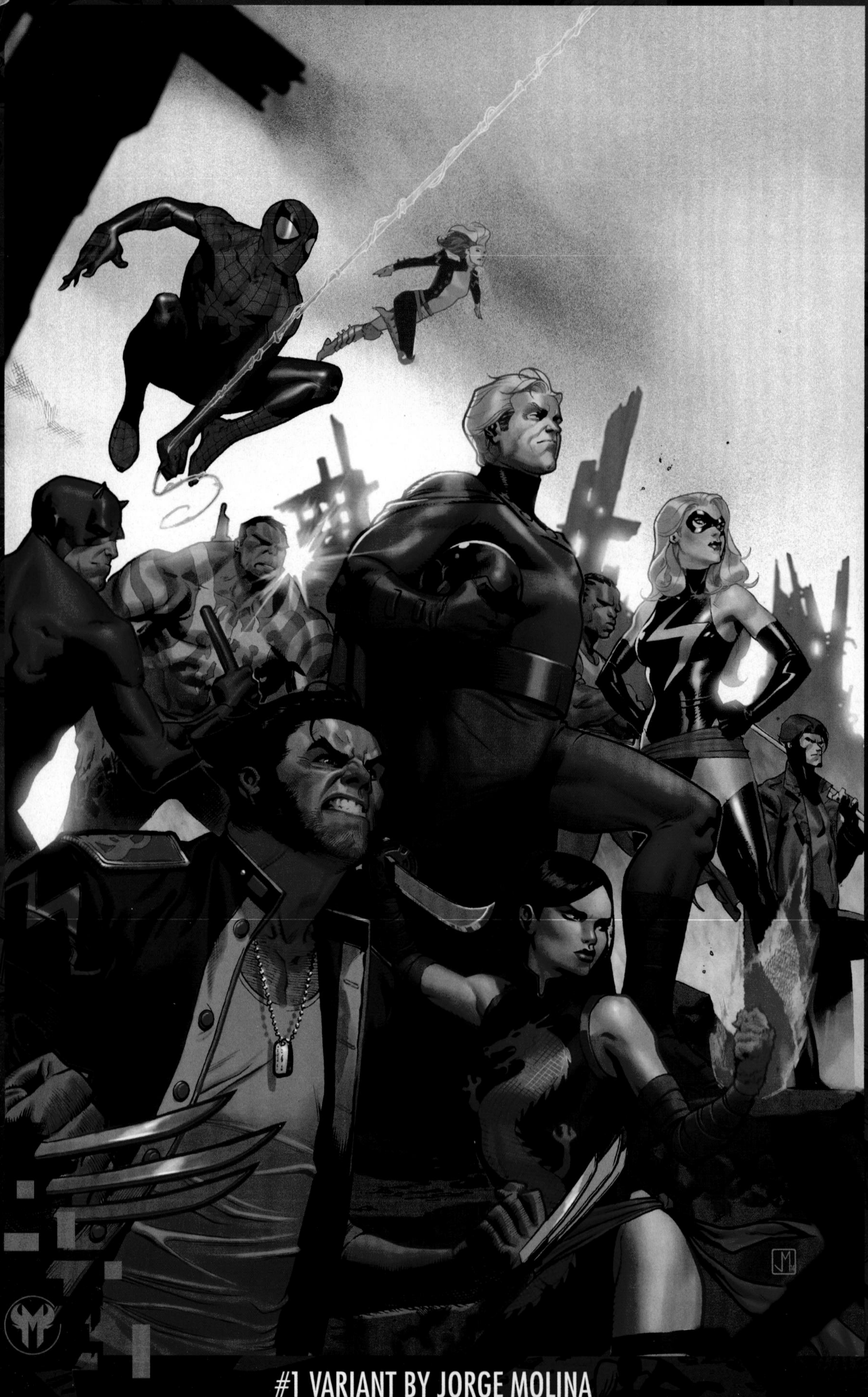

#1 VARIANT BY JORGE MOLINA

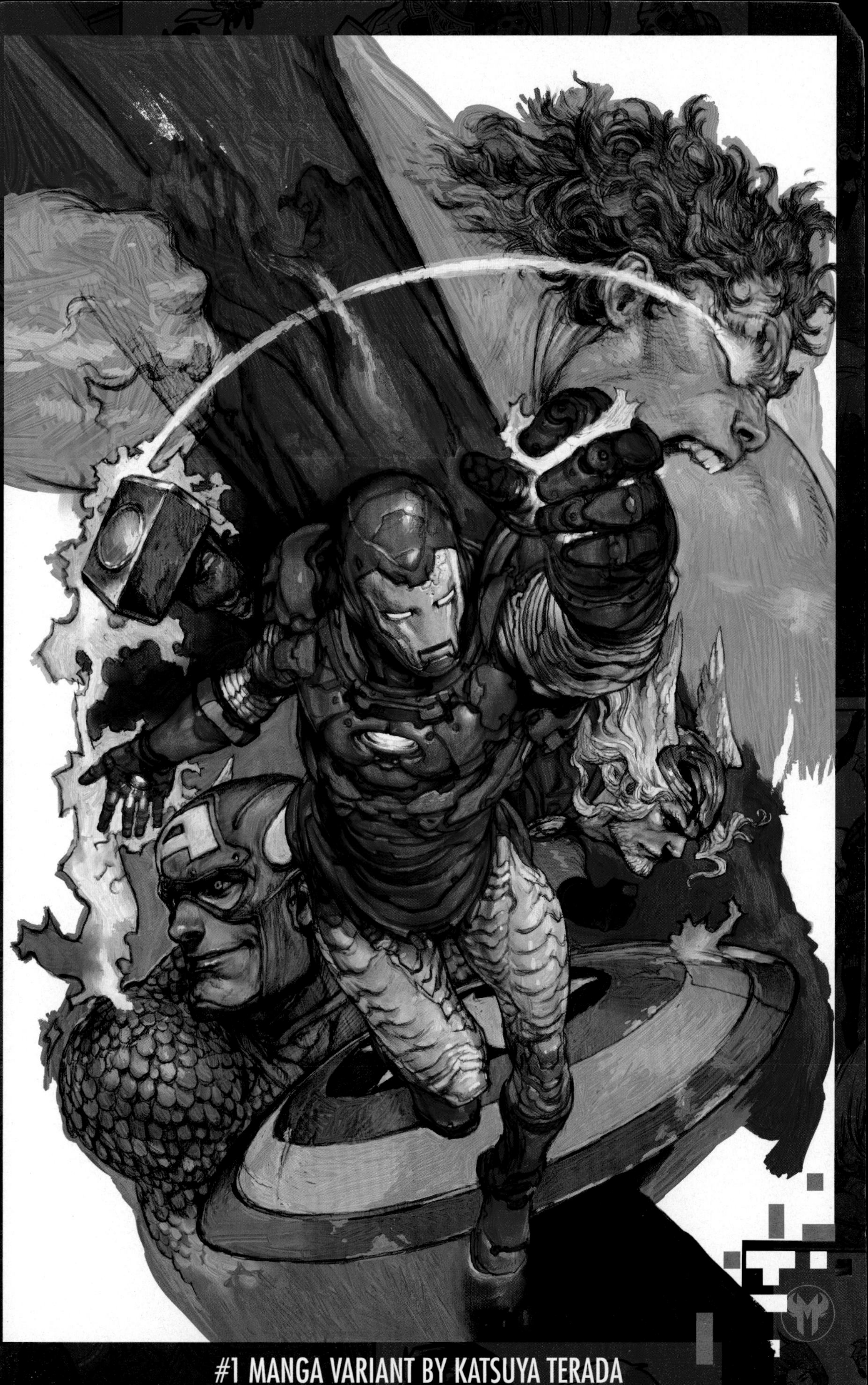

#1 MANGA VARIANT BY KATSUYA TERADA

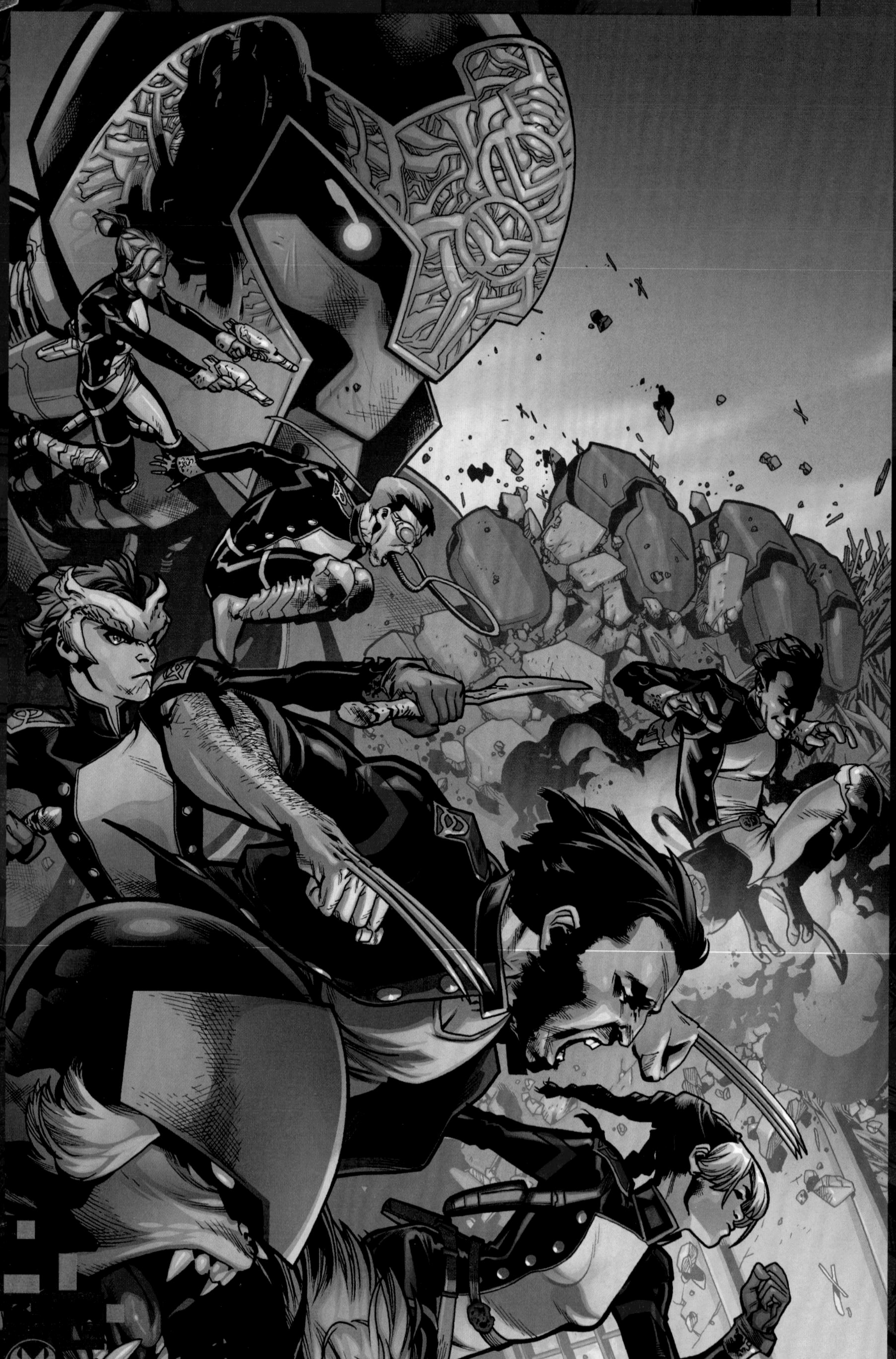

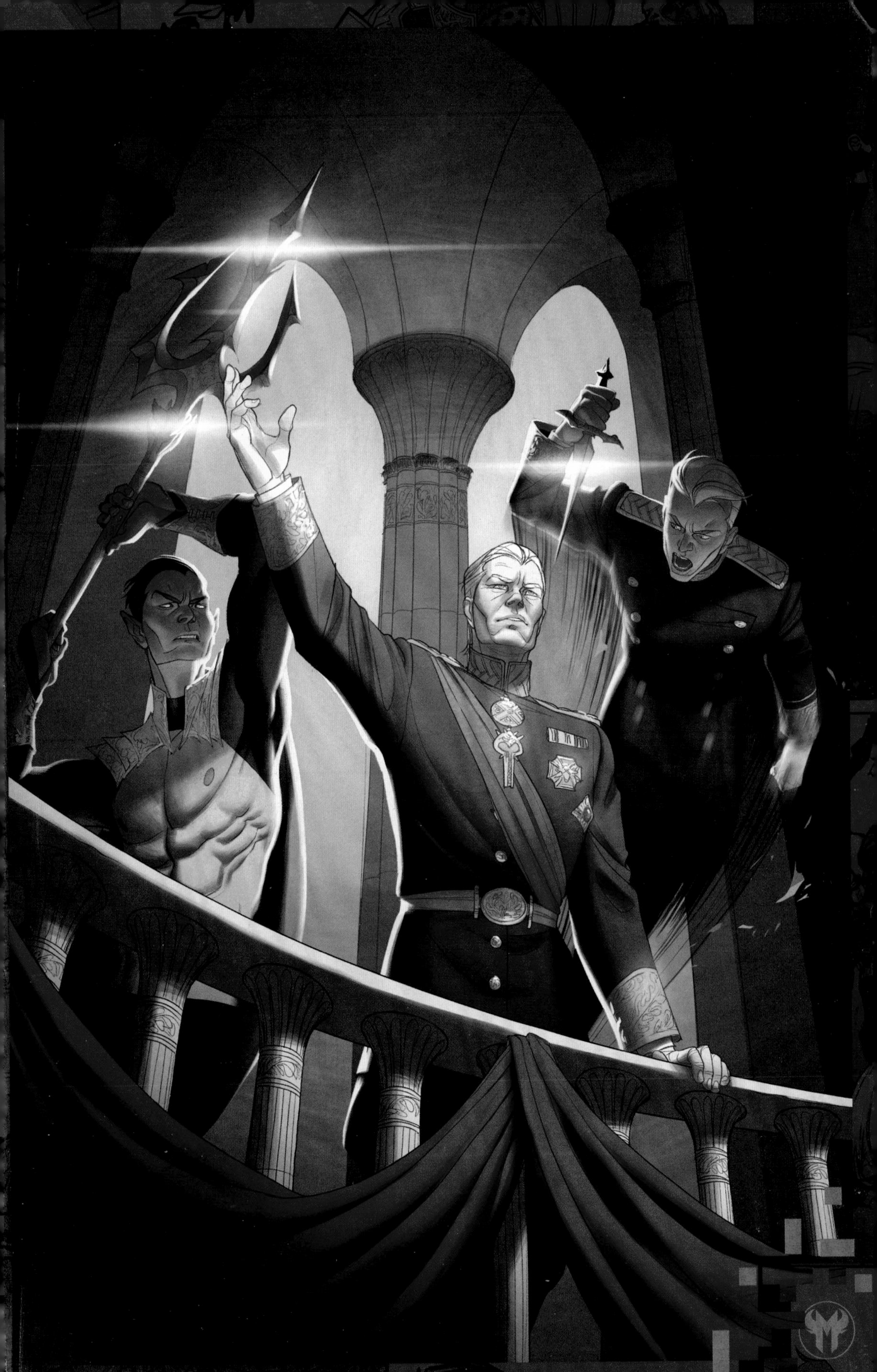

#2 VARIANT BY CLAIRE HUMMEL

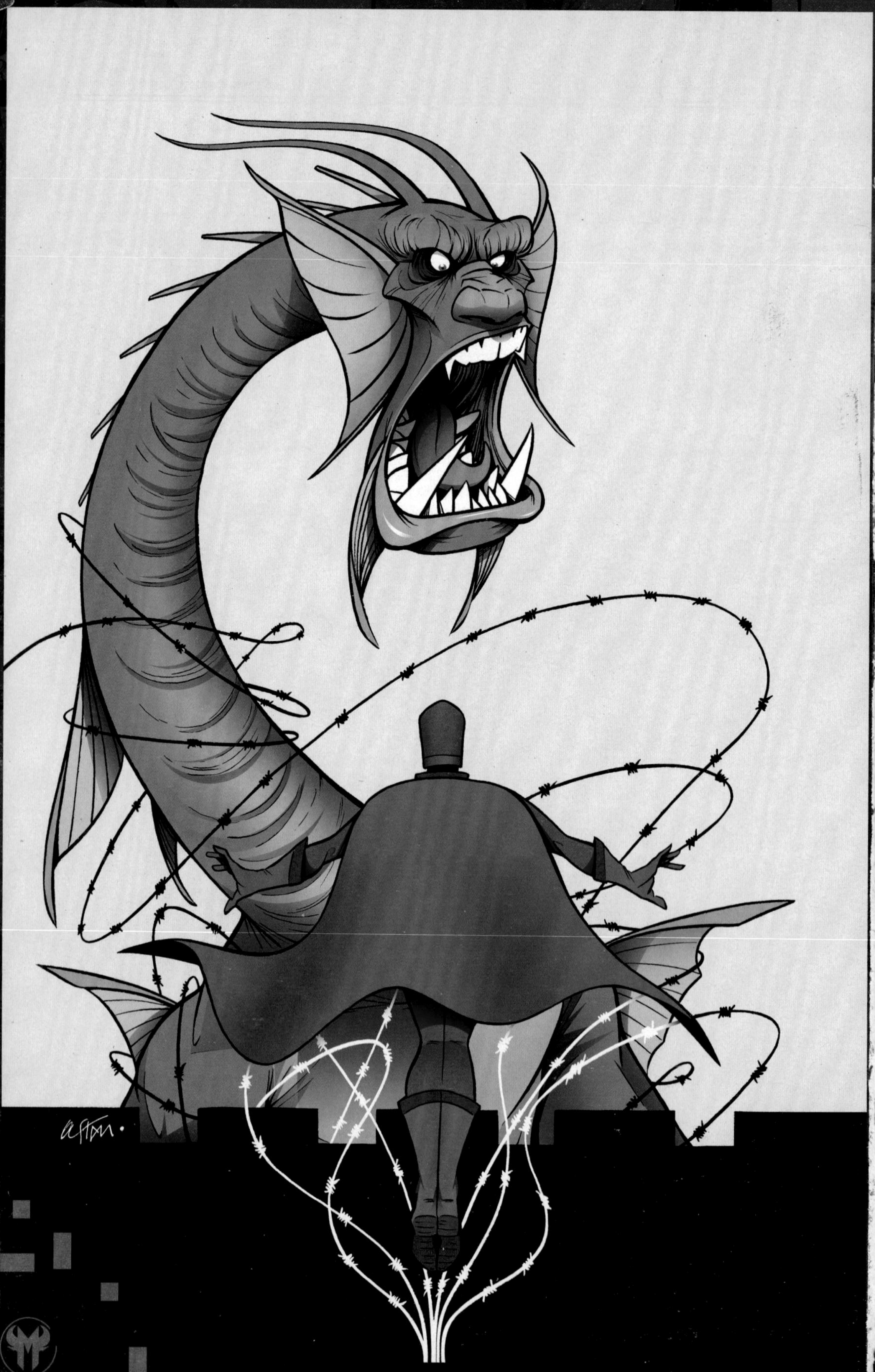

#3 VARIANT BY GUSTAVO DUARTE